MW00811002

Permission To Sparkle:
Claim Your Desires + Spark Your Dream Life

FIRST EDITION

For information about special discounts for bulk purchases,
marketing collaborations or interviews with the author, contact the
author. She loves to play with the book and the game publicly to inspire!

ISBN 978-1-7361778-0-8 (PAPERBACK)
ISBN 978-1-7361778-1-5 (EBOOK)
Permission To Sparkle card deck
available via AstridMueller.com

Cover, end paper design and book design by Astrid Mueller
Sparkle background image by NaMaKuKi via Pexels app

Astrid Mueller LLC, PO BOX 3205, Palmer, AK, 99645, USA.

AstridMueller.com

2-26-22

For Forest

Find what makes you
sparkle and follow
your dreams !!

Big hug from a
sparkle queen ;)

Astrid

permission to
sparkle

claim your desires ✚ spark your dream life

an interactive play book

by astrid mueller

Astrid Mueller Publishing

a message about this book

I LOVE this book, and I LOVE Astrid. Who wouldn't? She takes you on a very personal journey to open up your biggest joy and sparkle. She gives you permission to live fully, design your life to your desires, and open up to manifesting and magic in your world.

What does it take to actually do all that?

This is a real-life story that you most likely will see yourself in. Relatable inner voices, situations, and breakdowns that sound really familiar. Astrid does not hold back. She shares the whole story. The ups, the downs, the "aha"s, the triggers, the heartbreaks, and the missteps, as well as the deep spiritual growth that comes from owning that you are Queen of your Universe.

She never lectures you on how to be, simply gently plays with you to take the next step that your soul is calling for and then opens up celebration, joy and SPARKLE as the outcome. This is the PLAYBOOK to the life of your dreams.

When I met Astrid, I knew she was a kindred soul, a soul craving a world that understood that play and sparkle are not for children (in fact, they do not know its power!), that play is for Queens. Queens who summon their bidding, truly serve their people, and collaborate with other realms and queendoms.

Astrid and I bonded over play, playing a game I had invented to open up intuition. Ironically, it was following that intuition that bonded us into a friendship, partnership, and multiple collaborations to open up play with authentic lives attached. It was in one play-session where we were doing intuitive drawings (one of our shared superpowers!), and I declared, "I have a message for you, Astrid! I have the title of your book!"

She said, "What book?"

"The one you are writing," I replied.

"I'm not writing a book," was her response.

"You are now."

I have found the messages delivered through me are some of the most powerful and usually mean that the person receiving the message requires my support too. One of the many things I love about Astrid is her willingness to trust, to trust the messages, heart resonance, and signs. She knew in that moment that I was right — she felt it in her whole body. I could see that she was glowing, and all of us in that gathering had goosebumps.

And, it takes courage to be that vulnerable to share your story, your process and finish it and share it with the world. I am so proud to be part of Astrid's Queendom, and I know you will be too.

Follow Astrid's invitations to play, dive into deeper curiosity and insights, and find the courage to follow your heart into that sparkle land. When you do, you will be blessed with a life that is aligned with your deepest heart calling. As you begin to serve the world in the way that feels effortless, engaging, luxurious, and joyful, I hope that you will circle back and send blessings to Astrid's Queendom and her generosity of spirit to share this amazing journey with you.

— Jean Berry, Game Inventor, Mentor, Intuitive Artist

hello there, sparkle-seeker!

I'm dedicating this book to you. All my younger selves, and you in particular, your unique magical self! As you are where I was, seeking to give yourself permission to fully sparkle!

The journey I went through while writing this book (which is deeply reflected in this memoir) has been monumental. I went from wishing to wanting to <u>claiming</u> my Sparkle. I upleveled myself in huge ways to fully claim my own full-freedom and dream life in all areas of my life, including my dream business.

I upgraded myself from Princess of Sparkle to Queen.
Middle name Lightning.

I peeled off so many layers of limitations by fully embracing my desires, being ALL IN, and calling myself to FULLY SHOW UP.

The fact that you're here means you're ready. For the adventure. At least curious. I'm so happy for you.

Here's my wish for you. And a promise. And a dare:

#1: my wish for you:

May you benefit from this book in magical ways and uplevel your own dream life in bigger ways than you would ever deem possible. To your highest benefit, in your own journey, and your own time.

(Know that there IS no time. You can accelerate and uplevel and claim magic instantly. All limitations are only limitations of your mind.)

You choose your journey. You choose what you're ready for. Know that all your desires are possible.

#2: my promise

The more you PLAY with this book and play with it in your life, the more magic you will find.

Don't take this as an obligation. But as a commitment. To you. To your desires. Declare your wishes. Then make ACTING on your inspiration a priority. Make space in your calendar. Make this a THING. Then you'll find magic herein!

#3: the dare

Play BIG!

Challenge yourself. DO things. Don't just read. Do the scary things. You will find that you will ALWAYS win.

You only lose if you DIM your sparkle. And hide. So CLAIM YOUR SPARKLE.

side note

As I'm editing this book, I just came out of a turbulent inner growth time, where I felt I had NO CLUE of my sparkle. In fact, as I'm writing this, I'm thinking... wait, what? Me, queen? That's such bullsh!t!

You'll also find inner voices that will try to tell you you're NOT it. Don't believe any of it.

Me, as I'm here, I say: "You know what? I don't care. I'm committed to me. All you voices who say I cannot? Well, I can. I listen to me."

So be ready for all kinds of bullsh!t you'll hear! Have fun with it. May your journey be wonderful! And filled with magic. Your magic! And so it is!

another side note...

Here's an even more important thing I want to share. How it can feel when you come out on the other side. I just mentioned above that I went through a rough patch? It was DARK. I was catching all kinds of inner voices and discovering pretty sneaky and mean ways how these voices were holding me back. And judging myself! It SUCKED.

BUT... as I stayed committed, what happened was SO AWESOME:

Like when a storm blows over, all my inner clouds lifted. I can breathe again. I feel all warm, solid and HAPPY in my skin. I can see and feel that everything I did was perfect, and all is well. I FEEL AMAZING! I'm so much stronger. Shining. My sparkle is all kinds of sparkly.

You can do the same. Start with giving yourself "Permission To Sparkle" and keep going!

the chapters:

singing and dancing in the rain!

living a sparkle life

dipping your toes in...

(Foreword-like stuff. But not stuffy. Sparkly.)

how can you find sparkle here:

This book is not a normal, typical (aka potentially boring) book. It wants you to have fun. How do you want to play right now?

a. READ WITH YOUR LOGICAL MIND, from start to finish, the linear way

b. SPARK UP YOUR PLAYFUL SIDE: pick any play prompt in the book or the game![a]

c. FOLLOW YOUR HEART: go to whatever chapter calls you right now.

d. USE YOUR INTUITION: pick a page blindly and see what it inspires in you now!

---

[a] Visit AstridMueller.com to see where to get the game!

play list to
nourish your soul

how this chapter helps:

This chapter is to fill your heart with goodness and SOUL FOOD before you start the whole "Permission To Sparkle" adventure. Do this so you're ready for your trip! And to instantly start feeling good.

And to start a practice to <u>always</u> nourish your soul. Every moment. In all your choices. (Meaning, always choosing what you and your soul truly want. Sometimes that will be a long-term soul food, not instant.)

Real soul food takes time. AND you can nourish yourself all the time.

How? What? And why is this so relevant before anything else?

Well! It's like with a road trip:

If we don't first fill our stomach and tank, we'll soon lose energy and run out of gas. Also, if you're anything like me, if I'm hungry, I get hangry! And all I want is to eat! I wouldn't even start whatever trip I planned, no matter how enticing or how much I'd want it.

This chapter is short and sweet.

It will make you feel great, like really savory, darn good treats.

So take a moment. And EAT!

soul food prompts:
soul food feel-good play list

What things do you like to do that nourish your soul? Make 2 lists!

One feel-good play list for your mornings, and a play list for your day.

Starting the mornings in a feel-good way instead of just jumping out of bed and reacting to what gets <u>thrown</u> your way...? Huge difference. You can start with carving 15 minutes out for yourself and then play with your play list.

The other one is for whenever you need nourishment during the day. You can put things on the play list like, "give myself a hug." Or, "dance to a feel-good song" or a bit longer like, "meditate for five minutes." Or "go outside." Or put "lunch" on your calendar! Or silly ones like, "hop on a foot 10 times while patting myself on the head." (That will instantly shift your energy to good!) Taking three deep, slow breaths....

These will be your go-to soul food play lists! Write them on two separate pieces of paper, so you can keep them around when you need them.

Great! Now pick ONE of these things and "eat"!

Did you do something to nourish your soul? Awesome! (Otherwise, why not?) Do you want to sparkle or not?

Eat your soul food.

Now here's a two-second play prompt:

make it visible

Stick your list on your refrigerator. Or bathroom mirror.
Then decide to do one thing from it every day. For five days in a row.

If you fall off the wagon, simply start again. This will help you start and continue feel-good habits. And of course, every time you do it, it makes you feel sparkly!

Here's what I did: I made it into a card with a little soul food foldout menu inside. Then I placed it in a beautiful spot. Yes, you can make it pretty! Or just write it and pop it up. Do it your way, and have fun!

The soul food idea menu I did for myself, wrapped in a loving card.

soul food prompt:
pause. check in. breathe.

How are you feeling? Do you feel complete? Is there something else your soul wants right now? Take a moment to breathe.

Allow awareness to sink in.

What do you feel?

What do you need?

Here's what happened for me:

After completing this chapter, reviewing the last edits, doing the thing, taking a pretty picture, and placing it...

I caught myself jumping up, ready for the next chapter editing. Then jumping up to get more coffee, on autopilot.

Doing all the things. And I felt an unease, a heaviness creep in. For a moment, I kept doing the things. Coffee, milk, making breakfast, autopilot. Then I stopped. Realized that I was feeling heavy, like there was a cloud on my heart. And internally, I was beating myself up.

I paused. My hands on the counter, I closed my eyes and chose to LISTEN to all the voices. To FEEL it all.

It was a sh!t-storm.

"You suck. You're almost out of money. You're doing it all wrong. You have no one anymore, no boyfriend, and a the time of this writing, no hubby anymore either —you're all alone. No one is taking care of you. And you don't know how to take care of yourself. And your savings are almost gone. You don't know what you're doing with your business — what are you doing here? Wasting all morning? You're doing NOTHING!"

Whip crack, bully attack, ratt-a-ta-tatttttt machinegun fire in my head!!

I kept breathing. Starting to become aware it was just my inner critic. Not real. I stayed with it. Felt my feet on the ground. Let the voices barf it out. My breakfast was crackling in the pan.

An awareness began to emerge for me as if I was the eye of the storm, the voices circling around me, yet nothing was happening to me.

I kept breathing. Asked for universe support. Saying gratitude for all that I already have. And brought my awareness back again into my body. My heart. My womb. My feet. Facing the voices, calm.

And then something really awesome happened.

They passed through me, and the storm calmed down.

My heart stirred awake. Of COURSE I am taking care of me. Whatever happens, I'll be okay. Yes, it's scary, but I'll figure it out.

I started feeling this in my body.

Then I chose to walk mindfully to the stove, telling myself with each step, while breathing, "I am always taking care of myself."

Step, repeat, breathe, feel. Step, repeat, breathe, feel.

With each step, as I breathed this nourishing decision into myself, instead of the wild voices I had allowed to bully me earlier, I started to calm down and feel more and more peace.

Then I focused on my cooking again, slowly, while staying present.

Things got better and better. Not only was I not feeling the pressure on my heart and voices in my head anymore, I was beginning to smell the yummy food, and even in my current reality, feel the nurturing.

In everything I did for myself. Inside and out. More and more peace.

Then, with my heart open again and calm, I began getting awareness. Started finding gems. I remembered that I had run my mother's voice in my head! The things she used to tell herself! She had so often been stressed out. Worrying about money. Hustling to cook. Always stressing the crap out of herself (and not allowing us to help her — yet complaining we didn't help).

My dad had been the "breadwinner" (what kind of a term is that, come to think of it???), she always told herself. "He had the job; I was just the housewife," she would say. She never gave herself permission to do the things she ALSO really wanted, like singing, on stages.

He would have totally supported her — in fact, he did! All the way! It was herself not fully giving herself permission to dare, so she didn't.

And, because she saw herself as "only the housewife," not fully feeling her own value, she kept hustling, always trying to prove to herself. Not fully feeling like she deserved to be taken care of.

I realized, there in the kitchen, that my inner voices and inner stress had actually simply been a regurgitating inner story of my mum.

Heck, I even manifested boyfriends and a husband who took care of me, paid for everything while I hustled in my business, thinking I'm never doing enough and also don't really deserve being taken care of!

So much crazy. All in my head. All in my mum's head.

It wasn't even my own story! I simply re-manifested it! Because I kept running on auto-pilot. Not catching the voices, until this day. And the moment in the kitchen brought it all clearly back to me again.

I want to dedicate this book to all of us and our ancestors who have NOT given ourselves permission to be free in our hearts. So that we choose to DO what our soul wants! DARE to do all we want! KNOW our value (which is limitless)! And freely RECEIVE all support while also claiming our own dream-realizing (and own money-making, as we desire!) superpowers.

Without your inner bully. But with sparkle.

reflection moment.

What did you realize from what you just read, as you now pause?
Where have you been holding yourself back? Not nourished yourself?

How do you want to live instead, with love and Sparkle, from now on?

What does your soul want you to do as the first step to start this now?

For me, it was eating my breakfast. Mindfully, slowly. Absorbing this moment and my <u>choice</u> to always take care of myself like I am now.

The soul food nurture breakfast I savored, feeling how I am fully taking care of myself.

I'm aware I'll fall off the wagon again. But I choose that I'll simply do this again: Pause, looking the voices in the eye, becoming the eye of the storm, learning, integrating, and letting go.

Then starting the nurturing again.

And this, by the way, is how you play the "Permission To Sparkle" game!

why sparkle.

how this chapter helps:

This might be your first step into owning your sparkle, and actually, most likely, the most important part of the book. Do this, and you already win. Skip it, and you may miss out on the whole game.

So hello there, Sparkle adventurer!!

If you're anything like me, you like to know <u>why</u> you're doing things.

(I actually used to drive some of my bosses mad by questioning EVERYthing. Ha!) Maybe you can relate. If something doesn't make sense, you don't want to do it? Yea, that was me.

Here's the even bigger thing and a remedy:

If we have a really big WHY behind why we're doing something, and we feel that our heart calls, we'll do it anyway.

If we don't feel the gut and we don't have the big why, then we won't.

See where I'm going with this?

Why did you pick up this book?

If you have no good reason to step into your full sparkle, your true you, you real power, you probably won't do much with this book. And then, well... nothing will happen for you.

You'll literally drop it. Abandon it.

No additional sparkle for you!

Which means you'll pretty much abandon yourself.

Wouldn't that be terribly sad?

OMG! I agree!

You deserve to fully sparkle. We all do. But the only way to sparkle is to <u>decide</u> you want it. You have to start with YES to YOU.

So! Are you a YES? Then go on...

(Otherwise, I'm so sorry to hear you're not game for that. Come back when this book calls you! You now know where to find it.)

play prompt:

Close your eyes, and ask the universe to show you some of your heart's desire here.

Why are you here? What do you hope to get out of this book?

"Because I said YES to giving myself "Permission To Sparkle," and to fully play with this book, I now show up like this in my business / life..."

_____

_____

And this makes me feel (describe):

_____

And this is why this REALLY matters to me (what's behind it all): (Why? Why? Why? Get to the bottom of it.)

_____

_____

Great! Now you're ready. Stick this page up somewhere or write it behind your ears, as my mum would say. (We forget!)

Here's mine (I'm sharing this too, trusting it serves to inspire):

"Because I said YES to giving myself "Permission To Sparkle," and to fully play with this book, I now show up like <u>this</u> in my business / life..."

Limitless. Brave. Expressing all my desires. Living my dream life. Being fully myself. Inspiring tons of people on the planet. I walk in my strength & full truth. Take fearless action even if uncomfortable — aligned with my soul.

Calm, powerful, magical, shining! Love.

Because it's what my soul truly wants.

Now let's play.

this book is a portal to
possibility + power
and here's a first key

---

how this chapter helps:

This chapter shows you what this book can do for you. And how it's not more work on your plate, but a gateway to power and true ease. Where you get to find your inner POWER, do everything from the energy of HEART PLAY, and claim your unlimited POSSIBILITY.

So, if you have a notion that this may require a lot of work, take a breath and let this thought go. That's simply an inner fear that is trying to hold you back.

You always have the present moment to choose your next action. And you get to design your life exactly how you want it. Which ultimately actually leads to ease! Because you'll act from your heart-center, your place of power, and how you truly like to live.

Before you continue:

If you LOVE hard hustle, don't WANT to find more ease, and like your life as is just as it is, this book is not for you.

This book is for you if you're ready to find what your heart truly wants for you, how it wants you to live. It's if you're ready to find your pure inner freedom and operate from a place of power, from choice. Not autopilot, not force.

To get there, you have to be willing to question everything.

To be curious. To try something different on.

> "I feel I should be doing something. But I
> don't feel like doing something."
> – G (my hubby)

Whatever mind voices don't feel like heart-inspired action, you can choose to let go. And whatever mind voices seem to have you AVOID heart-inspired action, you can also let go. ;-)

That's exactly how I want you to play with this book. That you only do what feels purely right. And that you practice that.

Disclaimer: Sometimes, our heart wants us to do something that doesn't feel easy at the time. In fact, sometimes, you might get hugely challenged! Especially if you've lived a certain way your whole life!

You might really not want to do something your heart nudge says — for whatever reason our mind has.

Be aware. Be on the lookout. Keep acting from your heart. True happy, sustainable happiness (not just short-term pleasure fixes) always comes from there.

And as with everything, there's no right or wrong. Life's an adventure.

You always get to choose. Just ask: Am I following what my heart wants? What voice am I listening to?

Choose what — to you — feels right. Choose listening to your heart. Anything else will not serve you.

And you don't want to live someone else's life. ;-)

I've taken many detours. Listening to others. Making my answer depending on other things. Anything outside of me, avoiding my own wisdom, again and again. Why? Because it was easier! "Just give me the answer! I'll pay for it!"

And literally, I did haha. With money, but also with betraying myself.

By one, I wasn't honoring my own true desires, and two, when I made "mistakes" and something didn't turn out well, it especially sucked when it wasn't even my own idea! Three, I totally missed my true inner wisdom and universe guidance that would have been my own personal best steps forward. My path to magic. My sparkle path.

You'll find many such stories in this book.

Off the sparkle path and on it. I found diamonds in both paths. The shadowy one and the heart-follow sparkle path.

What I didn't do yet when I started writing this book was actually take the time to integrate the learnings and take new actions. I kind of just breezed through my life, got great awareness, but then moved on. Without integrating and embodying my gems.

And because of that, I kept recreating situations in my life that brought me the same learning lessons again and again.

So, make it a point to not just read and breeze through this book, but to sit with the gems you find, feel your wisdom land, and then take the actions you get inspired to take from your heart.

There will be lots of play prompts in this book. And some of my real-life shadow stories. Whatever you see, use your own inspiration and discernment.

There isn't one single path forward.
Choose to do things your way.
Play. From your heart.

As you play with this book, you'll start to practice a new way of being: Your personal "PERMISSION TO SPARKLE" paradigm for your life — and you get to define what that means.

And as you take new actions in your life, from the new truths you find from your heart, you'll get to create your own dream business / career, your dream relationships, and your own dream life. Find your sparkle!

Anything you'll do with this book can lead to feeling sparkly, magical, and your power. Even the deep stuff. It may not always feel that way in the moment — but it's always at your fingertips.

This will help you with everything:

a magical key:

This key works anywhere in your SPARKLE adventure and your LIFE:

The key is to "LIVE CURIOUSLY."

Here's what I mean by living curiously:

1. Get curious about what you make things mean.

2. Dare to "act curiously." (Meaning, it doesn't matter if others deem it "curious" — or silly! Dare to fully be yourself.)

What this can look like:

Whenever you notice you're feeling bad or thinking negative thoughts, get curious. Ask things like:

"Hmm! I wonder what story is my mind telling me here? Is this still true or useful for me? What is my body telling me? What is my reality reflecting to me here that I can learn about myself?"

"What does MY HEART want?"

Be curious, and then listen for a moment. Maybe you really do need a break. Or you may catch a limiting belief! Like, "This is impossible!" or, "You're not good enough!" Anything is possible. Get curious.

How does this kind of curiosity help to become more sparkly?

It flips you from feeling powerless (which always sucks!) to becoming the hero of your adventure again and getting ideas.

Curiosity connects you to your superpowers. Because it helps you get out of your (limiting) mind. See new things. It helps you access your brilliance and also see universe signs.

It always moves you forward and, eventually, leads to your sparkle.

Use any play prompts in this book to access this key. Actually, you already have that key at your fingertips. Use it any moment. Just stop yourself from running on autopilot, and give things a think.

And what about the other meaning of curiously?

That one is all about giving yourself permission to be silly, to appear silly, and simply do you. To be yourself. Do what your heart wants.

One time I had a boyfriend who told me, "if you dye your hair a wild color and dress super bold, I'll move over to the other side of the street and will not walk with you."

He was really stuck in shadow here and afraid of what others think. And back then, I adapted. Not sparkling either, fitting myself in.

Now I know better!

So WHAT if you dye your hair a crazy color!

Please do! Live curiously.

To unlock the wall in front of you whenever you're struck, stuck, or things don't feel right: Live curiously. Live sparkly! Shine your light!

This whole "STOP and GET CURIOUS thing" also helps you in another super magical way:

You'll begin enjoying your life in the NOW. Because you pause and practice listening to your heart — instead of running on autopilot.

In those pause moments, the NOW, is where we get to choose what we want. We get to tune back into our desires. Feel if something is leading us to what we truly want. Or simply a distraction. It's in the NOW where we get to choose our actions.

It's right here that we have all our power.

With this book, you give yourself permission
to PAUSE. To PLAY. To BE.
To rediscover what you want.
What brings you joy.

What will make you SPARKLY.

It's a practice. A playground. And you don't have to play alone. b

Welcome to your sparkle path of fun, freedom, and

play-light(en)ment *

* This word came to me as inspiration here. To me, it represents the experience of this book: you get to learn and grow through an experience of deep and meaningful play.

And the sun has risen.
Just as I finished writing "play-light(en)ment."

---

b Get access to my resources and playgrounds on www.AstridMueller.com

November 22, 2018 sunrise in Kodiak Island, Alaska, over Monashka Bay

play prompt:

What does "living curiously" as in "daring to be different" mean to you, right now? Where in your life are you holding back? And what small action are you choosing to do right now to change that?

_____

_____

the big magic of this book

how this chapter helps:

This is about a dream I had while writing this book, and it has a super powerful metaphor for the deep, magical walkaway you can get with this book. Several huge gems for your life.

This dream that I just had was intense. I got abandoned and lost everything.

I was in a foreign place and supposed to meet friends. Finally, we managed to somehow meet, and then they left me again. And they took everything I had given to them for some reason. Even my cell phone. I didn't even have money, no credit card, nothing.

I was in one of those Las Vegas-like hotel entertainment strips and casino halls where all blends into each other, and eventually all looks the same. At first, I was just looking for my friends. Then I got lost. I was starting to get desperate. I realized that I had nothing. I was stuck. I didn't remember anything, no home, and no phone numbers. I didn't know what to do. I was starting to freak out!

I started crying and talking to people. Telling them my desolate situation. And people seemed kind and curious to help me.

I remember there were two people who tried to inspire me, saying: "Everything has a purpose. What can you learn here?" And somewhere along my path, I found a penny, and it had a skull on it. I was thinking, "Wow, this must be a sign." I was curious.

When I woke up, I sat with this dream. Meditated on it. Asked it, and the people in it, questions while it was still fresh.

I realized the dream had to be in this book.

decoding the dream:

(the way I interpreted it right after the dream, back when I was just beginning to write this book)

There were two things that I always had in the dream that no one could take away from me. (I didn't realize that yet in the dream.)

Two things that would always save me and keep me safe:

Knowing myself, and trusting the universe[c].

As I was pondering, half-awake, I realized that these were two huge gems.

They may be the biggest essential foundational survival things in life!

When you have these two, you can do anything, create anything, and experience all the universe's treasures. And you know you're always safe.

How so?

---

[c] In this book, I'll mostly say "the universe." Let this stand for whatever you believe. Your religion. No religion. Christ Consciousness. Or simply something bigger than ourselves.

gem #1: know yourself

If you truly know yourself, you know how magical you are. You know that you can do anything. You <u>trust</u> your own magic. Your sparkle. You feel and know, deep inside, that even if tangible evidence isn't here, like in the dream... you are unique. And magical.

In a card I pulled for myself for today, I got "UNIQUENESS"

"UNIQUENESS" from the "Be You" Oracle Card deck by Rachael Thompson Phillips

From the card description: "There was a time when your thoughts of being unique equated to being different. And different wasn't acceptable. Life experiences have led you here to this very moment to know that your amazing quality of uniqueness is a truly attractive quintessential element that makes up your constitution."

That was a mic-drop for me. I did indeed once see "unique" as just cool, and, yes, that you need it for branding, and, yes, it takes bravery to be truly you.

But there's more.

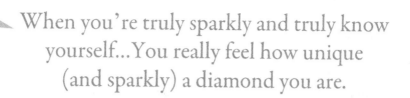

When you're truly sparkly and truly know yourself...You really feel how unique (and sparkly) a diamond you are.

And when you have THAT, all the world around you can fall apart and everyone may disagree with what you do, say, or stand for, yet you still know and trust and feel your own magic and uniqueness and keep following your heart.

You know you have magic and ARE magic.

You know that you can change the world.

And you know that no storm or comment or abandonment can really touch you.

When you give yourself "Permission To Sparkle," you change the world just by being you.

Eckhart Tolle describes what happens when you own your sparkle in his book, *The Power of Now*. He writes, "You become an observer."

You're not fazed by circumstances. You're not triggered. You don't get drawn into drama. Or feel like you have to defend yourself. Or blindly do things just because "that's how they're done."

You observe, are curious, and take charge of your mind.

You choose your choices. You become the decision-maker. You start taking action from what really serves you best, which includes your whole being. Your heart, your soul, your body, your destiny. (Not just from what your mind says on auto-play.)

You get off the hamster wheel.

You also only start playing with who and what lights you up.

* You know and feel that you're PRICELESS.
  Not worthless. Not "good enough."

* You own your inner rock star.

* And you rock it.

* You become INDEPENDENT. You thank your "enemies."
  And walk on.

You know that even if you're on the street, if you have nothing, if all your friends desert you, like mine did in this dream, you're okay. And that there are people who will appreciate you. There are things that you are and do that are freaking cool. That only you hold the key to.

You know and feel in all cells of your being that there's only one you.

That's the kind of knowing yourself that I'm talking about.

So even if you're in a rough patch, seemingly alone, you're not walking around as a victim; you're curious. You may hear your mind saying things like, "Hmmm! Who could I talk to who lights me up? Who might be an awesome ally? Who might see gems, truth, and humor in my predicament and also sees me in all the magic I am?"

Yes. When you know yourself — even when you just get curious — you can find humor, even in the darkness. You become the observer.

As you're curious, you face the truths of your heart.

And as you do that, you begin to know yourself more and more and spot what's not true. You begin to see more and more of your sparkle. More possibility. You begin to see through inner limiting thoughts, fears, or whatever is not true to your pure desires and your heart and take actions, through all that.

And then what happens? Your shadows and all those fears, limiting beliefs, and also the things in your life that are not aligned with your uniqueness and heart? They more and more melt away.

Your life becomes more and more sparkly.

All that is super powerful, yes?

I'm in this space right now where I feel I'm coming out of the muck. I'm getting better at decoding my mind. Getting to be okay if someone doesn't like what I do or say, or even says things that formerly used to trigger the crap out of me.

Like yesterday, a former boyfriend saw me as full of myself and arrogant. I was totally okay with that. Because I saw that was HIS story and his shadow. I was simply stating my desires and setting my boundaries. That was such a huge win for me!

I used to bend over backwards to NOT be seen as arrogant. Or this and that. Now, after having played with the concepts of this book, my coaches, and inner awareness for a while, I've released so many of such inner voices of why I CANNOT do something. Of why I WOULD NOT BE OKAY.

All illusions. All inner voices.

It is SO freeing to be yourself. Of course, we're always okay. Even more than before, I now actually fully take care of myself. By speaking my truth and by more and more being my sparkly, unique self.

I now have a practice to find (or at least become curious, then look for) the gem in everything! I feel peace. Even excitement!

And because of all that, I'm having WAY more fun.

We have all the power inside of us. The more we truly know ourselves and claim that the power we have in all choices, the more we claim our sparkle (and our brilliance.)

Now about the second gem! Let's decode that.

gem #2:
trusting the universe

When you have the pure trust into the universe, what does that mean?

Why is that so special? That's a huge topic that you'll have to experience for yourself. Let me sum it up for now:

You'll be free of worry, and you'll feel deep trust and peace.

Compare: sleepless nights of worry vs. sleeping in peace and knowing you're always taken care of. That's how your life can feel. Worry-free.

Compare frantically hustling all the time because you think you "have to," vs. doing very little and seeing things come together easily, in big ways, while you're coming from JOY. Knowing and trusting that the universe is also doing its magic in the background.

Whoa! You agree, that's a huge gem? Even if you're not there yet and can't fully feel it, that sounds mighty sweet, yes?

With Knowing Yourself and Trust (in yourself AND the universe), these two things alone, you can build your dream palace and your dream life. Knowing you're always going to be okay.

And these are the two huge gems you can find by playing with this book. There's no end game here. It's an evolving journey. This is for your life.

And here's another cool thing. This book is not linear. Like time. It also doesn't have to be linear. You may find big sparkle celebrations tomorrow! This minute!

In fact, if you want to play with this now, you can!

play prompt:

Close your eyes, and ask the universe to show you some of your own sparkle. This very moment. Then scroll blindly in the book and point a finger. What do you see? What does it inspire to right now?

Finding more of your sparkle can come in spurts and at any time. If you're open and pay attention to signs, that is.

The universe gives us signs ALL. THE. TIME.

For example, some people love to notice "angel numbers," like 4:44 or 1:11, as signs that they're supported by the universe.

I see signs everywhere now, reaffirming that I'm on the right path or giving me inner answers. Like painted rocks in the forest that have just the right symbolism for what I'm thinking about. Or I hear answers on TV on a topic I was just thinking about. Or I point my fingers into books to ask a question and then get inspired to just what I needed to see. Or I simply pause and listen to my heart.

You can get universe inspiration in any way you like.

How did I start getting my heart answers and seeing inspiring signs?

I started out following what inspired me. Being curious. For me, it started by finding just the right books. Or just the right person to help me with something. Or got just the right email at a time.

Follow the breadcrumbs that inspire you. You'll move ahead on your sparkle path and find more and more of your sparkle.

As you play with this book, you'll have epiphanies. You'll also be thrown on to the "no fun path" (where life happens, as they say).

Know that you may think you're back at the beginning. But you never are. It's always about finding new gems and releasing more dust from your sparkle diamond.

Of course, also pause, integrate, and take NEW ACTIONS. Out of the hamster wheel. Into choosing from your sparkle — your heart and your power.

And — even if you don't know this next piece yet or don't trust it yet —

Deep down, you know you're your own unique diamond. And very likely, deep down, you know that a higher power has your back.

That's what you knew as an innocent child. When you started your life. Remember? As kid? When you felt unstoppable? Dreamed limitless dreams? Where anything was possible?

This book will help you get you back to that.

Start dreaming. Big.

There's one more huge gem in my dream
(and in the magic of this book).

gem #3: ask for help

Remember what I did in my dream when I didn't know how to go any farther? That's when I started asking for help. I was never alone. I had people leaning in, wanting to help. And I started to allow support.

Knowing yourself and owning your sparkle also means asking for help. So give yourself permission to be fully supported.

When you know yourself (or when you're starting to become curious!), you will catch when your ego-mind tries to dictate things: "You don't deserve help/you have to do it alone/you need to make money first/this is too expensive ... (whatever your mind says.)"

I lost many years running such short-circuits. Without even noticing.

Catch such "you can't" voices. Make it a game. That's you finding gems.

Then keep only what's your sparkly you, and ditch the rest.
You'll do this automatically the more you play with this book.

And guess what. You are already doing it now!

play prompt:

Where are you not allowing yourself to be fully supported?
What resources are in front of you where your heart says yes, but your mind says no?

_____

_____

In what way does your mind object that you cannot have this support?

Spoiler alert: all the voices you just caught are all illusions. As long as you believe they're true, they will remain a limitation. If you shift to curiosity and let go of the how, you will begin to see possibilities.

This book will help you give yourself permission to be fully supported.

So you can be your very unique one-of-a-kind magical, world-changing, inspiring, amazing, fully sparkly you. Just by being you.

When you give yourself permission to be fully supported, you also give yourself permission to fully sparkle!

How does that work when there's a "real" limitation, you ask? Like when you don't have enough money in the bank? Or when you're born "on the wrong continent?" Or "don't have enough alone time with all the work around your kids and family..."

play prompt:

Observe what your mind says! Are you catching objections?

_____

_____

_____

This is great! This is you again catching limitations. Catching voices. In a moment, I'll give you a 1-2-3 to help you forward.

Just as heads-up: For this to work, you have to play with it. So roll with it. Give it a shot. WHATEVER limitations you just got.

You have to de-condition your mind bit by bit. De-dust your diamond. Give yourself permission to take time. Just take one play prompt at a time. There's only the present moment. No pressure. No rush. (Only the pressure your mind may try to put on you.)

You've got all your life to live and learn. And that's what you get to do with this book. So! Are you ready to get your 1-2-3?

This is how you give yourself "Permission To Sparkle:"
(aka "The Shadow Catch Game!")

1. STOP. Whenever something feels icky, you get triggered,
or feel stuck, observe your mind + catch what it says.
You catch the shadows.

2. Get CURIOUS. Rediscover (and ask!) yourself what your
heart truly wants. Discern between what's your heart's truth
and what feels true and what's your mind trying to hold you
back.

3. YOU CHOOSE which inner voice you listen to.
(Hint: choose what feels true and your power) Then allow
yourself to be fully supported by the universe and yourself.

Live CURIOUS-LY. Be curious.
And be your sparkly self.

Ready for an analogy that may boggle your mind?

$$1+1 = 11$$
$$1+1+1 = 111$$

When you team up,
your possibilities expand.

Whenever I team up with someone or invite someone in to help me, more ideas fly, and we inspire each other. We mirror things we can't see ourselves. Things become easier!

Everyone's possibilities exponentially expand.

(Obviously, this doesn't work with everyone. But the magic does happen when I choose someone who feels great, as I follow my heart.)

There's more. The energy rises. Ever been in an amazing, exciting brainstorm session? Where ideas flew like ping-pong balls? And everyone got more and more excited?

When we play with the universe and with others, we open portals of possibility.

Or, as my co-creator coach Jean Berry says, "portals of miracles."

And that's another magical thing you can learn in this book! :)

The more you play with it, tune into curiosity and into what is possible, the more you WILL find your sparkle, your possibility, and the more you will be living your dream life.

decoding the dream II:

(interpreting it now, two years later, as I'm wrapping up the book)

A lot has happened for me since I started writing this book. I went through a lot of challenges, learned a lot, and, instead of always staying on course and integrating my learnings — truly following my heart and my new knowing... I often prolonged my learnings and made things harder for me than necessary.

Until I ended up kind of losing myself. Also kind of like in this dream. All kinds of things around me seemed to break. And fall away. A car accident. Relationships. Me judging myself for lots of it.

Me thinking I was all alone. And hating it.

I'm realizing today that of course it was me who caused all of this. By not listening to my heart. Prolonging stories where I already felt it was NO. Recreating same-old-story scenarios.

I made things harder than they needed to be.

Yes, you can say that also kind of served me. I chose this. Chose more learning experiences to learn something. Truly land my soul lessons.

However. We also always have a choice. We choose our adventure. You can choose to listen to your heart right here, right now, or ignore it and then take some longer paths.

You choose when you're done with an experience and ready to play a different game (i.e., you learned something and then live differently.)

The heart voice is definitely the fast track. Not always the easiest. But the one that truly leads to your sparkle.

And the more we do that, the more the REAL FUN BEGINS.

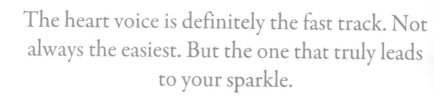

play prompt:

What experiences / feelings / things / people in your life do you no longer want? What do you want to experience instead?

_____

_____

Is your mind throwing any shade at you right now? Objections / judgments / voices as to why you cannot do or get that…?

_____

Catch the voices. Then take whatever tiny little action toward what you WANT right now that is COMING FROM YOUR HEART.

Now let the book and the sparkle adventures begin!

how I transformed my life into sparkle

how this chapter helps:

I wrote this chapter after finishing this book. Interestingly, I had "forgotten" to write this chapter when I sent it to my editor. The title was there, but not the chapter. Oh-so perfect. (Another synchronicity, perfect timing.) Now I get to write this to you in hindsight, after upgrading myself from "Princess" to "Queen."

Read this to get my key points on how I got here!

So! Let me begin intuitively, just like I also let this whole book roll out. And what intuitively comes to me is to first share a few highlights and stories. (For the full experience, keep playing with this book!)

Then I'll give you some KEY INSIGHTS and big sister tips.

Here's where I was and who I was at this book's beginning. And how I used to dim my sparkle.

I was in a marriage where I fit myself in (though I didn't know that yet.). I was not fully speaking my truths, and I was putting myself second. Literally, in so many areas of life. Being the good girl. Polite.

I was limiting myself to happy social times on Fridays, where I got tipsy with friends — good times, but it didn't <u>really</u>, fully feed my soul. I fit myself in. Wasn't really expressing my own interests and stories. (My limiting story was "they don't care — they're not spiritually interested or not entrepreneurs, not creative like me, not...")

I was also <u>not</u> treating myself to things I wanted because I felt that I couldn't afford them yet... Buying cheap stuff. Not eating well. Not buying my own stuff. I was truly, and in so many ways, hiding my light.

Actually AFRAID of my light. Thinking I wouldn't be relatable if I was fully me. People wouldn't understand. Wouldn't care to hear me. My ultimate fear behind it was that I'd hurt people by outshining them (too much! Too rich! Too all kinds of things!) — and also that THEY wouldn't love me as all of me, and I'd end up alone.

So I hid behind ALL KINDS OF THINGS. Internally sabotaged myself.

For example, I collaborated with others rather than fully trust my own power. "You do the sales; I'm not good at that." "Let's do marketing together; it's easier." Or, "You see the magic of this client, you say it. (I'm not as intuitive as you.)"

I wasn't trusting my own intuition and heart, not daring to speak it yet, and also taking all kinds of easy ways out.

Which, of course, conveniently kept me small. In hiding.

Sex? Love? Oh my god, I told myself I'm too old; I can be okay with little. ("Isn't it normal that it becomes less once you're together for a while?") No more hand-holding or cuddling...? I thought, "It's okay." I literally saw myself as "prudish" and saw that as part of my identity. I just accepted things as they were. It was comfortable. "Okay."

It's NOT effing okay.

You do not have to dim ANY of your desires.

You do not have to fit in.

You do not have to silence yourself and not even <u>speak</u> your desires.

I had so many voices in my head. Like we all do — it's normal. In my case, I grew up thinking it's a good trait to be humble, be nice, be agreeable... saying "it's okay." I wasn't used to even listening to my heart or what I really wanted. Total auto-pilot. "It's okay." "You say!" "Sure!"

Of course, I'm painting a bit of an extreme picture. I also enjoyed a lot of it. Made choices. Selected restaurants. Camping adventures. Followed my heart to move to a whole different continent. Started several businesses.

Yet.

I had stories like, "oh, but I can't have everything. I'd be demanding. He's already so nice to me. How much do you WANT, Astrid?"

If you translate that, it's like a mother tells her kid, "be happy with the birthday gift you got. You don't get to have what you TRULY want."

What kind of mother is THAT?

I was betraying my heart again and again. The things seemed little (my mind telling me so), but they added up. And it was a deep, inner hurtful thing for my whole system that I kept doing again and again... And it started piling up.

Not only did my reality begin to feel stagnant, it also started to feel more and more separate. I literally locked myself in my room, trying to create a world-changing, heart-open spiritual business while my then-hubby was watching war movies in the living room. Put to the extreme, that's how the contrast felt.

By not speaking up, I had created my own birdcage and imprisonment.

We are meant to shine our BRILLIANCE.
Meant to speak our desires.
Meant to <u>experience</u> them.

We are meant to have the whole freaking
birthday, Christmas, and Easter experience.
With all the chocolates, sex toys or whatever
the heck we want. We are meant to live our
heart's desires, our dreams fully alive.

To experience that, I had to learn to give myself "Permission To
Sparkle." Which began with giving myself permission to speak.

Once I started doing that (you'll see many examples in this book), my
desires ALWAYS manifested. Sometimes instantly, in an "of course! I'm
glad you told me!" way, and sometimes taking longer. Yes, sometimes
things shifted in my reality, and sometimes people did fall away. But
always, ultimately, things worked out. And always better than I could
have imagined.

I always ended up BETTER than "okay."
I always ended up upgrading my reality.

play prompt:

What makes you happy? What do you want? Pause for a second and think where in your life you may be dimming your light.

_____

_____

> You'll manifest what you ask for.
> So better ask for what you <u>really</u> want.

P.S. All the people in your life who care about you will thank you. They DO want to know your true desires. Not guess. How else do they even stand a CHANCE to fulfill them? Or to experience them WITH you?

Yes, it takes guts sometimes to speak our desires. But surprisingly:

> Giving in to my limiting voices and fears
> ALWAYS hurt me more than
> me speaking my truth.

What else was I experiencing BEFORE I claimed my sparkle? And before I claimed my queen?

Ridiculous prices. Not seeing my value. Offering my work for peanuts. Getting butt-hurt when no one would show up. Feeling I had to prove my value to people. Feeling I wasn't seen. Not appreciated. Where ironically, it was ME not truly revealing or appreciating myself. ;-)

Doing. All. The. Things. Yet not really seeing my business moving forward. Not in significant ways.

I was not aware and not in control of my mind games.

What's happening now is I'm starting to live in my true power. Following intuition. Taking inspired action. Being in balance.

Listening to my heart, and taking actions from joy.

Okay, so how DID I get from no-sparkle to sparkle, and then to QUEEN? This sounds so simple!

The first step was that I decided to give myself permission.

To fully show up for myself. To no longer hide. Not believing my inner limitations. But choosing to heal them. Transform them.

I started saying YES.

I started listening more and more to my intuition. And acting on it.

And because of that, AMAZING resources started to show up for me, which often challenged my bravery. But every time I followed my gut, I hugely benefited.

I started to release more and more limitations I was holding in my mind, my energy field, my system — even from past life experiences — ANYTHING that was (or still is) in the way of me shining my light.

I wanted to be free. To create my dream life. To <u>live</u> my full life adventure and all my inner soul's desires and dreams. Not just dream.

I began to actually SPEAK MY TRUTH.

Became curious about what I TRULY WANT. In all life areas.

play prompt:

Getting triggered by this? Where in your life do you think you cannot have all you want? What are your mind's voices?

What stories have you been telling yourself?

_____

_____

_____

What stories do you WANT to START telling yourself? (Ignoring the "how" — for now. Ignoring worry. Worry actually keeps you stuck.)

In the game of All Is Possible, what are your voices now?

_____

_____

Yes. Following the gut takes guts.
And. Things always work out.

A deep gut feeling that I needed to leave my marriage? I followed that.

Even without knowing where I'd live, how I'd pay rent, or why and what. Just trusting and following my heart.

We never really know anyway, right? We only THINK we do. We are comfortable in apparent securities. We give away our power to comfort. To appearances that make us feel safe.

Those trust funds? The job? Anything can change. Right?

Are you <u>really</u> in danger? No.

As I learned to SPEAK my truth, TRUST my truth, and trust MY SELF, the next puzzle piece always showed up.

And what's happening NOW in my life? As "queen?" I'm a new person. I more and more fully express myself. I cranked up the volume. Keep cranking it.

This is a photo I just posted yesterday on Facebook:

Me showing up fully, as my new me, awakening my inner queen, February 22, 2020

I went platinum. Will get black ombré. Because I feel like it. Because it feels INTUITIVELY RIGHT. And LIGHTS ME UP. I had no idea what it would look like. And didn't care.

I got my nails done. First time ever acrylic nails. Having so much FUN! Seeing myself as canvas. Why not! I LOVE it.

I'm becoming my own Pinterest board.

You THINK you cannot have all the things. WHO SAYS?

What else is happening?

I have a super magical love life. Like, amazing. Ah. Mah. Zing. AND I have all the freedom that I wanted.

Whenever something doesn't feel right, I decree my new desires, and my reality upgrades. No attachment to "how." Things always land again more magical.

My business?

Well, as you're reading this now, my book is published, and maybe you're in one of my programs. You'll see that I actually went from ground zero and nothing to having whatever you see now going on.

Question is...

HOW BIG do YOU WANT TO PLAY?

get your feet wet.

(In these chapters, you prepare to play,
and find things to get you going again.)

(Also. Literally. When you're stuck, get moving.
Go outside. Even if it's raining. Like it is here today.)

make space to play

how this chapter helps:

This chapter helps you feel safe and start allowing more sparkle.

To embark on your sparkle adventure, here's an important first step:

play prompt:

Create space to play.

* Physically: a place to journal, play, get creative and inspired about how to bring more sparkle into your life.

* Time: space in your calendar. Time just for you that feels good, spacious, and sacred. Where you don't feel pressured or distracted.

Why?

Well, if you don't have time and space that feels inspiring, without pressure, and it's not anywhere in your calendar or held as sacred "me-time," by you, do you think you'll actually use this book?

Neither do I! It didn't work for me either!
So, do this first.

Having an inner "hell, no!" moment?

And you're here and did not put it in your calendar? That's okay.

play prompt:

If your mind is giving you objections as to why you cannot make <u>any</u> space to play with this book... It's for you to question it. And then again, put your own desires first. You want more sparkle in your life? Then stay curious. A few thoughts you might be having:

★   Holy crap. What did I get myself into? Do I have time for this? Yes. You'll actually have MORE time the more "sparkly" you are. Peace and freedom are part of this game — and you'll find it if you stay to play!

★   OMG. JOY? Play? I don't know how to play! I'm not used to journaling or the, like... Ah! The famous "I'm not enough." I get it. It's one that shows for many of us when we embark on new dreams! All good. You're perfect just where you are. And you are enough. You don't need to know everything — or ANYthing. Just be curious. :)

★   "I can't work and play at the same time." (Is it even possible to have both?) Yes! I'm living this now, every day. This will be one of the huge benefits you get, as you become more "sparkly!" You design your life to feel more and more great!

★   Or your mind might slam full **STOP! On the brakes!** And have something else to say as to why this is a bad idea...?

All this is normal. Whenever we embark on a dream, our mind (or our body!) has something to say because change is uncomfortable. That does NOT mean you have to stop. On the contrary. It's an awesome opportunity to notice, tune into your heart again, overcome any limiting beliefs, bad feelings, or fears, and grow.

The universe just brings all these up so you clear them.

Basically...

Whatever is not the frequency of your dream + desires will come up for you to release!

So! If your mind is telling you some "can't" stories here, just write them down, and for now, simply acknowledge them. Sometimes that's all it takes to release them — getting them out of your system!

_____

_____

_____

play prompt:

Then make SOME space to play. It can be five minutes a day. What's your favorite time? It can be in a corner of a room when everyone is out. That's how I started out. It can be in a coffee shop 15 minutes before going to work. You pick! Take dominion over your schedule. ;-)

PERMISSION TO SPARKLE – a play-lightenment book by Astrid Mueller

fun fact:

"Who works out in six minutes? You won't even get your heart going, not even a mouse on a wheel."
– Hitchhiker, in *Something About Mary*

We actually can shift into SPARKLE in less than five minutes.
And we can change our brain and our habits in just five minutes a day.

All it takes is a true desire, and then put that "darn fun thing that will make your life more sparkly" in your calendar. ;-)

play prompt:

15 minutes tops. Pick one and do it. You'll feel more sparkly right now.

I. Your calendar. What can you CLEAR that doesn't feel good? What feels unnecessary? Can you group things together, and suddenly you have a free spot?

What time could you SET as ME-TIME for yourself?
What can be your SPARKLE PLAY TIME with this book?
(P.S. My editor had the great inspiration here that you could put sparkly stickers in your calendar to save sacred sparkle space. Or stars! You pick! Fun!)

2. **Your muse space** Where would you love to learn/craft/read/get inspired? Where would you love to sit with this book and play with it?

Can you clear a spot or make a little room?

If you don't have a full space, you can grab a bag. I have my laptop and magic "play bag" for writing this sparkle book. I sometimes take them to the beach or to the coffee shop.

play prompt:

More declutter for more feel-good! It's AMAZING what clearing space can do for our energy field. Two more suggestions if you're on a roll:

1. **Your computer.** How does your computer feel to you? Like hard work? If yes, delete some stuff and make some space. On the outside or any area that you don't like associated with it.

Example: I just grabbed a Windex bottle, cleaned my computer, and cleared my desktop, so I only see my pretty background picture. It feels SO FRESH, FREE, and GOOD now.

Also, I ordered myself a laptop shell that I loved (mine has a funky orange and green ombré going) and a keyboard that's all kinds of unicorn-fart rainbow colors.

2. Your closet. Is there any piece in there that you can give away to charity? Picture how you'll light someone up with it. Feel the love and gratitude. And how good it feels to make space! Then put it in bag to drop it off tomorrow.

feel safe to sparkle

Whenever we pursue something new, especially big dreams, we stretch our comfort zone. When we stretch our comfort zone, we get uncomfortable.

Great! This is normal. It means that we're growing.

When we stay in a box, we stay small. When we grow, we bust out of our boxes! Of course! And that's naturally uncomfortable.

A bit like growing pains.

You don't have to play alone. Find access to support spaces on my website. Find play buddies. This is a safe place to learn, grow, share, and support each other, with others who also play the "Permission To Sparkle" adventure.

We're all born fearless. Babies fall. So, what? They get up again. They are practiced in falling, so it's no big deal. As we grow older, we fall out of practice of falling. And then we start playing it safe. We get complacent.

The longer we don't dare, the less we dare.

So practice daring. Again and again.

Also, almost worse, we start telling ourselves that it's NOT okay to dare.
Not okay to play. NOT okay to sparkle. For all kinds of reasons.

It's time to debunk all those BS voices that don't serve us anymore.

It's time you dare to play again.
It's time you reclaim
your sparkle.

play prompts:

* What thoughts, if any, came up for you? Any freak-out voices of why you cannot play? Or sparkle? Of why whatever you want right now is not possible?

* How would you let your younger self know that how your mind is holding you back here is cold coffee? And not helpful?

* What beliefs or old experiences can you heal, or let go of, to dare to play bigger again and just be you?

_____

_____

_____

What can you do (that might be a little uncomfortable, a little dare) to make your life more sparkly right now?

_____

_____

<u>how</u> do you like to play?

how this chapter helps:

It's time to rediscover how to play. This unlocks your own inner treasure chest of joy! Your engine forward. Your path to happy. Here, you connect with the EXCITEMENT and SPARKLE of being YOU!

So! You have set sacred sparkle play time in your calendar. (If not, go back to the last chapter and take that play prompt there to do it.)

play prompt:

Put yourself in the shoes of you as a little child for a moment and ask: How did you like to play? What did you love most to play with?

_____

_____

_____

For instance some of the things I've always loved are clear transparent, bubbly-shaped things. And that is STILL the case for me. It still reflects in my choice of pens, journals, and generally, what fun things I like to surround myself with (or let go of) in my office.

How about you? What kind of writing or drawing things make you want to play? Get creative?

play prompt:

Now if you think about yourself today, as grown-up, and about playing with this book to bring more sparkle into your life, how can you take your child play fascinations forward to play with this book today?

How do you love to learn about yourself?

Do you love to journal? Draw? Doodle? Have a cool sparkly folder to collect inspiring things? Scrapbook? Take notes? Just read? Learn by doing? Learn by movement? Anything goes. Surround yourself with tools and things that inspire you to play, and get a little creative.

Creativity is magical. You'll find a lot of pondering prompts in this book. If you use art materials to play, color, process, journal, express yourself, and think, they'll get you out of the spin-cycle of your mind and help you find your best wisdom gems.

Also, it helps to have things around you that inspire you to take breaks, play, and get silly — to STOP thinking. Your best ideas will always come from your heart.

play prompt:

Now get your play tools. Like markers, a journal you like, and any embellishments or paints and tools and things that feel inspiring to you.

Manifesting tip: Collecting your play tools can be easy. And cheap. Play with manifesting magic! Manifesting is easy when you SPARKLE.

Here's a quick story and mini-manifesting master class:

I'm really good at manifesting awesome things in thrift stores. Why? For me, that's an easy area where my mind does not get in the way. I literally manifest anything and everything I need there.

And that's even here in the boonies, on remote Kodiak Island, Alaska.

You'd think you wouldn't find cool things here? Wrong. Anything is possible. Anywhere. (Key is that you don't believe otherwise.) I've even found designer stuff, sparkle, glitter, tropical island stuff, millionaire yacht-feeling stuff... anything.

play prompt:
magic manifesting shopping!

Go to a thrift store or shop that you like where shopping feels easy (you feel no money pressure.) Make a wish (like: crafting stuff that totally lights you up to embellish your sparkle journal or things that make you feel like your most happy abundant sparkle self!), then walk into the store, curious. That's it! Allow the universe to surprise you. I ALWAYS find exciting things that fit my wish and light me up.

find your guides and play buddies

how this chapter helps:

This chapter gives you the foundation and support you need to fully sparkle and realize your dreams. This is especially for business owners, but you can also translate this to your life. Use it as inspiration no matter what — we all need powerful support in our life adventure — here you get inspired to choose + find it powerfully!

Believe it or not, this was one of my biggest blocks in my business — AND life for many years. I stood in the way of my own sparkle path, my own adventure, because I didn't give myself permission to be fully supported.

In my case, I had a HUGE limiting belief: "I cannot afford this."

I had already "failed" (in my critical mind) with other businesses. I made it mean something about me. And then made-up beliefs to protect myself from the risk of repeating such stories. Such bullsh!t we tell ourselves.

Nothing is a failure. I actually <u>chose</u> to move on. And had gathered a lot of learnings. (Side note: calling ourselves a failure is judgment. An inner shadow voice. Hello, inner bully!)

Also, money always shows up. My scarcity fear was just a mind game. When you say yes, the universe (and resources) always show up.

Remember the magical key of living curiously? State your desires, then let it go, and simply stay curious. And shift back to living curiously! Expressing yourself, enjoying yourself, being all you.

When I told myself, "I cannot afford this or that training/group /resource that I felt I needed," I was effectively and energetically blocking myself from moving forward.

And guess what: as the energy-matching universe rolls, because I didn't invest in myself like a queen, I also didn't attract queens. I attracted non-clients who also didn't invest in themselves.

This isn't about money. It's about energy. It's about trusting. When something feels like SPARKLY SUPPORT to you, follow your heart, and say YES TO YOURSELF.

And then the universe will make that happen for you.

Anything becomes possible when we give ourselves permission to be fully supported. That means we are open to fully receive.

Now I'm not saying you have to purchase all the coaching and resources out there and that you cannot do anything on your own. I'm saying that when your heart, instincts, gut, and whole being are telling you YES to something (insert universe halleluiah chime) —^ and you totally feel "YES, this feels perfect," and you may not even know why or how this will work out, but you just have to do it....

Then follow your hunches.

It sometimes takes bravery!

Our mind might not see how this can work yet. Sometimes it can't!

That was another one of my limitations for a long time. Not believing something until I see it. And letting this thought hold me back.

That's so silly now that I think back to this! Imagine only believing that a cake is possible when you see the whole cake, and you cannot trust it when you just assemble the first ingredients?

Me holding myself back kind of was like saying, "I'm not going to bake, it's no use, I don't see a cake, so I don't believe it works… SO I WON'T DO IT."

Ha! Now I laugh! Back then, I believed it.

And that's how we tell ourselves tons of bullsh!t.

When you notice yourself saying NO to something that feels YES, catch those voices. And be brave. Even if what you feel called to doesn't immediately make sense.

Here's a stepping stone for you — this one is free (actually you're getting it because you already paid for this book, so yay! See! How saying yes pays off?) Here's some support for you, coming right up:

Remember *The Wizard of Oz*? Here's a warm welcome from Glinda the good witch, and me.

That was one of my favorite childhood movies. Glinda, the good witch, is also showing up here in my "Permission To Sparkle" story. She's welcoming you to your adventure!

Know that all is well, and whatever happens, you are safe. As Glinda would say, "You've always had the power, my dear!"

Whatever fears and old stories you picked up in your life, starting from when you were a kid, are all (at this moment in your life) illusions. They may or may not have been accurate warnings at the time. Today, they're simply relating to old stories. And whatever you made things mean then.

You're the hero of your life adventure. You've got everything you need to take care of yourself now. And the universe is always, always by your side. You'll also get some magical play tools in this "Permission To Sparkle" game! And... you don't have to walk alone.

play prompts:

Meet your guides + find your play buddies! Many are already here! All you have to do right now is take a small inspired action. PICK ONE (you can always pick more, but start with one and get 'er done.)

1. Find a support group. Come to my website for access to support spaces or find another group that FEELS powerful and SPARKLY to you. Where do other dream-chasers like you hang out who fully say yes to themselves and their dream?

2. Find play buddies. Who do you resonate with? Make it a point to connect with someone as you follow your heart. And if you resonate with them, see if you want to become an adventure play support buddy with that person or them!

Fun idea: Share your wins and gem-find celebrations in the group you're both in. That way, you're celebrating AND being seen (i.e., growing your network, and clients may also see you).

Pick people who LIGHT YOU UP. And people who are lit up by you as well. Don't be afraid to say no if it's not the right vibe, right time, or right fit. Nothing personal.

"Be an energy snob. You choose
who gets another second."
– Jenn August
(one of my favorite coaches)

3. Connect with your universe support team Depending where you're at in your spiritual growth journey, you may be used to calling in Archangel Michael, your guides, or another spirit support team. If not, no worries! Just be curious. And ask for universe support in whatever way feels good to you.

One of my dear colleagues, mentors, and friends, Lois Warnock, helps people get messages from their spirit guides in her coaching. She also just came out with a Spirit Guide deck that's super magical, where you can play and get wisdom from your spirit guides on your own. Find her at www.LoisWarnock.com.

Or, you can simply ask from your heart, "Who is my spirit guide or divine support team right now?" Then see if you feel your heart tells you something. Maybe you just notice that you feel good. You might get a message. A word pop in your head. Or you see or hear something around you.

Whether you believe it or not, the universe supports you. The more you look around yourself and celebrate, with gratitude, all the things you already have in your life that support you, the more you'll notice your support, and the more it grows too! (Yup, what we focus on grows! True!)

4. Play with this book + the "Permission To Sparkle" game. You'll get powerful answers as you pause and listen to your heart.

5. Coaches / Teachers / Mentors / Consultants / Guides ... When you are READY for your BIGGER dreams to take shape, allow yourself to find a guide. I do that all the time. To heal old energies, learn new skills, mirror blind spots and superpowers (Hello! Sometimes it's the hardest thing to see our own brilliance), for strategy, and for helping me train myself to see through my (not real) limiting stories. Also, to be in spaces with other dream-chasers and business peers!

TIP: As with everything, pick coaches not because you feel you "have to," or by "what you think you can afford" (or whatever else your mind tells you cannot do), but from your heart.

Also, be careful with coaches who do GURU-STYLE coaching (who might tell you that "you have to do it this way or you won't succeed!").

Nothing works for everyone. If you don't listen to your heart and think you "need" someone's system in order to make it, that can be totally counter-productive, totally STALL you, and you may even blame yourself later for not moving forward. And pile on more inner-critic shadows.

I found the only "system" that truly works is our intuition and following our heart.

That may guide you <u>to</u> someone's system <u>for something</u>, but you have to keep trusting your own heart. That's where you'll find your best inspired ideas to create the most magical things that light you up.

Choose what works for YOU. Again, you only find that by listening to your heart, your intuition, and your gut. Not your limiting mind. I've limited myself before by trying so hard, someone else's system, and then trying to figure it out... yet, I've found the most amazing answers listening to my spirit guide team.

Like a brilliant new marketing strategy, while I was looking at the sun by the ocean, just sitting with it!

Get resources and a support team that LIGHTS YOU UP, empowers you, and helps you find what works for YOUR life/business. Not everyone needs a million-dollar marketing system. Not everyone needs to do Facebook Live. Or even be on Facebook. Do what serves YOU.

6. Mastermind groups. Peer groups or mastermind groups can be a great idea — if the members match your intentions, your values, and they genuinely care about your success. And if, like you, they also say yes to themselves! Look for a group that feels amazing, where your heart says, "heck yes!"

(Then use whatever input you get there as inspiration, while following your own instincts and desires.)

hot tip:

Whatever you choose, if it feels like "should," don't do it.

You don't even have to do everything on this list. Pick what feels right and what lights you up.

But do take at least one action inspired by one of the points in this list. Without a support team or peers, it's a long and lonely ride and easy to get hung up or procrastinate. Also, with others, it's way more fun!

★

how to **get going** with this book!

how this chapter helps:

Is your mind telling you that you need HELP to get going...? Is that even true? You already came this far, right?

This chapter helps you to KEEP going. And expand the fun. And get your mind on board <u>even more</u>. So that you will be excited to <u>keep</u> going. And to spark your dream life even more!

Why is getting your mind on board so important?

Well, if your mind won't say yes, you won't take any steps!

It's like getting permission from your parents to play again. Only this is even more important than going to your favorite amusement park...

You came here to give yourself permission to LOVE UP and SPARKLIFY YOUR DREAM LIFE.

play prompt:

Notice how you feel. Where are you at right now?

If you just want to get going with this book (and your mind may have been beating you up why you haven't done so yet!), you're in the right place. This chapter helps you get started in an easy way.

If you feel you're not even in the mood for sparkle and your mind is going in circles, you'd like to snap out of it, go to the nourishment chapter for quick tools, a hug, and a cuppa chai.

If you're feeling like SH!T!!!, go to the "when sh!t hits the fan" emergency chapters or get help. (Disclaimer: this book is magical, but sometimes we need more. Call 911 or a professional.)

Here's the place for you if you're all kinds of stuck or feeling non-sparkly (even like sh!t! but ready to do something about it).

Ready?

I'm glad you asked!

First, here's something sweet.

a lollipop!

(Because you're here to enjoy yourself.)
Did I just see you crack a smile? Good. Sometimes we just need to snap
out of our head and start getting a little silly.

Now, a little creative action: have

a doodle-pop!

Color it! Or doodle your own. Make it purposefully JUST ALL ABOUT PLAY. Not perfect. Even ugly. Use any colors or materials or even the good old blue pen. But the premise here is to have fun. And get you out of your head. Express yourself! Have at it!

play prompts:

mind "snap!"

What if your mind just keeps saying things like, "I've got no time," "This is silly!" or "I should be working, not playing"?

First of all, know that EVERYTHING your (rational) mind tells you is kind of limited. If it did not come from your inspiration and intuition and your heart, it's based on the past.

In reality, anything is possible, and you always get to choose. The logical mind — especially the inner shadow voices — only see what's been and limitations. The big picture always comes from the heart.

Also! If your mind tells you "you should be working" — this might be your inner bully acting as your inner slave driver!

Do a quick all-body shake-off, then mellow out, take a few slow breaths, and close your eyes.

What does your heart say? What does it want you to do for yourself right now? Is there an action? An ask? A desire?

Follow that. Take action from there.

body hurrah!

This is a great activation of your superpowers to see and feel that you're actually really in the perfect place and doing amazing.

1. Stand up and celebrate yourself with a pose for showing up for yourself and being here. Make it a good one. Really feel that pose for a minute. It will activate your whole system with whatever they call the body chemicals that sparkle up your energy and mojo!

2. Do ONE tiny thing that makes you feel sparkly. Like putting on a hot lipstick. Or whatever your heart tells you to do. Go.

   (What I got inspired to do was take a break, eat a snack, more water, and relocate with my laptop outside. Now I'm here, like at a business retreat, posh hotel, with snacks by my side. Nourishing myself AS I do business things. Feeling sparkly.)

3. Now ask yourself when do you want to bring more such ME TIME SPARKLE TIMES into your calendar for yourself? Like another time today? A time every day? When do you want to dedicate sparkle moments to use this book to play? Then make it sacred. Set a timer. It will bring you magic, new energy, and new inspiration for everything in your life!

And then, whenever your energy drops, stop. Do a nourishing thing. Or another play prompt in this book. Whatever your heart tells you to do.

It doesn't matter WHAT you do — it just matters that you do take moments to feed your JOY. Make it a practice. Put up some kind of playful reminder for yourself that you see every time you walk by.

Do something that will inspire you to snap out of your routine and play several times a day.

It doesn't matter how long your play moments are. But the more you allow play-bursts to be a THING in your life, the more you'll sparkle!

(I just had some bubble tea. Sucking up those berries made me giggle. One actually made a squeaking sound. Perfect. More SPARKLE VIBE!)

Did you just do a play burst that made you feel real good? Share it with your sparkle play buddy or your support group! It will help you make it a habit and also inspire others! I'm currently sending my singing teacher a quick text message every time I sang and practiced.

Time for another celebration pose!

Well done.

your why.

Why are you here? Why and in what way do you want your life to be more sparkly?

This is a great journaling prompt for a coffee shop. It connects you to WHY you're here in this adventure and to what really matters to you.

Most of the time, many people run on auto pilot. And then one day they wake up and wonder where all the time went. You came here to sparkle.

So pause, and listen deeply to what your heart says.

This gets you off the hamster wheel and back in the driver's seat!

Be gentle with yourself. Sometimes when we think about our desires and dreams (especially the big ones!), fears, intense feelings, or even body reactions may come up. (Hello, kink in the neck, or pit in the stomach!) Allow the emotions to just be. Don't run.

Trust there will be sparkle.

possibility journaling:

I'll give you a bunch of journaling prompts in a moment.

Take one question at a time, then pause, and be curious. You don't have to journal all of them, just start and see which ones inspire you. Notice what thoughts come up, how your body feels. Is there an area in your body that has something to say? Be curious, and take note.

You can journal, record yourself as you're talking out loud, go for a walk, or doodle! Craft! Or play with a play buddy! Any kind of self-expression as you ponder these will help you process + find gems!

Ask yourself questions like:

* What does my dream life look like when I dare to play full-out, owning and rocking all my superpowers, doing what I love, loving everything about my life, feeling in flow... all is easy... feeling like I fully SPARKLE?

* Is it okay to SPARKLE? Why not? What is my mind saying?

* What happens if I DON'T SPARKLE?

* Where have I been telling myself NOT to sparkle? Why?

* What happens if you only sparkle PART TIME?

* What happens to my relationships when I sparkle?

* Can I make money while sparkling?

* What scares me about being fully sparkly?

* How may it affect my abundance flow if I don't sparkle?

* How may it affect my HEALTH?

* How will other people view me while I sparkle?

* How may it affect others when I sparkle?
  How may it affect them if I don't?

put on sparkle shoes.

A mini visualization. Get in a comfortable position, then take a few slow breaths and close your eyes. Then imagine looking down on your feet and seeing your magical, sparkly adventure shoes that give you superpowers to access and find your most magical you!

What do your shoes look like?

Do they have a message for you?

Close your eyes + listen.

(My visualized shoes looked pointy and long, and I got this message: "I'm magical and a (good) witch!" Of course. Lol.)

sparkle feeling connection

Set the intention to connect with your SPARKLE.

Imagine a moment in your life where you felt totally lit up, happy, sparkly, daring to be fully you. This can be a childhood memory or an imaginary scenario in your dream future.

Note how you feel. Write down three to five words. Keep these in your heart — we'll call them your SPARKLE FEELINGS.

Your three words are: _____   _____   _____

Now! Keeping your SPARKLE FEELINGS in your heart...
Pick any of the following that excites you:

* ★ Dance to a song that makes you think of these sparkle feelings! (Just close your eyes, take a deep breath, and ask the universe, "What song can make me feel these SPARKLE FEELINGS?"

* ★ Make a collage of what you being SPARKLY feels like.

* ★ Dress up! Go to your wardrobe and pick out clothes that feel like these sparkle feelings (and get rid of others that don't)!

* ★ Go to a store + be curious: What might you find that makes you feel the power of your true sparkly self? This doesn't have to be expensive. I love doing this in thrift stores!

* ★ Create a doodle-dala[d] and see what emerges. Just play – even with your eyes closed! That's how I do my intuitive drawings.

* ★ Pick your own idea _____

The last one is a special gem, because it comes from your own "sparkle generator" — your HEART. Close your eyes and listen to your heart, then pick your own sparkle action!

P.S. You can also raise your vibe by asking yourself, "What do I need to see or do for myself right now?" then go to any page with your eyes closed. And take action from whatever inspiration you get.

---

[d] I got this idea to make doodle-mandalas, which I call "doodle-dalas." They're powerful frequency-shifters and fun. See here how to make one https://youtu.be/zpA6t6nHxnc

pause and let it go

Still not fully on board with your mind to keep going with this book now?

Cool. Time for a break.

(You'll know when the book calls you again to keep going!)

The harder you try to do something, the harder it won't happen ;-)

What do you want to play with for more sparkle right now?

You can do things like...

* Go for a walk, or a run, or enjoy nature...

* Take a shower — I get so many great ideas there!

* Sleep! Yes, sleep! You can ask a question to your subconscious before you sleep, then be curious what you'll wake up with!

* Take a vacation day, until you feel rested and excited again!

TIP: Always have something to write with you, to catch whatever "a-ha"s and gems you'll suddenly find. Stay curious.

I've often wanted a notepad in the shower.
(Has anyone invented that yet?)

jump into the puddle!

(Let the bigger sparkle game begin!
Disclaimer. There will be some deep dives.)
(ooooo shadow voices trying to make it scary.)

Spoiler alert: I survived.
AND came out more sparkly
because of the deep dives.)

me at the edge of a cliff - **and my sparkle**

how this chapter helps:

This is another real-time account — a crazy-ass one. Me literally facing mission impossible, stepping through it, and coming out on the other side, out of the shadows.

Read this as inspiration that anything is possible.

As I'm writing this, it's August 8, 2020. I thought I was done writing the book. Just doing last edits, wrapping up. Yet, it just hit me that where I'm at, this needs to be in here.

Where I'm at could be — in a human perspective — seen as ridiculous. Me on a cliff.

I know I'm in a pickle. And I <u>decide</u> to pull out of the shadows.

story time.

About three months ago, some of my inner circle coaches lovingly yet firmly showed me that I was in deep, crazy-ass shadowland.

I felt I had it all together in my business and life, was showing up in calls cheering others on, feeling as if I was sparkly!

Yet...

Deep inside, hardly admitting or realizing it myself, I was feeling like a pressure cooker. Not happy. My relationships and financials actually felt all wrong.

I was in a relationship that I didn't REALLY want anymore, still entangled with my ex-hubby emotionally, not having fully processed being alone. And my bank accounts: a disaster! (That, of course, is a voice of judgment. But also, here's a human reality. Which can simply be. Without inner judgment. It was time to do something.)

See for yourself. My bank accounts as I'm writing this:

ASTRID ACCOUNTS
Aftermath of shadows on the loose.
And me now reclaiming me.

assets	owing	owning
PayPal		0
CU1 personal checking		160.44
CU1 biz checking		272
CU1 personal CC	7265	
Bank of A personal CC	10500	
Bank of A biz CC	2250	
Swiss personal checking		1500
Swiss personal CC	1500	
Swiss savings		100
TOTALS	21000	2000

income sources / mo	now	potential
dog walking	500	1000
house sitting (covid n/a)		1100
some business thing now		2000
me		unlimited

If you're in the USA and it's around 2020 as you're reading this, you get the idea that I'm running out of cash. And see, that 500 per month (from my doggie sit side gig) most likely will NOT cover my expenses.

From a "rational" view, I'll be effectively at 0 at the end of the month.

So! Where am I at in all of this? And what am I doing about it?

Well, this morning, I woke up with anxiety, even before putting the numbers on paper. Heavy cloud on my heart. Inner voices going wild.

"You're not safe! Alert! Alert! Get up! Do something! Fast! You're running out of cash! EVERYTHING is disappearing. You spent all retirement now, you have no clients, and now you'll also have to stop working with your coaches... you DEFINITELY can't pay them $1,500 per month at this level. You NEED to DO something!!"

It was not a good feeling in my body, as you can imagine. In fact, I felt a sense of PANIC!

So what did I do?

One, I STOPPED. I got UP. (Instead of staying in bed at 6 am in this mind-spin craziness.)

Two, I opened one of my meditation apps — the "CALM" app — and did a few meditations. Two on anxiety. Another one on heart-opening.

In the middle of that, a lot shifted. In fact, my world shifted.

Then I took another action. I messaged my coaches about my inner situation. Not hiding. Full truth sharing. They gave me the homework to make that asset list and another one about my inner voices. They'll help me do a strategy and reclaim my true inner strength next week.

So I was already taking three actions that moved me out of my mind tornado and toward getting control of the situation again. Beginning with my inner game and activating my resources and support.

Because of the calming meditations, I started to get the bigger perspective. Started realizing very tangibly in my body that — again! — the panic doom voices are just voices! Catching them is always the first step.

If you're feeling off, step back!
Are you listening to shadows?
Or your sparkly self?

Yes, my current situation requires some action. Yet it's not the end of the world — it never is. But to find my best actions, I first had to get out of my fears!

Acting from fear creates more fears.
Acting from sparkle creates sparkle.

I also asked for spirit support. And soon after, had a dream of Dennis Quaid (??!) speaking to me, heart to heart, saying, "I want you to claim your inner power, be you, and then in one to two months, you come see me." The energy of the message and dream was just what I needed. It powerfully sparked my slumbering inner badass.

Of course. I can do ANYTHING. We all can.

So here, present moment, I'm sitting in the sun, on a beautiful, perfect, nothing-is-wrong Sunday morning. And nothing is wrong, really.

No, it isn't!

Because I got two crazy realizations one after the other:

First, I realized that I had created the SAME scenario that I'm always creating. Repeating pattern! My money numbers are adding up EXACTLY to "ground zero" per the end of the month. This time, it includes having used up all savings and maxed out the credit cards, so it's the very same pattern I've run a LONG TIME.

Except now it looks like the end of the railroad.

I used to muse about it — how is it possible that whatever I do I always "make ends meet?" it was kind of a joke to me, many times! I was never able to change the outcome, though — until soon after this story.

(Subconsciously, I was telling myself things like "I don't really WANT to become big and famous and rich, because ..... — it scared me! I'd lose friends / family / become unrelatable / alone / ..... the UNKNOWN..... boooooooohhhh!!")

(Ghostly echo)

So now, sitting here, I'm seeing this again.

$2,000 plus $500 from dog walking would LITERALLY cover all my expenses. To literally. Ground zero. To the cent.

Suddenly it became just ridiculous.

Like, "this is not even real!" ridiculous. How the heck did I manifest such precision in getting down to zero?

It was like me being in a nightmare, but instead of still running from the ghostly unknown and echo, I stopped. Stared into the darkness.

And then I smirked. Seriously, shadows? Seriously, me? Is that even real?

Yes. We are that powerful.
We manifest exactly what we believe.

Then my smile got bigger. Like I realized a prank was pulled on me.
And I started to actually, really, wholeheartedly laugh.

That, of course, shifted the whole energy.

You can't be scared and amused.
If you see humor, you can't feel fear.

(If you see things with humor, you'll see *behind* the fears. See deeper gems. What's really here for you to see.)

And I just did another big laugh as I'm typing it.
Feels good. (Try it!) So THEN.... Something else happened.

I said, "the heck with it."

(Suddenly I was back in a more powerful space.)

And I decided two things:

a) If this were to be the end of my road (which I know it isn't, because I see through it), I might as well enjoy myself.

b) This reality is not going to be my truth.

Taking back my reigns. Actually showing up in my full sparkle.

(I'll come back here with a chapter after this one where I'll describe what happened next!)

Before you go on, I invite you to pause, though. This is about YOU.

play prompt:

Reflect at this moment first for yourself:

If ALL that you held dear, right now, would disappear, and you felt "at the end of the road"...

What would you make it mean about yourself?

_____

_____

Which of those meanings do you now decide to let go?

_____

_____

How would YOU approach YOUR "end of the road?"
With sparkle, from your power?

_____

_____

me after the cliff moment – sparkling.

how this chapter helps:

This is a time-tunnel magic-view chapter that I started during my cliff-moment (see last chapter) and am now finishing in September 2020. I'm reflecting here how my life did NOT end. How what I wanted (mostly) became real. And how I took back the sparkle and power steering wheel.

On August 8, 2020 (my cliff moment! See last chapter!). I <u>decided</u> that by or before August 31, I would enjoy the following in my reality:

- ★ A financial payment plan agreed on with my coaches and next month's payment made.

- ★ Feeling fully nurtured in my body, having fully expressed myself creatively, and also started to express ALL my hidden desires.

- ★ Having made music with a musician and sang, having had a blast!

- ★ Having wrapped this book and sent for last proofreading to editor.

- ★ Having paid all invoices, including coaches, AND $2,000 spare.

Turn the page to see what happened, from my view of September 2020:

I did an "end of inner-shadow drama stories" funeral ritual by the sea.

Deciding that I'm now staying in my driver seat. No more inner bully.

This enabled me to connect with my creative juices. I got inspired again. Clear and excited about what I want to offer in my business.

(All the objections of drama stories were now out of the driver seat!)

I followed inspired actions, moment by moment. While keeping nurturing myself as a foundation. Biggest win walkaway from this:

A monumental shift into feel-good grounding and my own power.

I did schedule that singing session with the musician on the island, and we had a blast. And want to do more. Also fed my soul. Sparkle.

I'm actually wrapping the book today. 1 day before my decided date.

I actually do have $2,000 spare, after paying all invoices. (Not all through my business, but it's a start. I'm rolling.)

My big takeaways and realizations for myself:

It feels SO GOOD to have dropped the inner-shadow dramas!
All shadows look so small from this viewpoint! And I totally only see them as stories from here!

It's only when you BELIEVE the stories that they SEEM real.

Even if it sometimes felt like it would take forever to find my true sparkle... I realized that "forever" was also simply a drama I had made up.

Whatever we believe and see as "real," we allow to become real.

Change can happen in an instant.
We, in our mind, can flip the switch.

What made the difference was my decision. And wholeheartedly saying yes to moving on.

Even so, I did get challenged a few more times. I still am! (After all, life is a learning journey.) But it got yet easier to catch the voices, do something about them, and take back the steering wheel. Back to sparkle. To following my heart.

By the way, the more practice you have to notice your inner limiting voices, the more power you have to say no to them! (One of the reasons why playing with this book is so powerful: you practice catching your shadows instead of running on auto-pilot!)

And here's what that looks like now in my reality, and how I feel now:

I'm actually sitting at the Anchorage airport at the moment. (This is September 2020.) Scheduled for in-depth breast cancer screenings this week. And... I'm okay. Calm. In power. Deciding and knowing that I'll walk away okay soon — or that I'm already being — in full health. After a short freak-out, I was even able to even flip the whole thing in my head to see it as a retreat. A cleansing. "A spa experience into love."

Whenever I spot fears or inner pressure, I embrace them, then shift them to love. Focus on taking care of myself. One step at a time. This allows me to mostly stay calm. No matter what's going on!

I'm excited (and a little nervous, but game for the adventure) about my next things in life and business (including the cleansing of my cancer-story, whatever magic that will bring.)

With me in my sparkle and power, the skies are again open.

first-aid tools –
when sh!t hits the fan

how this chapter helps:

This is quick-access to my personal toolbox of things you can do when you're going down a rabbit hole. Like when your mind is spinning, you're feeling down, and you want speedy help.

Note: If you're in acute emergency mode, please get professional help.

Note also: Stay curious, and you might find big gems! And you'll see your reality change into more of what you want to experience!

emergency prompts:

sparkle breaths

Quick version: Take three deep, slow breaths, and give yourself a hug. Know that the universe has your back. Trust that. Love yourself up. Keep breathing and focus simply on where you're at. The ground. The room. The air. The things you see. Reconnect yourself with the present and breathe all thoughts down, out, until you feel relieved.

Sparkle version: Visualize healing sparkles as soothing waves flowing into your body as you breathe and breathing them out in a different color. That instantly creates calm. You can also try focusing on the tip of your nose while you do that. That zones your mind to Zen. If thoughts come to you, simply see them and allow them to float away, then focus again on your breath or your nose.

Sparkle tree version: Create a picture in your mind of a magical sparkly tree of life. Imagine it in front of you, giving you healing, refreshing air to cleanse your body and mind as you slowly breathe in and out. Visualize breathing in sparkly air from the tree and breathing back used air to recycle and cleanse. Like real trees, this tree also loves to recycle your air and has healing energy! I love this one!

do a meditation for anxiety

Google or YouTube search for an anxiety meditation and treat yourself to one that speaks to you. It will get you out of the spin-cycle of your head and back into your heart, where you see and feel clearly.

And find best, true, and feel-good answers from there.

I used to not think I have anxiety, but one day I got inspired to try one of these meditations, and it was EXACTLY what served me.

The fact that you're here right now, in this chapter, you'll probably really enjoy one as well. Like, right about now.

have compassion with yourself

Since you're here, you might be doing a pretty good job at beating up on yourself. WE can be our worst enemy. Those people you're concerned about that you hurt? Things you may have done "wrong?" Are stories YOU are telling YOURSELF right now.

You might be surprised that the view on the other side may be quite different. Always is! We all have our own experiences. Maybe people are actually indifferent to what you supposedly did. Like me, I was just beating myself up for leaving a relationship, having been such a "bad person," only to hear that days later, in his words, "he is 100% okay."

Forgiveness moment:

Complete this sentence:

"I forgive myself for _____."

Then say this aloud, and repeat three times.

Then say: "Now I let it go."

love yourself UP

This is so simple, yet a practice to reclaim. To love ourselves in every moment. Loving ourselves leads us back to our hearts. It is only from there that we feel, see, and create sparkle. Create our dream lives!

As I'm writing this, I'm actually in proofing-mode of this book. Can you imagine? I almost forgot to add it! Yet it showed up in my life RIGHT NOW to reclaim and remember it. As essential, any-moment, go-to, for when things really don't feel good.

For instance. I just left a relationship. I felt relieved, even <u>light</u> at first! I felt in my heart that I needed OUT! Yet after I left (my mind kicked in), I went through moments of feeling really low. Looking at my shadow voices, I realized <u>I was making myself wrong</u>. Not loving myself. Not being kind to myself. Not trusting the voice of my heart. It felt heavy!

Does something feel EXPANSIVE and LIGHT? Or heavy?
Are you listening to your HEART? Or to your shadows?

It can be that simple! Follow the expansive. That's the voice of your heart. Then stay the course.

Yes, things can sometimes feel heavy as we process. But if we start giving IN to shadow voices and doubts, and STAY there... We just add unnecessary drama.

Honor and celebrate yourself for following your heart.

What can you do right now to celebrate following your heart?

Take a nice long shower? Give yourself a hug? A glass of water? A pause? Honor and treat yourself as the most precious thing in the world.

Because you are. And we deserve and must claim that love for ourselves. What can you do right now to love yourself up?

embrace the "wind" with love

This worry-stopper helps you get out of those negative spin-cycle mind-storms and into flow.

I just had a dream in which I noticed myself running from an uneasy feeling. In the dream, I realized, "Hey! I'm running from discomfort! And it's time to stop running!" So...

* I stopped.

* I turned around, as if I was facing into the wind.

* And then, without even knowing yet what exactly I was running from, I just sent it love. Stayed with the feeling. Stayed curious.

And it started to dissolve! Get much smaller. It was as if a storm turned into a small wind that just makes paper flutter. Like party confetti. No more tornado.

I stayed with it and kept giving it more love, being curious, and just loving it up. Until I felt complete. This being present turned my unease into feeling much better, even warm in my tummy, and I also got some awareness. I started getting a sense of what was behind it.

> When we face our worries, they stop haunting us, and we start finding gems.

And I even got back into inspiration mode! (In my case, it was to get up and write this play prompt!)

stop and step back into joy

When you catch yourself feeling off, stop whatever you're doing, and take a step back. Take a break and do something to nurture yourself.

Chances are you're in a shadow mind spin wheel. If you stop, you get out. Get a glass of water. Get some colors and color up a crazy-ugly, whatever-comes-out, quick-expression painting. Go where your heart says. What does it say? What serves you best to do right now?

move.

Move out of your mind and into your body to find sparkle again.

Any movement will do. And you're allowed to have fun! Or let the madness out! Whatever feels good to you, jump into it!

A few ideas to jump-start your brain (Quick! Pick one!)

   ★   Jump around! Like in that song! Jump. Jump. Jump around!

- ★ Throw a pizza. I did that once after my fourth immigration visa application had just fallen through despite all promises of my (expensive) consultant. Another year! More thousands of dollars! It turned out he had consulted me — like all the other consultants before — for a visa I didn't even qualify for! I was SO mad. So I threw a frozen pizza on a wall. It felt SO GOOD.

- ★ Strike a pose! How do you WANT to feel? Then strike a pose for that feeling. Add some sound to it! Get into it! It's super powerful! Instantly changes your body chemistry. It will actually generate those feelings. Feel it? Do it a few times!

- ★ Dance it out! Pick a song that calls you, and dance all out!

- ★ Go outside. Take a walk or a hike or a run.

- ★ Take a class. Go to the gym, or yoga, or Zumba.

What kind of movement feels good to you now?

Now get up and do it. :)

inner voices meet-up

This is a more deep, cleansing, amazing release valve and clarity creator. I've done this many times. It's like a spa for the mind — awesome for whenever you feel funky or even regularly, to check in how you feel!

Here's how I used this in a recent situation in my life:

A few weeks ago, I woke from a scarcity dream. (Yes, that can still happen to me too!) My inner critic was throwing sh!t storm.

How do I make money? I need money! I need to get a job! Ah! All kinds of fears. My mind was throwing bombs at me.

I tried a bunch of things to shift the energy — mind you, while (house)sitting in a house worth millions, with a sea view, sweet doggies, and all the food and toys I needed... even having my dream lifestyle and dream business ... none of it enough to placate my fears!

(It was so great. This meant that new things were coming up to release.)

So I went for a drive! To nature, to take the dogs out. While in the car, I started talking to myself. I gave my inner mind-storm (aka inner critic) a voice. I talked. I let it out! I did a lot of repeating myself. Even just single words. Just let her blah, blah, blah it out.

And I made an effort to HEAR her out. Not dismiss her.

I instantly started feeling better. The more she spoke, the more warm and fuzzy my stomach felt.

I gave her gratitude and looked for her superpowers. I found several!

Then I let my other inner voices speak. I even asked, "who else is at the table here?" (This may vary, just be curious.) I had my inner grown up and my inner child, and of course, my heart is part of that.

From there, I knew what to do next. I had reclaimed the steering wheel. And guess what! I let my inner child (now with grown-up wisdom) lead! (By the way, that's part of the secret inner happy sparkle recipe!)

I felt a ton lighter.

All was actually pretty well. AND I had found some gems in the form of old limiting stories that I now got to release.

A glimpse into my journal afterward — my inner voices meet-up.

Here's the quick how-to for the inner voices meet-up:

1. Let your inner shadow voices out. You can just talk out loud to yourself or journal; pick what feels easy and right. You'll get them out of your head — and stop the mind-spin.

2. When you feel complete, stop. Don't let this drag on. (Your inner critic can take you into a downward spiral.)

3. Give all your voices gratitude. What do you see as their superpowers? What are you grateful for from the share? Where's the truth behind the criticism, if any?

4. Let your power voice — your true you — your heart, speak. Speak what's really true to you. You have the big picture. You see through the fake fears and illusions. Imagine yourself as a parent speaking to all your petulant inner bullies and children.

What does your heart say now? Are you good?
What does your heart want you to BE, PLAY, or DO?

your magical game tools for every day!

how this chapter helps:

In this chapter, you're getting magical tools for your everyday sparkle adventure. Like James Bond at the beginning of his movies, you're now going to "Q" to get your adventure tools, woo-hoo!

All these tools will help you in the "Permission To Sparkle" card game[e] and as you play with this book, as well as in real life:

 A Sparkle Mirror (Connect with your sparkly self and see what's your true you.) STOP. Discern your shadow voices from your truth. What is shadow. What is your truth? Then take an inspired action through your fears

 Intuition Spark Receiver (Find guidance, self-love and inspired actions.) Connect with your intuition and listen to your heart. Breathe. Feel the peace. Then do what your heart says and sees. (Even if it doesn't make sense.)

 A Magic Wand (Make wishes to the universe to realize your dreams.) Make a wish! Speak it out loud! What's your desire? Then let it go + take inspired actions as they'll show up. (Without forcing it. Follow your heart.)

---

e On www.AstridMueller.com, you'll see where to get it!

Holographic Facet Glasses (See beyond what's happening; find new superpowers and gems.) Look at all angles and energies. See through. What can you learn here? What's yours? What can you learn about YOU?

 A Sparkle Meter (Measure your frequency and reclaim your power.) On a scale of 1–10, how empowered are you feeling right now? First number you think of. What can you do to claim more of your sparkle and feel good now?

 The Sparkle Miracle Formula Be, Play, Do Ask your heart: Where can you open to more flow of abundance? Are you called to BE or to PLAY or to DO at this time? Do that. For more details, see the book.

You can whip out these tools at any moment in the game or as you read this book. Need a superpower? Grab a tool! Soon, you'll automatically use these tools in your life. Helping you overcome your challenges and find more and more of your sparkle!

Talking about sparkle... here's this first tool explained in detail:

game tool: your sparkle mirror.

What does this tool do?
This tool helps you to discern your shadow voices from your truth.

See THROUGH shadows and see your true you! And reconnect with you — your most sparkly empowered, TRUE version of you.

You can imagine this mirror or craft one (see the following pages).

This mirror has two-sided magical glass: you get to see yourself and all your inner voices, inner parts and thoughts. And, if you imagine it being see-through, you get to see your future sparkly self on the other side!

What can you do with it in real life?

* A magical creativity moment. You get to do self-care, forget any worries of your life, and connect with your future happy self. When we're creative and focus on a topic, we really immerse ourselves and find some deep answers!

* In this case, you'll get to emotionally and energetically connect with your inner sparkly diamond that you already are, and you also get to feel into who you get to be as your future self again, giving yourself "Permission To Sparkle!"

* A beautiful meditation tool. By creating a tangible piece, you'll be able to gaze at it when you meditate and reconnect with your sparkle any time.

* A play tool for your mind: Simply by listening inside, with or without a mirror, you can observe. "What do my inner voices say? What would my true sparkly me say to me here?"

I've done this for myself and for clients, in visualizations and meditations, and also in coaching sessions. It's magical. It shifts things within you because it goes deeper than your conscious, awake mind can. And it helps you find diamonds, your wisdom gems!

If you want to get answers from your true sparkly self or clarity about your inner voices, but you have trouble doing it, you can use this mirror and ask it for help. Then see what it says. This helps you hear your heart!

play prompt:

1.

Craft a magical mirror. Print one of my drawings (see next page) or draw, doodle, or craft your own. It doesn't have to be perfect. See it as a creativity play moment. Express yourself. Follow your heart. Have fun.

Pick colors, materials, and tools that feel like you as your most sparkly (powerful) you.

You may also be drawn to incorporate materials/colors that represent your non-me. The shadows. All will come through in the mirror.

While you play with all this, observe. As always, be curious what your mind says. Anything feels like "not possible?" Or your body doesn't feel good? Be curious, and you're bound to find learning gems!

2.

Play with your mirror. Ask the mirror (and yourself), "Who am I as my most sparkly true me?" Listen deep within. Then journal as inspired.

You can take a picture, print, color, or embellish this doodle from me...

Even better: make your own.
It will be most meaningful, and the whole experience of making it will help you feel your sparkle.

Play. Be bold!

Here's what I just created. I just used what I had close at hand. Which happened to be paper, watercolor pens, a cool frame stamp-out thingie (that totally got me excited!) and duct tape.

A glimpse of my journal that I stuck my paper "mirror" into, and my sparkle creativity moment.

I used duct tape on the front of the fold card, symbolizing a mirror. Folding it open, On the left side, I boldly and messily splattered some colors, representing my shadow voices (that I get to see through.)

On the right side is my sparkly me, where I used yellow, kissed it with pink lipstick, and put a heart on it.

In the journal, I expressed how I experience myself as sparkly me, energetically. It feels powerful!

How about you? What did you experience through this creativity moment and sparkle mirror reflection prompt? What magical thing did you feel and find out about yourself?

What's the deeper magic here?

So you know that this mirror connects you to your true, fully sparkly self. Which you already naturally, deep inside, are. So, how come you're not just like that today anyways?

Through life, we simply accumulate some disempowering things.

For example, limiting beliefs like "we're not good enough." Or "we can't do this." Or "we don't know how to play."

What are some of your voices you instantly think of?

We also pile up limiting paradigms and beliefs from our families or culture, our environment. Things that may have once served in a context but may not personally serve us anymore. Like "Don't eat meat on Fridays." — "Why?" — "Just because." (We might not even remember why.)

As we move through life, we start picking up all kinds of rules and believing all kinds of things! That's okay. If they still benefit us.

We also pick up fears, negative emotions, negative stories we make up... These can get stuck in our system, our energy field, even our body. If not released, they can even create diseases.

So, this mirror helps you spot anything that is interfering with you being your most sparkly diamond, AND it helps you get free!

Wowsers! How? You ask?

You know! It helps you use the key of living curiously!

As you gaze at the mirror (or close your eyes and imagine) and ask, "Who am I when I am my most sparkly self? And who am I right now?" compare. See through the mirage. See your true you.

You can ask yourself things like,

"What does my mind say? Who's talking here? An old fear? My inner critic? My inner child? Is it even real? Is it still serving me?"

Listen, and have a conversation. Then you get to choose.

You don't have to force this. Simply become curious. Whenever you have something in your life that doesn't feel good or catch your mind saying things that aren't sparkly, like: "I can't do this...", pause and come back to this mirror.

You'll always find your truth. Suddenly you might say...

"The heck with it!" — see through it, and then dare to do it anyways.

And... swoosh, you let go a limiting thing that didn't serve you anymore.

Every time you spot such a limiting thing (i.e., thought or feeling or belief...) and sit with those moments, you can have big "a-ha"s. That's you finding gems. Then you can choose to not live by these old rules anymore and release them. See through them. And choose a more sparkly way of living.

Sometimes you may also find gems <u>behind</u> such limitations. There might be soul lessons. Like learning about love. Or learning to trust yourself.

We're collecting gems. And de-dusting our inner "live limitless" diamond!

game tool: intuition spark receiver △

This tool helps you hear your intuition and your heart so that you can make the best decisions for your business or career and life.

(I'm closing my eyes and listening to my heart, inviting the universe to tell me what to write:)

This is a little different for everyone. Start with your heart. Close your eyes, and do this mini meditation to start.

(Or record this, in your own voice, and then listen to it!)

Intuition Spark-Receiving Meditation:

Take a few deep breaths and get comfortable as you sink into your chair. Feel how you're feeling more and more relaxed. Get ready to enter your sparkle fairytale.

Above you, you see a sparkly glimmer: imagine there's the universe intuition spark receiver!

It's coming closer to you, like a soft landing, and you may see it in your mind's eye coming into your hands or simply showering you in sparkle rain.

Take a few calm breaths, just being with it.

Feel the peace. The quiet. The sparkle drizzle.

Does it have a color? Is it a golden rain? Do you hear a sound as you imagine this happening? Does it have a smell, this sparkle rain? Just observe. And observe how you're feeling.

Now tune into your heart. Can you feel it? Feel your chest expand? Is it feeling warm? Like love wants to burst out, to share with the world.

Allow it to happen. Whatever wants to unfold.

Now. As you're sitting in this magical sparkle space, with your heart bursting with abundance, love, and sparkles... or a glimmer of that feeling...

Let's land your magic! Let's connect it to earth!

Imagine wherever you're sitting, your sparkle rain also connects deep down with mother earth. You may feel it in your sitting area or your feet — you're rooted, connected, ready to speak!

Your heart will speak. For now, just sit.

Feel that connection with earth and feel your magic within.

You may also feel your first chakra, in your buttock area, buzzing.

Yes, you're landing, and the magic can begin!

From this space, ask your heart:

What does it want you to see at this very moment? What message does it have for you? What does it want you to do for yourself?

What simple thing can you do today, when you end this meditation, to nurture your soul?

Breathe. Thank your heart for this moment of wisdom.

Is there anything else it wants you to hear, know, or do?

Just listen.

And then trust that you'll remember easily, right after this meditation.

Now, when you're ready, thank your heart, thank yourself for being you, thank your sparkly universe spark receiver for having connected with you... and know that you can always access it easily!

Through your body!

Where do you feel your spark receiver now? How does it want to be recognized by you?

Is it a place in your body where you can always connect to?

What's your superpower to easily feel it, hear it, or sense it and connect with your heart's wisdom in the future?

Some feel it in their heart. You may feel it somewhere else in your body... just observe, and thank your body for that wisdom, too.

Now when you're ready, give yourself a hug and breathe into your heart. Take as many breaths as you need,

And then when you're ready, open your eyes!

You now are connected to your intuition spark receiver!

Take a moment and write here or journal what you want to remember from this meditation. Where in your body did you feel your intuition spark? What message did it have for you just now?

_____

_____

_____

_____

Can you also access your intuition without doing this meditation?

Yes. It's always accessible to us. It's just a matter of us noticing it (again) — like we originally did, as children.

How do YOU typically notice your inner guidance?

You "just know" or kind of "hear it" (turn left here, not right) or feel it in your body (this doesn't feel right), or you see things or sense things or get guidance in your dreams?

What's your most typical way to notice? (Ultimately, we can learn all ways to hear intuition and get better and better at it! But begin with what's easiest for you now.)

Then practice paying attention to it in your everyday life. Be curious. Signs are always everywhere!

(And you can also ask your guides for help, answers and signs.)

game tool:
a magic wand!

What does this tool do?

This is you making a wish to the universe! Playing with your wand (or even just making your wish) will set the universe in motion. Making a want (ha ha! I wanted to write "wand" but typed "want" — that's also a universe sign, and kind of funny. Get it?) A wand is a fun tool that helps you in the game, and in real life, to get what you want.

What can you do with it in real life?

Literally, manifest magic. We manifest our dream life with intentions and with energy. As you'll wave your wand or meditate with it (or even just imagine it and make a wish!), you get to have fun manifesting and setting your wish in motion!

Feeling odd about this? Ha! Maybe there's a fear or limiting belief? If yes, be curious if you want to keep that belief or if you're ready to play!

This is crafting fun. To help you manifest and activate your sparkle feelings, aka, your "sparkle frequency." Fun + also magical: what we focus on grows. So come have fun and focus on your wishes + dreams.

This is a fun creativity prompt for everyone.

Yes, you, too. This is you giving yourself "Permission To Sparkle" again (i.e., play again) — to connect with your younger you. To fun!

You don't need to be an artist. This is about feeling good and having fun. And you WILL also find some inner wisdom gems!

You can simply embellish store-bought wands, like the ones you see here. I found these in flower shops and the thrift store.

Or be as creative as you want,
and make your own.

Bottom line...

follow the fun!

How you can make your magic wand:

1. Set an intention. Here, because we're playing the "Permission To Sparkle" game, choose as your main intention to "become your authentic awesome powerful self, when you're fully sparkly!" Focus on how you'll FEEL when this is happening. (You can also do wands for anything, like for the intentions for your year... keep this in mind for later!)

2. Collect stuff that FEELS like your intention. I love to go to thrift stores. Whenever I set an intention (aka make a wish), let it go, and walk in, curious to see what I'll find... I find the coolest things and in perfect synchronicity. Things that are like "OMG! That's perfect for what I wished!" Follow that with curiosity. Don't look hard. Stay curious. You can do the same thing going into craft or fabric stores.

   Look for beads, wire, ribbons, hair embellishments, crystals, fabrics...with your intention: what feels like YOUR MOST SPARKLY YOU? Pick what lights you up. And get some basic crafting stuff like sticks, hot glue or wire — done.

3. Set space. In case you have a tendency to think you're too busy for this, this is perfect. Just make space and lay things out. When you see your sparkly things and have your space ready to craft, you'll sit down and have fun with them in no time!

4. • Have fun! Keep your intention in mind and play! Lay things out, glue pieces onto your wand, and just allow it to take shape. This is not about perfection and earning a design award. It's about FEELING SPARKLY.

What to do with this wand, now that you have it?

Keep it in a place where you're LIT UP to see it! You can also use it in walking meditations or rituals. I've done a new year's intention ritual with wands for several years! I created sticks symbolizing things I wanted to let go (and then burned them or tossed them into the sea) and wands to represent things I wanted to call IN. The crafting alone was very soulful and also powerful. And every time I did it, my intentions manifested super soon after the ritual.

Why? Because what we focus on grows.

As you craft, you focus on what you want.

So call in your desires, and have fun!

game tool: holographic facet glasses.

What does this tool do?

This tool helps see different facets of any situation, see beyond what's happening, and find new superpowers and gems.

Become curious. How does your situation change if you look at it from different angles?

What if you view it from the receiver? Or look at it upside down. What from the past or the future — how may it look from a different time paradigm? In what way may you shake your current view up to see your highest wisdom?

For example: Have you been in a situation that felt similar to something that happened before? What's the FIRST time you felt this way, ever? What did you make things mean then? Is that same story angle still relevant and true for you, with the wisdom and desires you have today?

Be curious, listen within, and you'll find your answers and gems!

What did you just realize as you pondered this? Take a moment to journal or just listen inward to what comes up. And then celebrate! (I bet you just found new gems!)

game tool: your sparkle meter.

What does this tool do? It gives you an easy reference point on how sparkly you feel and helps you reclaim your power.

Are you on the sparkle path? Or spiraling down a rabbit hole? Are you in manifesting frequency? Or in a dense, heavy-feeling moment? Are you the best version of yourself, empowered, with your heart in your driver seat? Sometimes we're running on auto-pilot, unaware of how (not) sparkly we feel. This helps you STOP, adjust, and get back onto the sparkle path!

Before you jump to reading how to use this tool, I have a small disclaimer from me and the universe — to make you feel good. And to give you permission NOT to feel sparkly.

Every state and emotion holds gems, and everything serves a purpose.

If something sucks, we can learn from it. If we eat something that tastes bad, we learn at least what we don't like and what we appreciate.

There's also the immensely important part of BEING.

In today's society, we've been conditioned to run, do do do, and often we don't give ourselves permission to just enjoy, be, rest — even eat!

So know, very importantly: your sparkle meter also includes permission to BE. It's not just about "pure sparkle blast feelings of productivity." There's a place for everything. It's about balance. Find out how you roll.

This is about you nourishing your soul, feeling aligned with your destiny, feeling whole, happy... that kind of sparkly. Sometimes we're on the fast lane and rolling with ideas... sometimes we're happiest when we rest.

(Important side-note: we need BOTH. And we can also manifest magic while we sleep. The universe is always at work.)

Full sparkle happens when we give ourselves permission to do what lights us up and ask for and receive what we need.

play prompt:

On a scale of 1-10, with 1 being "not sparkly at all" and 10 being "I love my life and feel fabulous!" where are you on that scale right now?

1   2   3   4   5   6   7   8   9   10

Now what to do from here?

First of all, don't judge yourself. This is not a competition. (Are you playing the sparkle game or the judgment game?)

This is about you listening within and hearing what your soul needs. Take a moment, and listen:

What does your number mean to your heart? Are you in a good place? Is there something you can do for yourself right now?

_____

_____

I'll give you my example. I listened to my heart for where I'm at, and I'm a 7. To me, right now, I feel very good. It's midnight, and I'm in writing flow and very grateful. I played with "what would it feel like to get to a 9? What could I do for myself right now to get there?"

I realize that I'm happy with a 7 for this moment in time. I could get up and dance or do some high-vibe play thing to raise my frequency (like one of the inspired tools I have in my game! You can always use them!) Yes, I'm currently calm and happy with the 7. And even just thinking about the 9 and dancing made me feel great and giddy and slightly raised my frequency.

We always get to choose. And yes! I can also raise my frequency by just sitting here! All good. Just listen within for what you need.

What if you WANT to raise your frequency? Feel better?

Ask yourself first: What can you do for yourself right now? Is there an inner part of you that needs something that you've been ignoring?

_____

_____

_____

(Hint: Do not follow anything that feels like "should." That's our inner critic. As always, go with what your heart wants. Your heart will lead you to your best next steps. Even if it might feel like a challenge and NOT what your mind would choose... it will lead you to more true sparkle.

If you feel heavy and unsure WHAT can help... STOP! You're probably in your head!

Pick a SQUIRREL PLAY card from the "Permission To Sparkle" Game!f

Or just JUMP UP! And do a wiggle dance! Then sit back down and listen to what your heart wants. The first thought will be it.

If you're still stuck, ask for help! Come to my group, ask your play buddy, ask one of your inner or in-the-world guides, ask me — or whoever you're inspired to ask for help.

Give yourself the support
your heart asks you to receive.

game tool: the sparkle miracle formula "be play do"...

This is so powerful and essential and has EVERYTHING to do with what I had to learn about "Permission To Sparkle"... that I ended up making it a whole new chapter!

Get ready! Fasten your seatbelts!

---

f If you didn't get the game with this book, come to AstridMueller.com to get it.

the sparkle miracle formula "be play do"

how this chapter helps:

This chapter is about manifesting miracles and co-creating with the universe. It's also about being your most effective AND nourished self. My BE PLAY DO miracle formula allows you to live your dream life and be happy. Manifest your sparkle life!

I didn't invent this. I'm crediting this concept to multiple inspirations, from coaching by Kavita Singh to Jean Berry's 100 Days of Miracles game to thousands of years of philosophy that's been around...

But here it is, with my own spin:

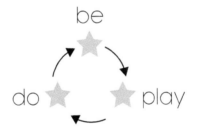

* BE (Pause. Simply BE. Listen to my heart and my desires.)

* PLAY (I do something playful. Enjoy. Get out of my head.)

* DO (I take action, as inspired.)

If it doesn't work, it simply means we have inner interference. Where we get to learn something. Find gems. See how we stand in our way. And then clear that.

Once we're clear of any inner limitations, the road is free for us to manifest all our desires!

Why?

(Catch any inner contradictions you hear here as inner voices! They're all shadow! See the chapter "Manifest All Your Desires" to go deeper.)

Because when we have no inner resistance, we don't hold ourselves back. We freely take action. Are resourceful. Allow ourselves to be fully supported. We know and trust things WILL work out. All feels like it's already done. We simply take inspired actions, one by one.

What can this look like when you manifest without interference with my sparkle miracle formula BE PLAY DO?

Here's an example of how I recently manifested magic in a thrift store:

1. BE. I enjoyed a beautiful Saturday morning breakfast and then decided to find camping stuff at the thrift store.

2. PLAY. I went to the thrift store and simply played a fun discovery game. Fully trusting I'd find cool stuff.

3. DO. I simply picked up the perfect items as I spotted them, knowing this was EXACTLY what I wanted.

I manifested a set of camping cooking pots, a large plastic camping water jug, a large freezer bag, a barbecue grid for onto the fire, cute skull ice cube trays, and even free milk for my morning coffee. All for $23.

I've been loving manifesting through thrift stores. I'm really good at it.

How come? Because I have no inner doubt, resistance — I simply KNOW, with all the cells of my being, that this happens. Every. Time. I do it.

This is exactly how you manifest ALL THE THINGS.

It simply gets trickier when the things are more dear to our heart, more important to us, and more complex.... and when we have "stakes!"

Then our shadow voices come out. And the miracle circle gets broken.

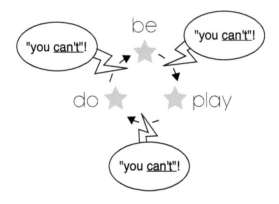

Our system doesn't like changes. Especially big changes. They can be scary, different, and therefore uncomfortable. It's like we have to come out of our cave. Dare to venture.

We'll get voices like why we can NOT have what we want! Maybe it's dangerous! Or we shouldn't have it! Others also don't!

We have to look at those voices so we keep venturing.
So we can get what we truly want!

play prompt:

Most likely, you also have areas in your life where you manifest magic with ease. What areas are those? What things come EASILY to you? Where you merely state a desire, and it happens?

_____

How do you see that you're <u>already</u> using the "be play do" formula there? Think of an example, if you have one. What happened? How did it feel?

_____

Where in your life do you currently have a HARD time manifesting?

_____

Where do you hold yourself BACK there? The BE? The PLAY? The DO? What are your "can't!" voices? Your interfering stories?

_____

_____

_____

Those trickier areas can now be a wonderful playground for you to amp up your sparkle powers and manifest your next desires. If you feel called to go deeper here, go to the chapter "Manifest All Your Desires!"

I'm doing that myself, right now, to manifest with the same ease and power through my business.

Which is simply another playground. To release more stories. Find more gems. Learn more things about myself. Claim more of my sparkle and bravery as I'm moving forward.

So how do you use the BE PLAY DO formula to manifest your dream life now? And maybe you don't even know where to start? You don't have to have all ducks in a row. Or work hard for years until you can...

Here's a story about receiving. And living my dream life now:

story time:

As I write this, I just came back from an almost seven-week trip around the world, where I visited Austin, Switzerland, Hamburg, Barcelona, more Austin, then Houston, then Seattle.

Most of it was travel experiences and fun, with family visits, yet I also had one of my most successful months since forever in my business.

I had the best ideas and next action steps AND client sessions while splashing in pools or lounging under birdsong, poolside, in a bathing suit.

I stayed in a mansion, got chauffeured in a Tesla, and danced with a world-class dancer in a private session. I was driven from and to airports without even asking. Received full fridges and an $800 voucher from Airbnb... I was invited everywhere AND upleveled my dream business.

I also danced my ass off, met one of my soul-mates, and made peace with a lot of old family stories.

Why did all this happen in such big ways? Let's look at the formula:

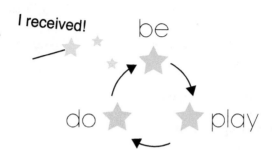

I received!

be

do ★ ★ play

1.
BE. I nurtured myself. Rested. Did what my soul wanted. This part is VERY important! If we're burnt out, we will NOT get inspired. If we're not nurtured, we're frustrated. And that's also when our mind goes into overdrive!

2.
PLAY. I played. Pools! Dancing! All the good stuff! P.S. There's a reason why rich people golf! They have fun, BE, PLAY, which then helps them find their best ideas!

3.
DO. I took inspired action steps from the heart. Then I stepped back. Trusted. Made room to receive.

Also, very importantly: I embraced my shadow voices and released them, like those old family stories. Like stories about not deserving to receive. Like stories about not being able to do big things with my business!

Once I believed and trusted, of course, I was able to. I received. Because interference was released. You can do this as well.

play prompt:

Where are you NOT giving yourself permission to live sparkly and receive all kinds of sparkle gifts, in your reality, right now?

_____

_____

And what stories are you telling yourself as to why you can't?

_____

_____

Find your gems. Change your stories. Design your dream life.

second story:

Back when I had just left my hubby, I had nothing. (Said my mind.)

I had no idea how I'd finance living on my own in Kodiak, Alaska, with my young coaching business! I was barely making enough to cover my bills. (Talking about not yet having been fully open to receive!)

While married, I had been pampered. I didn't have to pay for living expenses. Not even for a car. Nor food. He had fully supported me.

All that was gone after the divorce. I didn't know how I was going to live. YET — I didn't buy into any fears.

During that time, while doing a house-sitting gig for a dog owner, I was savoring a dinner by myself, with good wine, feel-good food, and dogs around me. Doing self-care. Feeding my soul, grateful. For all the goodness in my life — despite the divorce and all the unknowns.

I was in the BE and in the PLAY mode.

And guess what happened? In that savor moment, I had a brilliant idea of how I can live AND have my financial needs met AND more.

When we are nurtured and en JOY, our best ideas can come to us in convoy :)

DOGGIE LOVE KODIAK! As business side gig was born.

That literally came to me as flash inspiration, while slightly tipsy at that. The universe gave me a perfect solution and an easy business idea.

Here's the idea: I house-sit for pet owners, live in amazing houses, surrounded by dogs that feed my soul, AND get paid... for doing and being what I love. While continuing to grow my purpose work, my coaching business. (Which is online. I can do this from anywhere.)

In that moment, staying curious about how I could get a website live with EASE... I also found the next action step:

Inspiration hit again!

It was easy! "Duh! Just make a Facebook group!"

Next thing I knew, I just made a Facebook group called DOGGIE LOVE KODIAK! Saying simply, "Hi, this is Astrid. I love doggies and pretty houses, and hey, let's share pictures here of doggie love moments! And you can come here whenever you need a sitter, too."

As easy as 1-2-3.

That whole thing went live, while I was tipsy. Savoring that dinner.

See how my Sparkle Miracle formula BE PLAY DO was at play here?

It all starts with first feeding our soul
and taking care of ourselves to feel good.
That's when we access our inner genius
and find our best next steps.

Had I gotten into action mode while trying hard to figure this out, how to
live on this island after my divorce, where living cost is easily $2,000 a
month, while I make around a $1,000 at this time with my purpose work
and world-changer coaching business...

Guess what.

I would have freaked out, not seen a way... hustled... worried... and would
have totally missed this brilliant idea and opportunity.

So!

BREATHE.

Take self-care.

BE. PLAY. Then DO.

(Then step back, and also allow to receive!)

finding the right DOs

The right actions don't come from SHOULD energy but from
INSPIRATION. We have to be in "the right" energy. Meaning no
shadow voices. No inner critic. But a clear, no doubt, "of course!" energy.

Think about it. If I had taken actions in fear and survival energy, all
actions would have resulted in NOTHING. Why?

People sense energy. Words written in fear don't smell good.

So, how do you get into this "right" energy? The CLEAR, sparkly one?

Here's the BE PLAY DO formula in a bit more detail:

1.

BE. Zen. Center yourself in your heart, and tune into your
desires. What do you want? Your true desire? (No obligation.
No comparison. Pure desire.)

SHADOW CHECK! Do you feel any fear, doubts, or
resistance why this can NOT happen?

If yes, your energy is NOT clear. Go to the chapter
"manifest all your desires." Or ask your heart what page to
go to in this book for inspiration, and point your finger.
What awareness do you get? What inner voices are in your
way? Choose to see through them, and clear them, before
anything else. You can use PLAY for this! See how it helps!

2.

PLAY. You can do this by simply doing a SHAKE -OFF
body move. Or take whatever's at hand for a moment to
play. Or play the "Permission To Sparkle" game! Then
CATCH THE INSPIRATION from your heart.
The first thing you think of!

Note — inspiration doesn't always feel easy. Sometimes you're like, "oh sh!t!" But you KNOW that it's the right thing.

What did your heart say is your next step?

Before you take that action...

Do another SHADOW CHECK. Do you still feel any fear, doubts, or resistance about this action? If yes, go deeper, and work through those shadows. Embrace them with love. Stay with them until you feel them leave. Or check if whatever you said you want is really what you still absolutely want!

If you feel ready to move forward toward what you want...

3. DO. Take the inspired action! (And sometimes this means taking action through discomfort and old fears!) Follow your heart and your gut. You will be just fine, and you will win.

Why is the play energy relevant here?

When we're in play energy, we're not trying hard, but an open channel to hear what's truly aligned with our heart.

Play energy actually allows us to hear our intuition. Because we get out of our head. And those inspirations lead us to our BEST next action steps. Instead of AUTO PILOT or INNER PRESSURE action steps.

Those intuitions and heart prompts are actually the things that are helping us manifest what we want with way more ease and as direct route!

Because our heart and our higher knowing know best. It knows the shortcut.

So, when we BE and PLAY... we not only rejuvenate and enjoy ourselves... but we also find the shortcuts to the best action steps, instead of doing a whole lot of busy work!

A little adventure note for you:

Sometimes the inspired, universe-guided actions don't make sense.

It might literally be something like "talk to that stranger over there." And suddenly, it turns out they know someone who is EXACTLY the right resource for something you want to manifest.

Or, it might be an inspiration that does NOT feel pleasant — like me right here, getting the repeated inner nudge to finish this book and all the corrections in it (not so fun) — YET... it's also what I want, and it's to everyone's best benefit. (It simply doesn't feel as exciting as it did when it was fresh and new. Now it's a different kind of feel-good. The kind of finishing it.)

Listen. Hear your intuition. Then follow it.

So what happens if you don't do the BE part and don't do any PLAY? You don't hear your intuition and just take action anyways?

Here's a real story of what can happen and what you can do instead.

It's from my dear friend, abundance coach Lanie Smith, who is amazing at discerning her inner voices and inner critic [g]). She shared this story with me during a beta program I did for this book:

She noticed that the energy went down for her when she was not taking breaks from her work. "What did she need?" she asked herself.

"Space. Go for a walk. Eat. Fill up her cup."

But she didn't follow that voice. Her mind said, "You can do all this with a half-full cup, too! Just go half-full!" She followed THAT voice.

She could have easily gotten off a call she had committed to without affecting anyone else. But she still stayed. Doing what her inner critic told her to do.

(Our inner critic can be quite the bully!!)

And then, of course, she felt like crap.

From this experience, Lanie realized the power of space between business calls. And, of course, the importance of not listening to the inner critic and taking action from the right energy.

She also noticed that she falls into judgment when she's not the master of her energy. So not listening to her inner good voice, intuition, and what her body asked, but instead following the inner critic's voice, actually made the inner critic LOUDER.

She realized the times she gave her inner critic a stage were when she didn't take care of herself! Ironic, right?

---

[g] Learn more about Lanie Smith on www.LanieSmithCoaching.com

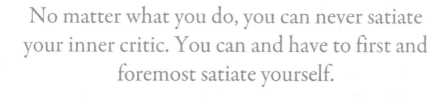

No matter what you do, you can never satiate your inner critic. You can and have to first and foremost satiate yourself.

When Lanie listened to her inner bully, shadow voices, aka inner critic (instead of her intuition, body + heart!), she went off the sparkle path.

When you notice a feeling of HEAVINESS, a SHOULD energy, or inner voices that make you feel like crap... STOP[h].

Then allow your voices to speak[i] — for a little. Then choose which voice gets the power. Like a parent would. With wild children.

So, when your body is hungry, and you have other voices saying something else... you'd register (as a parent) that you want to eat.

Be like your most nurturing parent to yourself. Listen to what your heart, body, and intuition are saying. Don't let your inner critic lead.

Or, to START to experience more sparkle, at LEAST treat yourself as well as you'd treat your own pet. (Humor coming. You're welcome. :))

Ever noticed how sweetly we talk to them? "Ahhhhh, good doggie! Aren't you cute, doggie! You hungry doggie? Here, eat! Pretty doggie! Good doggie! Good pee! Good poo!"

How often do you judge yourself for looking wrong? Being wrong? Doing something wrong? Not deserving something? On and on....!

---

[h] Side note: Lanie later developed a powerful STOPP acronym to stop your inner critic. See her book "Be Solid Gold" on www.LanieSmithCoaching.com for details!
[i] See also chapter "the judgment game & how to get back to sparkle"

Stop that inner judgment. Give yourself some love.

Follow the inner voices that make you feel good. Find your own inner "good doggie" voice.

Can it be that simple? It can be!

And that's the first step to giving yourself "Permission To Sparkle."

As we talked about it, Lanie spotted that she was running a pattern of punishing herself. Her inner SHOULD voice had been telling herself that "food was an inconvenience." Whereas what she would have REALLY liked to have done is go for a walk and eat.

So I said, "Well, let's play... What might happen if you instead play with a LOVE voice instead of the SHOULD voice?

What if you tell your food "I love you" and then eat THAT energy?"

play prompt:

Move the needle all the way — the other way.
Become the queen of yourself. Be your own best concierge — "IS there anything else I can do for myself?"

Lanie and I played with this question, and here's how she answered it:

Lemon for tea! What else? A snack for the walk! What else? A bubble bath! And entirely different inner conversation. And different choices.

How about you? Is there something else you can do more of right now to be kind to yourself and nourish yourself? What else can you do for yourself? And then what else?

_____

_____

Do those things right now. Go play!

As we played this game, Lanie realized that when she DOESN'T nourish herself, her inner mind drama shows up. Otherwise, her mind is at ease.

Being HANGRY does not usually result in healthy, happy thoughts! Nourishing ourselves does!

(And it will also lead us to the right actions.)

Can you think of situations where you tend to not nourish yourself but push yourself? What stories are you telling yourself then as to why you have to? And cannot do what your heart wants?

_____

_____

What stories and actions do you choose to start using now instead?

_____

a word from **merlin.**
the magic of play

how this chapter helps:

So you don't know how to play? You don't deserve to play? You don't have time to play? You don't know what play even is anymore? Or you want to find out how to play more?

This chapter helps you see, feel, and KNOW how magical and important this play energy is and reconnect with your inner child. (Not the one who interferes with work, but the magical child.)

Get ready for a message from Ascended Master Merlin!
And get ready to step into your magical play shoes!

Here, here! Welcome!

Here's the thing about play prompts.

They're like unicorns or rain. Effervescent. Yet magic is within.

You don't play; you stay.

You play; you sway.

In other words — you need play to get moving.

Forward. In your adventure, yes. Forward, in your learnings.

Also, you need play energy to create miracles.

Astrid talks about sparkle frequency. And that's what play helps you experience. That's the frequency where anything becomes possible. Because why?

Because you believe in it!

So!

Open your mind, back to your child's eyes.

Believe in miracles! And you can fly!

Now strap your seatbelts (if you want.)

Get ready to play. Pick any play prompt.

Or read. Jump in!

hopping <u>on</u> the sparkle path!

how this chapter helps:

First steps are exciting! You hop and play the sparkle dance from here, and your challenges and learning gems appear!

This chapter is the beginning of the "Permission To Sparkle" game. You can simply begin reading here (and learn through your logical brain) or start picking up the game (and let creativity reign!)[j]

I'm so excited you're (still) here.

This means you're a "hell, yes!" to your adventure!! Yay!

Now your life can become full Technicolor. Get ready to discover miracles. Your hidden superpowers. Universe surprises and delights! And hidden gems you didn't know you had.

Let's begin! Welcome to the adventure!

Turn the page for a ridiculously easy first step...

---

[j] Go to astridmueller.com to get access to it in case it didn't come with this book!

play prompt:

Hop!

Yes! Do an actual, silly hop!

Not later. But now. Get up! HOP!

You now officially ARE on the sparkle path.

Just like that.

Didn't that already make you feel sparkly?

(Giggles allowed.)

permission to
<u>not</u> sparkle

---

how this chapter helps:

This is for you if you're in a really crappy spot where it feels like everything sucks. Or someone sucks. Or the world sucks. Whatever's going on in your life, you're NOT feeling sparkly. Dog-darn-gonnit NOT sparkly. This chapter can help you be okay with ALL of that AND still find exquisite sparkly gems. In the fast lane.

There was a time I felt like crap. In 1998, I hated my job, hated that I was single, hated that my best friend (whom I had made myself dependent on) was about to leave the country, hated that I was racking up debt, and hated that I had too many boyfriends in a short sequence of time and felt like dirt. AND THEN... I encountered this super-happy person one morning in the supermarket at 7 am, and I was so NOT HAVING IT.

What did she do? She was beaming with happiness as she picked out some yogurt. Her happiness was palpable.

And totally pissed me off.

That's how miserable I was.

Did that wake me up to do some soul-searching?

Sadly, not yet. I had zero sparkle self-awareness. I didn't know how to get out of being miserable. I felt like I was powerless.

I didn't yet know how to look for my deep gems back then.

I kind of soothed myself, shrugged it off, eventually quit that job, and followed my heart again to other positive things. Not a bad thing.

BUT I did not stop to really dig deep to find my deep learnings then.

And because I didn't, I later recreated similar scenarios for myself, again and again. Many "poverty" money loss experiences. "Ground zeroes."

From "poverty" to "powerty."
(That auto-corrected itself and is brilliant!)

It took me to get to my mid-thirties, and especially my recent years, where I started to do "sparkle work" (inner work) on myself. Yesterday was such a moment, in fact. June 10, 2020. I was proofing the edits of this (so I thought) already-finished book! I suddenly paused. Dug deep. And found some long-time-coming key learnings and deep gems for myself.

Realizing things like... I had subconsciously been recreating a feast-and-famine, sacrifice-myself pattern to honor my mum. I had not really listened to my heart and spoken up for myself for what I really wanted. Thinking things like "I have to do this / be nice / grateful..."

I spotted several totally unhealthy unconscious mindsets where I had been sabotaging myself.

A big overarching pattern I found was that I have probably been recreating "poverty" or "ground zero" situations, again and again, to let others rescue me in order to feel loved! And also to avoid my own power. It seemed safer, more comfortable to play small. I'd remain relatable. (What if I were to suddenly be richer or "bigger" than others? Would I lose everyone? Would I end up alone?)

Ah, the mind-stories! All hypothetical! And I allowed them to keep me small! That's how bad it can get if we let shadows run our lives instead of catching those gems and claiming our true sparkle powers!

Now, as I'm writing this, I am committed to keep catching them, reclaim my full sparkle power, and step OUT of such patterns. Not just jump into sparkle play, but actually dig out those buried gems.

I'm not doing this alone. I'm working with coaches who see my shadows and hold space for me to find them. I chose to get coaches because a) I want to do bigger things in life, and b) I've had enough of recreating ground zeros (that's just not a way to live.) And c) because it can be tricky to catch shadows yourself — they can hide in the darkness sometimes!

You don't have to take years to stop your inner sabotage patterns.

You don't have to wait until you blow up to change your life.

You can find gems now. If you're feeling like crap (since you're reading this chapter, I'm assuming you are), you're in a great place to go deep and catch gems. You're HERE. Curious. So come play!

play prompts:

Feel-like-crap soul search moment. What bugs you most right now in your life? What were similar scenarios at other times in your life? Start listing them, beginning with whichever one first comes to mind.

THE SITUATION: YOUR FEELINGS THEN:

_____   _____

_____   _____

_____   _____

Are you beginning to see patterns? What's similar here? What stories were / are you telling yourself each time?

Shift into your wisdom: What do you think is BEHIND your stories? Why do you think you subconsciously repeated them? For example, I created these "ground zero scenarios," telling myself things like "it's not safe to be on my own feet." Behind that was me not trusting myself.

How about you? What might be behind your repeating stories?

_____

_____

Shift into your SPARKLE prompt: If you imagine going back to all the stories you listed, as your now wiser self, and with all the bravery it takes: How would YOU show up for yourself? What would you do differently?

_____

_____

_____

How can you apply this to your most recent or current challenging situation? And what do you choose to do about it differently now?

Be kind to yourself if this feels icky and hard. All is part of the journey. It's okay. Go for a walk or do something to get out of your mind, embrace the icky feelings, and then allow them to leave.

And remember

the magical key?

To live curiously!

This key works anywhere in your SPARKLE adventure. Any time in your LIFE! Whenever things feel hard and impossible, try it! Live curiously. Curious and bold.

Hint: the biggest key about this key is to remember it ;-)
Yes, don't lose THIS key. (ha!)

When you remember it, simply go, "hmmmm... isn't that interesting!" and look at whatever's happening in your life with curiosity.

It can snap you right out of feeling things are happening TO you to becoming an observer, seeing the bigger picture of what's going on.

play prompt:

If you spotted repeating scenarios in the last play prompt and you feel there's more to learn, play with this:

When do you think is the very first time in your life that you felt like this?

(Think early childhood, the earliest memory where you that felt like this. Close your eyes. And breathe into this. Be curious. Anything show up?)

If yes, you can then ask...

As that child, what did you make all this mean about YOU?

And then...

Knowing what you know now, as a grownup, do you think the meaning you gave the stories back then was accurate to what was happening?

This is powerful stuff. Here's the backstory to that. When we come into life, we're fully sparkly. Right? Innocent, brave, anything is possible.

And then stuff happens. We hear "NO!" "Don't do that!" Rejection. We may feel ignored. The child we are at the time, we don't understand everything. We think things mean something about us and make up all kinds of things, trying to make sense. Then, we store these beliefs, and we store these feelings. We store negative experiences.

Until we choose to let them go.

So then... fast forward in life, when we have similar situations, like when someone says NO to us, it may trigger those same kinds of feelings from wayyyy back when, where we were just a little child.

It brings back the same feelings and the same meaning of whatever we made it mean back then. As a child. When the world didn't make sense.

Like "you don't love me" when you say NO.

Or "it's my fault!" when you GO.

Or "I have to be a nice girl!" so you feel GOOD.

What stories did you make up as a child that you now want to let go?

_____

_____

_____

Did more situations from your life pop up now that seem similar?

If yes, go deeper with earlier play prompts, or take a moment to simply be with these stories and feelings. See the similarities. The deeper meaning.

Then choose what you want to do to let the old stories go.

It can be a ritual by the sea. Writing them as a word on rocks, then tossing them into the water, as a symbol of letting go. Or you craft it out and then burn it. Toss it. Or simply say, "you're done." And move on.

What's your way to let them go?

And what do you choose to do differently now?

How do you choose to SPARKLE from here forward?

from **crap!** to sparkle
_my story of burnout

how this chapter helps:

In this chapter, I'm sharing my SPARKLE NOW and also my story BEFORE I was feeling sparkle.

This is my contrast story of burnout and no spirit connection and no body awareness and none of all that goodness. A story of being a hard-hustle robot running in a hamster wheel, and not getting anywhere. A story of where I was before I got to sparkle and feeling awesome.

Go here if you feel your life feels like hustle and sh!t, and you want to see where I was. It may help you to relate. And to know that I got here to this sparkle place from THAT.

I love how this book flows together in such magical ways. I just had a super magical close-connection with two of my spirit guides, Merlin and JC (my way of describing Jesus,) and it gave me this huge feel-good clarity and big, bird's eye view that all is well.

Even as my world appears to be off its hinges, and I would have enough human reason to freak out — I'm calm.

Off hinges? What? What's happening in my life as I'm writing this?

This is the moment in time where I just experienced meeting a new soulmate, "D." (P.S. I've come to believe there's more than one soulmate.

My – at the time of penning this book, still current – husband is also one. But that's another story.)

It's Sunday morning, after a very interesting Saturday:

Yesterday I went from waking up at 3:22, restless and mind spinning to reclaiming my calm as I was writing the last chapter…

…to living from my queen-sparkle-heart-light and buying myself a latte and croissant to enjoy by the beach…

…to a super-powerful, long-distance, energetic sparkle connection with D, feeling a strong pull to be with him and see him again…

…to a brand magic moment where I quickly got a client's new website designed and live within two hours[k]…

…to a cozy feel-good dinner and movie night with my husband.

What? How can all of this exist in one day?
Without me going cray-cray?

Good question. Once upon a time, I would have asked myself the same thing! Except now I don't have to anymore. I'm very connected with my sparkle and inner and higher guidance, and because of that, I can stay mostly calm, no matter what's going on.

Instead of worrying (which honestly doesn't do much good, other than alerting me to check in with myself if I want to change anything).

If you're connected to your intuition and sparkle, you can be calm even in storms!

---

k Brand magic it is! Come to www.AstridMueller.com if you want some for your own brand.

But... you may ask... what do you mean? Don't you feel bad about your husband with all that's going on? And what does the universe have to do with anything?

I can imagine you may have all kinds of judgment flying, and that's okay.

Here. Let me share where I'm at, fully vulnerable (and independent of your opinion.)

First of all, being calm and Zen, no matter what is going on in my life, is a good thing. Thank goodness for that!

You WANT to be the calm captain on your boat. Not a freaked-out panicky captain. But one who is solid. Listens to the gut.

(That doesn't mean that I don't turn human here and there and also jump into the non-calm roles, feeling all kinds of emotions, of course!)

It also doesn't mean that there's no next step to my adventure coming — yes, this whole situation with my new soulmate and my hubby is about to get resolved. It's coming.)

This moment is a moment of gratitude. To show you how I'm navigating now. Even when sh!t hits the fan, I mostly have my calm, my sparkle.

I'm the captain of my boat — most of the time — because of all the inner sparkle work and release work I've done — and because I've opened myself up to be fully supported by the universe. And all human support.

It wasn't always like that.

I didn't always have this sparkle connection to my heart. Once I was literally BLIND. (Like in that song "Amazing Grace.")

I used to be on the other side of sparkle.

Hard hustle. No universe connection. Not empowered. Burning out.

story time.

I was studying in New York, with a full student load, while working long-distance on my Swiss international illustration + design business and also working on getting my new U.S. business off the ground in the wedding industry and making key connections while in the city.

And at that same time, my dad was in his last months of life, back in Switzerland, suffering, and I was not fully aware, but I was feeling it.

I hustled. And bustled.

I was reaching up while feeling small. Kind of like the skyscrapers in Manhattan. So symbolic. I felt like an ant below those skyscrapers. Not knowing myself. Running. But not getting anywhere.

Felt all kinds of not good enough. Had no clear inner guidance, just followed what other successful (or apparently successful) others did. I was giving my power away! To things and people outside of myself!

I didn't listen to my body. I had no connection. I was running myself into the ground. One day my body said, "STOP!"

And turned my world upside down. Literally:

Once, at 1 in the morning, I had just pinned a painting up on a wall for my art class when the whole painting tilted sideways. While still fully attached to the wall.

I was like, "What the heck just happened?!!"

I found out later it was my first small spell of vertigo.

And I kept ignoring it.

I ended up getting more and more spells over the next weeks. Suddenly in a restaurant, I would feel queasy. And then weird. And then dizzy. I'd barely make it home and had to fix my eyes on one point not to spin out of control. Then I'd sit on my bed, head against the wall, not moving, while the whole room spun wildly out of control.

I STILL kept going.

I barely made it home to Switzerland to see my dad one last time. Of course, to get to the airport, I had to get one of those international cab drivers with the driving style of stop and go, wobble, wobble — while my whole head was spinning and I was queasy with vertigo. That ride seemed like the longest two hours of my life. I was also playing scarcity then, not investing in a smooth, direct cab ride but a freaking shared van. Seriously! NOT QUEEN.

And I still wasn't listening to my body.

It got worse. I didn't know any better then. But I'm telling you this powerful story now so that YOU DON'T have to experience it.

I didn't know any better then. I thought I HAD TO fight hard. Work hard. I thought I had to do all these things! What else? Forward!

(Notice? I was massively internally bullying myself!)

I was also playing the "be an A student game."

Another thing I have since let go of.

The day my dad passed away, I actually went to school after I got the call. All was in shambles. I tried to go to class. I pinned my painting on the chalkboard for class discussion, keeping it together... when suddenly I just stared at it, froze, and my eyes filled with tears.

The teacher came to me and stunned me with a hug, which I wasn't even able to receive.

Looking back, I was a zombie. Yet feeling the pain. It was so bad.

And I kept going for quite a while longer. Scheduling lunch that same day with a friend, I remember saying, "Yes, of course, I can! I'm ok!" Keeping up all the "I have to"s. Not allowing my full feelings. Self-care was on another planet. In another universe.

I even kept a PHOTOSHOOT DATE that day. After school, I took a taxi to Brooklyn to shoot my upcoming wedding stationery line. The day my dad died.

Dude.

Not one of my glory moments.

But now, it's a powerful story in my life. And a reminder of a place that I don't ever again need to be at. And neither do you.

Today I'm operating from the sparkle space.

And I would love for you to choose that too.

So! Let's take a deep breath!

Shake this heavy story off (I'm actually asking my hubby to go for a yummy Sunday breakfast, and I will wash my hands with warm water first to release this story energy... after giving myself a hug of gratitude and forgiveness for all the big things I learned and am now sharing here.)

And then I'll tell you how I got here to this sparkle path.

Choose what you want next:

If you're ready for my intuition-awakening spirit journey, how I got from just a human-logic being with no idea about magic, psychics, etc., to freely co-creating with the universe so powerfully..., hop over to the chapter "from sh!t to sparkle."

If that doesn't feel quite right, go to the chapter index at the beginning, and pick what speaks to you there!

You're the captain. Navigate with your heart.
That's where the magic starts!

the judgment game.
how to get back to
sparkle!

how this chapter helps:

In this chapter, I'm giving you some tools to release bad feelings + judgment. You'll practice the habit of curiosity. And shifting from heaviness to light feelings and feeling sparkly!

Our inner critic gets a bad rap. However, its voice can help us spot thoughts and beliefs and feelings that we no longer need.

Whenever you feel inner self-judgment come up, STOP. And face it.

This recently happened to me in a dance class. I literally was facing mirrors. And my inner critic started bombarding me with shadows.

And then...
Ready? Grab some popcorn...

story time.

So I'm already a good dancer. And have a great body. Ha! Now I can say that! But right then, I did NOT feel it. I was playing the judgment game.

It really doesn't matter how good we are at something or what we look like. It only matters whether we're playing the "love myself" game or the judgment game.

Are you owning your brilliance and your magic?
Or beating down on yourself?

Did you ever see super charismatic people — maybe even in your family — who aren't really the best or prettiest (or whatever-est) but you were totally smitten by them? No matter what they looked like or how imperfectly they did something?

Now I want you to do that for yourself.

Because all the judgment we give ourselves is a bunch of baloney.

It's only self-bullying! Not helpful. And not healthy.

I am writing this in the airplane back to Alaska, after just visiting Texas, where I met a bunch of people (actually dancers!) who said you have to OWN IT. "Don't apologize," they emphasized more than once.

As a lesson for dance movements but also, of course, for life!

The Texans aspired to "be confident." Even if you don't know what you're doing. Or heck, even if your shape isn't the shape of your dreams.

So how to do that?

Back to my story with the dance class and the mirrors, in February 2019, at that dance weekend in Anchorage, Alaska, I had gone there to do what I love — dancing. My thinking had actually been along the lines of: "I'm so good I don't need this. I'm just going to have fun at this workshop."

Little did I know that I'd go from that feeling of aloofness to feeling like an old spat-out piece of chewing gum within 24 hours.

And I did it all to myself.

Gradually, over the weekend — in which we were learning couples' dances, western, two-step, and west coast swing — I started glancing in the mirror and seeing myself as… fat. I judged my hips, my thighs and compared myself to every other woman. I was vicious to myself. It was bad.

I literally felt heavy and bad in my body because of all the inner voices going rampant. Like a dark cloud was upon me. Know what I mean?

I kept looking at the mirrors. Then at others in the mirrors. Then at my hips. Comparing, comparing. Feeling less and less good in my skin.

By Saturday night, I had run out of all the clothes that made me feel good in my skin — I actually tried on about five different combinations of outfits. None of them made me feel slim. (Which is not even normally my goal! But it suddenly had turned into my measure of judgment that weekend!)

So here I was, entering Saturday dance night, facing all the big mirrors, when finally it hit me, "Hey! I'm feeling really bad! I feel like crap!"

Finally, I CAUGHT what I was doing to myself!

So what did I do?

I pulled full - STOP!

...and went outside. To the bathroom. To be by myself.

I did several things there to feel better.
You can use them, too — I'm sharing them as a play list here!

play prompts:

There are many things we can do to shift out of judgment.
I'll start with the ones I did on that evening, in that bathroom.

- ★ I took a few cleansing breaths. Closing my eyes and imagining I was breathing heavy energy OUT and clear fresh energy IN.
- ★ I counted to 10.
- ★ I shook it off, flapping my arms and shaking my whole body.
- ★ I called in Archangel Michael to release any heavy energy.
- ★ I washed my hands with the intention to cleanse not just my hands but also my energy field.
- ★ I put on new, bright lipstick.
- ★ Then I decided to not listen to the shadows but choose JOY. I set the intention to start over with a fresh positive attitud, and went back into the dance studio.

(See my list of additional tools at the end of the book for more ideas.)

So what happened after I shifted my energy in the bathroom?

I came back into the dance studio and actually started having fun.
Imagine that.

A song came on that suddenly EXCITED me. (The universe was also helping me!) I liked the song SO much that I didn't even look for someone to dance with, but just started moving, in JOY, and being me.

And then, what happened?

A most unusual thing, actually.

A WOMAN (who I didn't even know) came to partner-dance with me.

She told me my energy was so CONTAGIOUS that she just couldn't help herself but dance with me and join the fun.

This happens when we shift into sparkle and into our true being: Awesome people want to join us! We just attract them!

Whoosh! We become attractive!

at-trac-tive

As per an online dictionary, it means:

★ Providing pleasure or delight, especially in appearance or manner; pleasing; charming; alluring: an attractive personality.

★ Arousing interest or engaging one's thought, consideration, etc.: an attractive idea; an attractive price. Having the quality of attracting.

So what happened next?

I attracted a soulmate.

Holy smokes! I actually went from feeling like sh!t to being so attractive, as to attract a SOULMATE?!? How is that even possible?

It's a great and extreme example. And I see two deeper answers here:

* ★ ONE – I had ditched inner judgment (at least in that moment!) and shifted my energy. To SPARKLE. To JOY. To feeling clear. Me being me. That IS when we're attractive. No matter how we look^ or whatever the heck the circumstance. When we are ourselves, comfortable in our skin, and simply enJOYING ourselves, we become charismatic. Attractive.

* ★ TWO – I was ready in my life for this soulmate. Universe opportunities show up when we are ready for them.

So! What kind of person or experience would you like to attract next? Are you giving yourself "Permission to Sparkle " to experience this?

_____

_____

For this to happen... What kind of JUDGMENT or inner stories do you think you have to release?

_____

_____

loving yourself–no matter what

how this chapter helps:

Self-love is a foundation for sparkle life. And I almost overlooked to include it in this book. Because, actually, I wasn't fully embracing it myself (and hence, didn't even notice the chapter was missing!!!)

In this chapter, you'll lay your foundation for your sparkle — and your fireworks. Absolutely essential to create anything lasting in your life, from relationships to wealth to health, and also... your birthright.

If you don't fully love yourself, you also won't fully allow yourself all that you want. You'll keep saying, "meh, that's 'good enough,'" not, "believe in yourself," or, like I did, again and again, "give up!!!"

You might make yourself dependent on others, feel jealous of others, compare yourself, not trust yourself, not feel good in your skin, not do what your soul wants you to do to feel AMAZING!

And you actually may get sick.

You get the gist.

You want to choose this.

Before I'll go deep with this chapter...

Here's what happened JUST NOW. My book is almost done, mind you. I just got done with implementing my editor's notes and just began actually working through the book for myself from the beginning. Just to absorb it. A last look.

You'd think I'd have self-love covered by now? And that I'm actually fully, wholeheartedly, and completely loving myself at this point, right?

Wrong.

Here are two pictures from today to illustrate where I'm currently at. On the left: Me, with a dog I'm walking in the background, full of love. I love doggies! And I also love this one. That's Magnum's butt. He made me smile, seeing him in the background, and I <u>felt</u> the love.

Then I got inspired to take a photo of ME looking at myself, feeling in love WITH MYSELF. Loving me. See how that went:

Me full of love, seeing the doggie.   Me trying to see and feel the love for myself.

Holy farnuggels. Seriously? It's also not like I only took ONE picture. I tried this several times. This is the best smile I got. :(

And even that felt kind of fake. What the heck!

So then, at first, I paused, pondered, and started wondering. Why the heck am I having such a hard time loving myself?

I've already done a lot of work on myself. "I've been trying SO HARD to "get this!" (This inner voice, by the way, is (of course) me beating up on myself. Also not love. All kinds of shadows.)

Back at home, on the couch, I tried again to connect with the love for myself. I said to myself, "I love you! I love me!" and, raising a drink: "Cheers! To me!"

It still felt like bullsh!t.

A curious thought came to my mind: if you don't feel love for a partner, you leave.

But...
what do you do if you don't feel love for YOURSELF?

You're stuck!

It seemed kind of funny. I sat with this for a moment.

Then I said, "So be it. I guess I'm stuck with you."

"Here we are. We just have to get along. Cheers!"

Now, this was a bit of a conundrum. And humorous too, kind of.

Except this has been wreaking havoc in my life until now, and I've had
ENOUGH.

I've had so many people tell me they love me and all the good things, and
I haven't been able to fully receive. First, it was my body. I didn't feel like
I deserved it. My inner story was, "I didn't make it. How could I take
credit for it?" If someone paid me a compliment, I received it as
superficial. "How dare you tell me my eyes are pretty!" I literally thought
one time when a guy I was dancing with complimented me.

But it wasn't their fault! It was me not fully loving myself.

At some point, I accepted and even started loving my body and having
fun with expressing myself. (Also thanks to many inner awareness play
full-out adventures you get to read here in this book.)

Yet. There's still this photo just now! This look on my face! There's still a
gaping inner darkness in my heart.

Like, "Who the heck am I to even love myself." Like, "Meh. I don't even
care."

Whose voice is that? What the heck! It's my inner bully. Giving me a "eff
you" in my face. Then ignoring me. (See the last paragraph? Who talks
like that!)

As I write, that voice keeps sh!t-storming me with all kinds of bullying of
what I'm supposedly doing wrong. "You still don't get it," it sneers.

And yet, here I am. Stopping. Now looking this bully voice in the eye.

Standoff. Showdown.

I decide that I'm done with this game.

I'm done with the inner critic at the steering wheel. My mind already
knows I'm magical. For like a million reasons.

And I choose to now also fully feel that for myself. I choose love instead of inner war. And I'm choosing to feel that I AM love.

With all crazy sh!t storm that that critic ever wants to throw at me. I CHOOSE and decide that you know what?

I'm magical. I'm god-made. And with all hairs, wrinkles, farts, flaws, mistakes, not-good-girl actions, AND all the good sides, I now choose to fully, wholeheartedly love myself.

So take that, inner critic. I see you. And I no longer listen.

Here's a cheers to ME and MYSELF.

My "I see you, inner critic, and cheers to ME!" moment.

This moment shifted my energy. I stopped fighting.
I decided to choose love.

(And that "angry orchard" soon thereafter also left.)

This is what I want you to do for yourself as you go on with this chapter.

Decide that you are lovable. Decide to love
yourself. Decide you ARE love.
And keep choosing THAT game.

How?

You'll find your own soul answers and inspired actions.
(What does your heart want you to do for yourself in this moment?)

For me, the decision itself set things in motion. And saying it loud!
Instead of running from it, facing it. Like the story in the nourishing
chapter at the very beginning. If you run from shadows, they'll keep
chasing and bullying you. Face them. Feel them. Face them with love
until they shrink and disappear.

Then choose differently.

And if the shadows creep back in, STOP again. Catch what's happening.
Face them. Then take the wheel back again. Back to your sparkle, your
feelgood, your joy, your love.

By the way, on a soul level, there are no shadows. There's only love. Your
higher self, and all that's on the other side, is ALL about love!

All the critic stuff and inner mind games only happen on the human
world plane. Part of our game here. Our growth. Our learning experience.

soul food prompt:

soul food love breathing

Stop whatever you're doing, and breathe. Any slow deep breaths. Slowly.
Count to three. Do it for one minute. Breathe LOVE in.

As you do this, notice how all concerns flow from your head down to
your toes. Release them, and fill your whole body with love.

Keep breathing wholeheartedly until you feel nourished and loved.

If you feel you need more nourishment to truly fill your cup, go back to
the beginning of the book, to the chapter "nourish your soul."

reflection prompt

look into the deep pond

Take a moment to ponder. Where in your life are you currently not
feeling full, deep sparkle love for what's you're doing or what's going on?
What about yourself do you not wholeheartedly love? Perhaps even hate?

Call out your inner critic and embrace it all.

_____

_____

This is a great moment to clean out old cobwebs of mind games and connect with your own unconditional true self-love.

Up to recently, I've been in the habit to quickly jump forward and shift my energy to the happy, to sparkle! Which can be great! Unless if we're always just running and jumping and missing the whole point.

Does your heart weigh heavy? Does that keep coming back? Then linger a bit longer. Get curious. Stay with the discomfort. Embrace it. Talk to it. Be really present with it. Until you feel the discomfort leave.

Then...

Shower yourself (and your inner critic) with love. This will make the critic dissolve!

(Because fear and bullying can't exist when love persists. Try it!)

If this is really hard for you... and perhaps you have some deeper stories that weigh heavy... allow yourself to be supported. Go to someone who feels good to talk to or get healing from.

There is no shame in getting help. (Only the shame we keep putting on ourselves!)

I'm speaking from experience: Once, I kept spinning in circles over a toxic relationship, thinking, "I'm okay." "I got this."

FINALLY, after SIX YEARS, I went against the stigma of talking to a therapist (which then, I had in my head because going to therapy was a common taboo in Switzerland, where I was raised.)

Within a few months of therapy, I was free of my inner mind games regarding this guy. And it turned out — ironically! — I didn't even love him! The mind-games had been all about myself!

Seeing the therapist helped me clear my mind cobwebs and find gems. And new ways of thinking and being kinder to myself.

All was about my own inner empowerment.

Of course. All about sparkle!

play prompts:

ask for higher love support

Take a moment and ask for universe support. Call on your angels, spirit guides, or a higher power (whatever you believe in.) Ask for help to start seeing, receiving, and FEELING full love for yourself.

Then sit in silence for a moment. You might get an inspiration. It might feel like you hear a message. Or a nudge to do something. What does your higher guidance or your heart want you to see or do right now?

Allow yourself to accept whatever support shows up when it does!

Journal what you experienced. What are you feeling? Thinking? Sink into that space. Use your own journal if you have one. Let your emotions and thoughts flow. Allow yourself to really feel your gems as you integrate the feeling of love for yourself.

And take those inspired actions your heart wants you to take. Be brave.

go into nature and let go

Nature has so many healing resources waiting for us. From fresh air to body movement, good energy, even universe guidance. Because as we walk, of course, we start moving our body circulation, see other things than just our mind-games, and begin to get out of our head.

What do you feel inspired to do? Go for a walk around the block? To a park? Or for a hike? Give yourself permission to choose what feels right. No pressure on you. This is for you to love yourself.

Before you head out, see if you have a question on your heart. What do you want to get an answer to right now? What do you want to resolve? If you have no question, you can simply set the intention of finding self-love.

Make your ask to the universe, and then go.

Enjoy your time in nature, and observe. Be really present. Walk with the eyes of a child. Curiously. Imagine plants wanting to give you wisdom. Or even forest beings. Even a fresh breeze may bring you new inspiration.

Then come back here and journal your newfound wisdom.

where are you not receiving

Receiving is an experience of love.

Where in your life have you not allowed yourself to fully receive? Relationships / wealth / health / self-expression... Where have you limited yourself? In what way?

What are your voices telling you as to why you canNOT have this?

(These are non-love voices!) Face them, and dissolve them with love.

---

face your inner demons

Are there things about you or your life that you actually HATE? What things? Body, mind, soul, old stories, regrets, areas in your life now? This might feel uncomfortable. Be kind to yourself. Simply observe. Be curious. Where did that come from? Why do you feel hate here? Are those stories even yours? Allow emotions to process, and let them leave.

And then forgive yourself. Until you feel it.

If there's more energy in your body or inner mind-chatter, there's more to learn, more to let go. Stay curious. That's not a bad thing. It's good awareness. And it's simply coming up to be released. That's why there is the not so sparkly path. To heal.

Think of it like doing a mind spa! If we don't ever look at these things and only want to sparkle, grime accumulates. So go deep. Allow yourself to shift your negative guilt / shame / hard feelings to make room for your true sparkle.

setting new love standards

In order to claim your full sparkle and fully love yourself, we need to know our love standards.

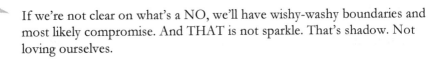

If we're not clear on what's a NO, we'll have wishy-washy boundaries and most likely compromise. And THAT is not sparkle. That's shadow. Not loving ourselves.

For instance, I just did that for my next dream relationships. Looking at what I loved in my previous ones and what was missing. Adding that to my new standards. I did it in all areas of life.

How about you? Pick a life area that can use the most love from you now: health / wealth / relationships / creative expression... then:

Set your new standards. The must-have qualities that you want are:

_____

_____

Then decide for yourself that you will hold them up, not compromise.

And if situations come up where you're challenged? Seek your pure truth. PAUSE. Observe where you are tempted to settle. Where are you giving up on your desires? Say, "it's okay? It's good enough?"

It can feel like an addiction! I just went through this!

Be strong. If you hear other voices, catch your shadows. Claim your sparkle. Choose to stick with your standards of love.

If needed, revisit your standards and rewrite. What feels TRUE to you, as to what you want? What are you willing to compromise on? What not?

For example, I would say yes to watching a movie with a friend if it interests me, even if it's not fully my thing — but I would no longer give up all quality conversation time to <u>only</u> watch movies all the time.

getting clear on your values

Knowing these helps us ask for, GET what we want, and have clear boundaries to say NO if something contradicts our values. This helps you fire UP your sparkle power!

How so? Not just because of others. But because of YOU. Your inner shadow voices will have a harder time — or even no chance! — if you know what you stand for. And therefore know when to say no.

For example, some of my values are "true joy" (going for my true desires, not quick gratification), me (being true to myself!), love, truth, savoring, self-expression, empowerment...

How about you? What are the values that are important to you to always have present in your life?

giving yourself soulmate love

Imagine for a moment that you have the most amazing relationship, a soulmate love. What would be happening in that relationship that you aren't already experiencing now?

_____

_____

Now ask yourself, with curiosity:

Where and in what way might YOU not be your own best soulmate lover to yourself? Think of your inner voices. And think of your actions! How could you be more of a soulmate lover to yourself?

soulmate lover creativity prompt

Doodle or craft something that represents you fully loving yourself as your own soulmate lover of your dreams. Feel the energy as you create it. Then keep the art piece around as inspiration as you live with more love.

write yourself a love letter

Write all that you love about yourself. Body, heart, mind, and soul. (If you still hate some things, write those hate pieces on a separate piece of paper and then, with compassion to you, crumple the paper and toss it.)

Don't rush it. This is for you to claim all of you. It matters. You matter!

love yourself up

Do something sweet to honor yourself and express and feel the love for yourself. Like a silent gratitude walk. Or a full date night for yourself. Whatever you do, do it consciously, savoring, choosing only things and activities that you truly love. Treat yourself. Savor the experience of love.

decide that you're awesome

Face yourself in the mirror. Truly. Fully. And decide that whatever you see, and you are, is awesome. Make it a point to see through inner objections and judgments and forgive yourself for human imperfections.

Face yourself until you fully feel how awesome you truly are.

Which, on a soul-level, we all are! Forgive yourself for being human.

the no-fun path & finding big gems

how this chapter helps:

This chapter helps you when you feel all hell breaking loose!

The bigger the storm, the bigger the gems — you may find your biggest learning gems and abundance freedom keys here. Hop on a ride with me: As I'm writing this, I'm in the middle of a deep dive + mind-storm.

story time...

You get to join me on my own journaling mind de-puzzling adventure. You get a seat in my mind. And witness how I find healing — aka go through the no-fun dark path to find the biggest gems!

Follow me! And keep your own pen and paper ready.

I just got the rug pulled from under me, and it's shaking up my entire life and belief system! What's happening? What am I talking about?

It started about two weeks ago, when I got a letter from one of the Swiss National retirement institutions, the "AHV," which is pillar one of the Swiss retirement security system. It's the mandatory "absolutely essential" account that everyone gets and has to pay into. Kind of like the social security system in the U.S.

Pillar two is the one your employer pays half, and you pay half, during your working lifetime. Pillar three is your own voluntary pension fund and whatever you can or want to save for your own retirement.

Since I started following my soul path purpose work and big dream, I started heavily investing in myself. In 2016, I invested pretty much my entire pillar two in myself. Other people use it to buy houses or keep it to accumulate interest. I cashed it out and invested in my inner growth, inner healing, and dream business.

That took all kinds of guts and tears. And then doubts. And fears. Then guilt! And disappointments when it didn't bring me the results I had in mind immediately! "Show me the money!" was one of my thoughts! But I don't regret a thing. I found bigger magic once I started looking.

feel-good hint:

The universe always brings us just what we need for our highest benefit. Stay curious. Keep walking. Keep learning.

The letter essentially said:

"You don't qualify to stay in that retirement insurance because you filed your ex-pat re-entry application too late."

What!? I won't go into detail, but there's some bureaucracy involved. Like them not receiving a letter and now claiming I don't fulfill the requirements to stay in it because I missed a date.

It can all be sorted out. Or not.

What happened for me because of that was:

Hello, FREAKOUT!

This is me potentially having *nothing* when I retire. Or so I thought!

After the first shock wave (because I know now that there are always gems and sparkle eventually), I switched to curiosity and took a deeper look at what's going on.

So I paused. Then took a few breaths. Then told my inner circle support system of co-creator coaches, my mastermind peeps who are also my lit-UP soul-cluster of dear, dear friends. And they started holding space.

I stayed curious. I journaled. I tried to stay calm.

Then, because I noticed heavy-weighing fears (aka inner shadows!), I booked a money-healing coaching session with TWO of my inner circle coaches to see what's going on and heal.

One is my dear friend, coach Kavita Singh — she's an amazing inner transformation and mindset coach, with all kinds of magic and energy-reading tools under her belt.

Kavita sums up her superpowers as helping change-makers see inner stories and old patterns that no longer serve and "connect the dots" so that they can transform into their most empowered leadership selves. She's also the person I describe as my soul-sister of many lifetimes and part of my inner support circle.

The other practitioner is intuitive energy healer Yola Mehmeti[1], a magician in her own right! She tunes into the energy and stories of people's present and past lives and helps them spot and heal inner limiting beliefs. She does deep transformational work way below our conscious awareness level. To put a label on it, her key modality is ThetaHealing ® (a method by Vianna Stibal). I also really love working with Yola. She's helped me big time with releasing money blocks before!

So I invited both of them into my room. This was December 17, 2018.

---

[1] You can find Yola on instagram under @yolabear17, and Kavita at www.kavitasingh.today

Heads-up: I'm giving you full disclosure here of my own story and how I saw things at that time. I'm not telling you this is how things are or how you should view things.

I'm not promoting any religion or truths.

You always get to choose how you see things.

Stay curious.

So! What happened in our session?

It was deep. I shared my story, and they intuitively tuned in, reading my energy and some of my past life things. They saw guilt. Some past life money-laundering thing where I did something "bad" (from a human perspective.) Apparently, I took some money that I didn't give back.

They also mirrored to me that I have some big beliefs about institutions and not wanting to fit into boxes. Um, yes! And there's some connection here in my story, they said, about resisting to pay those institutions.
So true! It just feels like victim energy! Like "I have to!" Not exciting. I really would prefer an "I OWN THIS — I CHOOSE THIS" kind of power freedom energy!

Can you imagine? I was born and raised in Switzerland. The land of rules. And institutions. And lots of "this is how you do it." The need for security was pretty much instilled into my genes.

This was going to be a big cultural + family belief makeover for me.

I wasn't there yet. Not feeling it, as I was in the middle of it all.

So! Back to what I was percolating:

About the money thing I supposedly did in a past life... I couldn't get full details; I literally hit a wall. I was so ashamed that Kavita wasn't even able to access my Akashic records! All she saw was, literally, a huge wall.

I didn't even want her, my dear soul-sister-coach-play-buddy of many lifetimes, whom I trust with all my life's details (and my life) to see it!

My whole system was ashamed. Can our subconscious be ashamed? How bad was what I did anyway?

Here's something you may not know about me: Coaches usually love me. When I show up for coaching sessions, I'm ready for anything. I'm always all IN. Heart forward. Bring it on! Because of that, I always have super powerful sessions. Huge walkaways. I'm open.

(Side-note, the more curious and open you are to find your inner truths, the more you'll find, and the more you move! I see this with my own clients. The more open they are to find magic, the more magic they find. Of course, all in good time. You have to be ready.)

So! This being said, with my history of being ready and open in coaching sessions, I was shocked to hit this wall.

My other dear inner-circle-soul-cluster-coach-friend Jean Berry had a great reframe for this later (she's always wonderful in shifting EVERYTHING into curiosity, playfulness, and seeing gems!) she said

"Isn't that interesting! You're playing the unforgivable game!"

play prompt:

This is a great powerful coaching question and tool you can use any time to stop your mind spinning and find gems: Ask yourself:

"Ha! Interesting! What game am I playing here?"

Yes! Indeed, what game WAS I playing? She totally nailed it! I felt that what I did was unforgivable, so I was playing the unforgivable game!

That emerged in bigger and deeper ways in my session with Kavita and Yola. They sensed that there's also some connection again with my late uncle, who in my current lifetime did all kinds of shady business dealings.

In fact, Yola felt his energetic presence as I wondered if he had anything to do with my story of that past lifetime. (Apparently, there had been other past life entanglements with him, where I had felt guilt.)

WHAT? I'd done shady things? How bad? It was all murky yet felt terrible and sent me into a mind-storm. Me, good girl, SHADY? What did that mean about me? I felt I was in an identity crisis.

Head's up: juicy family story.

bonus entertainment.

You're welcome.

Before I continue, here's a bit more about my uncle so you can understand my reaction and do him full justice:

First of all, he had a heart of gold.

He was also one of those relatives who brought glorious stories into our family that kept percolating at holiday dinner tables, where we reminisced and laughed and lovingly shook our heads at the same time.

Got one of those "crazy" relatives? You love them dearly, no matter how crazy they are?

For example: One day, he had some mafia-like guy coming to my dad's house with a bunch of gold bars to hide in the cellar for my uncle!

Yes really! Total movie material.

My parents were appalled and wanted to say no. They ended up saying ONE NIGHT only and that the next day they would put the gold out on the street, not wanting to have anything to do with it.

(Needless to say, someone did come very swiftly to pick it up again.)

My uncle was a kind soul and no mafia big shot — as far as I could tell — but he ALWAYS attracted sure-to-fail deals and shady people, and they always cooked up some oddball schemes. One time he even bought an entire bank! A whole building block across the street! Which then sat empty for months until he had to drop it again. It was so strange!

He was always talking about millions, getting strange bursts of money or big fat cars, then always somehow losing all.

He was the best uncle for me growing up, though! I even fought, as a seven-year-old, to get him, not the other family friend who had been planned for me, as my godfather. (Now there's a hilarious pun not intended.) My brother Marc and I were able to play with our uncle without limits. There was never a "no." Never a "this is too scary." Nothing was too wild, rude, or off-limits. It was great!

We sledded sitting on his back, him head-first, laughing so hard when we hit a tree (only then realizing how stupid that had been.) Sat on his shoulders, patting his balding head with silly sing-along rhyming songs. Giggled wildly as he was racing red lights with us in one of his Mercedes, while our parents had near-heart-attacks, following us in their car.

It was glorious. We loved him.

As I grew up and saw more of the shady side of the fun, his unsavory companions, and strange business adventures, I started to see the deeper side of it: He didn't feel he was enough. He kept trying to prove his worth. And no millions could do it! No gold bars. No bank deals!

This almost breaks my heart again thinking about it. I always saw him as lovable, just being himself, without any of all that stuff! Who cares! Now this session with Kavita and Yola suddenly suggested that maybe I also had my own shady past life story, where I, a self-proclaimed A-student and "Sparklegirl," did something shady? And possibly with my uncle!??

Something like money laundering. Spy stuff...? So shady that even my subconscious wouldn't want anyone to see it?

Ok then! Hello, unforgivable no-fun no-sparkle path!

My mind started tumbling. I questioned EVERYTHING. Questioned myself. Who I am. What else did I do in that lifetime? In other lifetimes? What does that all mean about <u>me</u>?

So then we had a big conversation in that session, me being curious yet also me playing the rebel. The dark shadow wall stayed.

They tried to give me consolation and pointers (I guess like I did with my uncle when I said, of course, you're worth gold! Just as you are! No matter what you did!) — to no avail.

I realized that I didn't believe I deserve! ANYTHING!
If I did something unforgivable? No way!

No wonder my money wasn't flowing.
No wonder I manifested this denial of my retirement.

I kept recreating lack in my reality because my belief system, and my subconscious, deeply felt that I didn't deserve a darn thing!

Talking about a past-life guilt trip!

My mind kept spinning. I started questioning <u>more</u>! How the universe works! What IS forgivable? What not? Are all souls inherently good?

What if I'd done something REALLY bad like Hitler?
(Yup, my mind went haywire!)

Is it true that we come to this life with pre-agreed soul-contracts, where we ask for adversaries, and adversaries agree to be our "bad guys" so we can all learn? (Only God would know!)

That's how I used to see things, but well, I didn't think I was such an adversary. That's a whole new story...! What WAS I in that lifetime?

Are there limits? Was Hitler an innocent good soul deep inside who had agreed to play a contrasting role? Really? What a crazy thought!

Or are there also genuinely NON-good people?

Which kind am I?!

Still going down a rabbit hole here.

To catch those old inner beliefs that started rearing their heads here, I kept digging. Curious. Antennas out to find gems.

play time!

So then I'll play the "good souls play different roles" game.

So, what if... in one life we play a sparkle-girl-good-girl-world-changer, and in the next, we play a contrasting harsh-bad-evil person sort of role... Doesn't that also change the world?

Every adversary brings about a superhero.
And a playground for world change.

Right?

Notice how so many revolutionaries, light workers, and good organizations have started to grow and thrive since Trump became president? This is not me taking political sides. It's me showing the other side of bad guys being in the game.

There's always a good side on the other side of the bad side. Right?

So, what if I — "Sparklegirl" — was a really "bad girl?" What if I had taken money from families who really needed it? What if people DIED because of this? Or went hungry? ... Ah!!! How do I even KNOW I can forgive myself if I don't even know what I DID in that lifetime?

More of the unforgivable game.

So what if "good girl" did something bad in that lifetime? I've also done bad things in this life. I'm no saint. Yet I've come to see myself as do-gooder-change-the-world "Sparklegirl." Slight conflict here!

I have no idea what I did in that lifetime with my uncle, but it feels really bad. And unforgivable. As I'm writing this, I'm feeling knots in my stomach. Nice awareness. (That's also my body telling me something.)

And, as I'm mind-dumping all this mind-drama... Live journaling... I'm also getting kind of tired of it.

Thank you!

The healing of this mind story (and the return of my sparkle!) has begun. (Because I'm letting it out! Bravely! Instead of keeping it covered up!)

Healing begins to happen when you start letting things out.

Digging deeper.

So, what if? What is the worst scenario?
Let's play the worst-scenario game.

What if I literally had lifetimes where I was a monster of the planet?

Now I'm here. With a big passion to (positively) change many lives.

And I feel compassion. Remorse. Guilt. I'm feeling "good soul things."
I'm seeing perspectives. I understand pain. Heck, I FEEL pain right now.
I'm living the human experience and learning.

Without contrast, I wouldn't feel pain. I would be in la-la land.

So, thank you, me, and contrast for that experience.

Also, I'm noticing that ...

I can't change the world from a high horse.

I have to understand and have compassion also for the contrasting side.

And this statement gave me a visual of me being on the ground. Literally
close to dirt. Feeling like dirt. Sitting in it. (This might also be a glimpse
of that lifetime that I got. Perhaps the end of it.)

So now I'm having a dirt party game.
Which just turned into a pity game.
And again, I'm tired of it.

Good.

(Journaling this stuff out really helps me get it out of the system!)

So... back to the core question on the table here... and how this all
ties into my whole sparkle quest:

I have a big dream. To really be my SPARKLY self, bring all my gifts
to the planet, being me! And inspiring others to do the same!
Changing lives around the world with my message:

We all deserve to be who we came here to be!
To be fully sparkly. To live our dreams!
To bring our unique gifts to the world!

We deserve to be free!

That's what I "preach!"

How beautiful that the universe brought me a huge new gem here: a huge limiting cloud that I can release, so I can BE THIS. And step INTO MY DREAM. Be what I preach. In bigger ways.

And obviously, I can't step into this dream if I feel I don't deserve it.

So I stay curious and play with that. (This is me live journaling again.)

Let's play the "I don't deserve abundance" game.

★ So WHAT if I stay ground zero with my finances? What good is that? Who benefits from that? The world? No. Me? No. It may even be selfish to cling to this guilt because now I'm not allowing clients who need me to become clients! No one wins.

★ On the other hand, if I heal and let go of this guilt... This alone will help heal others, even if they don't pay me. (Our healing and evolution inspire and affect the energy of others and the collective consciousness. As we sparkle more, we inspire more.)

★ Is that guilt even reasonable? Is it ever? And, is it even MINE? It's so obscure... past lives... who knows what happened, right? How can I feel guilt or pay for something I don't even know I did?

So now I'm holding on to a guilt that is literally stupid.

Well, BUT (devil's advocate) — let's say you created poverty with your greed! Maybe now that's your freaking karma, dude. And you deserve to really feel this. And to not get ahead.

Okay, curiosity! Well! Isn't THAT interesting then!

I have two choices.

I can stay victim to THAT belief or take back my power and choose what I WANT to believe. So I'm free to create all the goodness I want.

I choose what happens from here. Good or bad. Are you with me? If I don't choose good now (healing and changing the world, beginning with myself) and give power to the "that's karma" belief, I would perpetuate staying stuck. Perpetuating the belief that there's no way out!

And I don't believe in that kind of God or universe. I believe that we have choices. We can choose to do good. We can choose to change. And I choose to heal this old guilt so I can do all the good I want to while I'm here on this planet.

So then...is there ANY purpose still for this guilt?

I'm starting to feel that the only way this guilt still benefits me now is to see it. And to release it. And to give myself permission to DESERVE ALL and ANYTHING — including all my dreams. All my sparkle!

Because I believe in a universe of pure possibilities! And love!

"Permission To Sparkle" at its finest!

This is a huge healing opportunity from the universe.

I get to choose what I want from here.

I feel like I just put myself in a big courtroom with all my inner voices and lifetimes, in front of my own inner judge and the universe. While the universe (or God) gently observes, smiles, holds space.

Am I playing God here? That's quite ridiculous!
I'm pondering here what sentence I deserve!

Shadow alert! Snap!

JUDGMENT is HUMAN. It's not soul level.

Judgment means I'm fighting against myself. It's the anti-sparkle path.
Forgiveness means release, back to sparkle, to power, to love.

I get to choose. Drama or love. Guilt or thrive. Dirt party or Sparkle LIFE!

Also... wouldn't God want me to do good so I can redeem myself?

Talking about deserving abundance: isn't part of being a world-changer, who inspires and changes lives, also getting PAID abundantly so they can serve more and more people and in bigger ways?

Strangely, I notice that something in me is still trying to hold on to this — rationally pondered, quite irrational! — guilt somewhat. What??!??

So, then I'm playing the selfish game.

(See how I'm digging deeper to face anything else I can let go)

If I don't get to receive abundance, I don't get to serve clients who actually need my work!

So! What ripple effect do I WANT to create? Being a role model for change, bringing my gifts to the world, and doing good? Or staying stuck and inspiring others NOT to do anything either and stay stuck too?

Nooooooo!

All this has me curious... how does this relate to my uncle? Let me put the "facet glasses" on and take a look!

Now I'm playing the different angle + curiosity game!

My uncle didn't think he was lovable. He had huge guilt because of some things that happened in his lifetime. Tragic things. His wife and one of his sons committed suicide. And he flipped. That's when all the gold-chasing, shady games started happening. I totally understand this from the outside view now!

He may also have generated this guilt already in a previous lifetime. He tried frantically to make up for it. With his shady dealings and status symbols, he was trying to fill his heart, to prove his self-worth...

So, hello, I'm Astrid, and I'm playing a very similar game here.

What if I just STOP and forgive myself?
What if I just STOP and love myself?

As I wrote this, I intended to sleep on it and allow all these huge shifts to integrate. I stayed curious. Intending to heal whatever guilt energies I was still carrying here.

Why does it all matter??

If I don't heal this guilt and the belief that I don't deserve, I will keep self-sabotaging myself, spinning in circles, and also never help anyone else. Also, feeling guilty freaking doesn't feel good!

I get to heal what my uncle didn't get to heal in his lifetime. His hole in the heart. I don't have to carry that.

And what a beautiful gift is THAT. That I get to heal this! For me! And for ancestors, possibly also for him! And maybe other souls, too! (Our healing actually also affects collective consciousness.)

Can you imagine him watching over me, seeing me choose forgiveness, becoming fully sparkly, and be me?

And that, my friend, is a huge HUGE awareness gem and gift I just found.

Here's one healing prompt I used the day before writing this:

play prompt:

Listen to healing music as you choose to forgive yourself. Pick what resonates. Mozart? Monk chants? Pick something your heart loves.

Just four days later... I FOUND MORE BIG GEMS.

After sleeping on this, I first woke up still feeling heavy. I was almost rock-bottom. I felt I had the guilt of the world on my shoulders. It was ridiculous! But I embraced the feeling. And again, sat with it.

I pulled cards. Journaled... stayed curious.

I was ready to find more healing, but I felt I needed help.

The universe is always working in the background!

Notice that I stayed curious and asked for healing as I embarked on this whole quest since I received that retirement denial letter?

That curiosity and my ask had set the universe in motion!
To help me. To bring resources. To help release things.

Like Gabrielle Bernstein says: "The Universe Has Your Back."

What help? What resources? Universe what?
I love that you can be witness to this story.

Here's my sparkle journey for this particular situation so far:

★ The obstacle: Got the denial letter in November.

★ Asking for support: My inner circle supported me instantly

★ Curiosity + journaling brought me the first gems. Curious, I found guilt around money and not deserving and stayed present with the feelings in order to release them. Also, importantly, I knew I was NOT in the right mindset or energy yet to respond to the letter. (Energy affects things! Even letters!)

★ I played a "love my negative money feelings" game on Sunday, December 16, where I literally paused every time I felt bad in my body about buying what I really wanted (do I deserve this??) and loved the icky body feelings up. (Awareness + sending love energy to a body part heals. I felt better, step by step.)

- ★ I played an "abundance energy shopping" game next, actually buying what I <u>really</u> wanted (as opposed to following the old "I can't afford this" mind patterns). I stayed present with intentional good gratitude energy while shopping, even consciously paying forward and leaving surprise money tokens in the store and looking for signs. I found lots! Instant manifesting gifts! Savings!

- ★ The amazing past life awareness session with Yola and Kavita...

- ★ Mastermind love support from inner-circle coach friend Jean Berry on Tuesday, who made me feel good + brought the "unforgivable game" as new perspective to play. I felt seen, supported, and loved! There were some happy tears of release. Oh, and she suggested the "unforgivable game" and my story here as a priceless chapter for this book!

- ★ Universe support + meditating: In all my morning practices, I asked for help, stayed curious, journaled, and found clarity in cards. (They kept saying love yourself! And heal your heart!)

- ★ I asked for legal support: My tax expert in Switzerland surprised me with not just a quick answer but a whole letter to the insurance to copy and paste, and he offered it for free. Ah! Relief!

- ★ A coaching session with psychic coach Jessica Paschke (IntuitiveByTheSea.com), whom I lovingly call my "Mrs. McGonagall" gave me a big-picture view, more reassurance that really, I just need to trust my own inner wisdom. FIRST.

- ★ A healing session, gifted! The same day, I was invited to a live group call with Kavita and Yola, which turned into a huge limiting-belief healing session. It was amazing. I felt FREED!!

On Thursday, December 20, I mailed my response letter to the retirement institution, guilt-free, at peace, and totally ready to receive (yet now unattached to what would happen — trusting myself and the universe.)

And guess what! The universe supported me so big even while I was writing and mailing the letter. It was so beautiful!

> The universe is always supporting us. It's just up to us how open we are to seeing signs. (And resources, solutions, and support!)

Here are some of the signs I got:

★ The day I wrote the letter, my Merlin painting arrived. :) Several weeks earlier, I had booked intuitive artist and channel Lois Warnock (www.LoisWarnock.com) for a session and spirit guide painting. (P.S. She's amazing!) A magical treasure chest of universe wisdom! Turns out, Merlin was the spirit guide that showed up for me. And his painting showed up on my doorstep JUST when that universe support meant an extra special lot to me.

★ In the empty envelope I picked up to use was Queen Victoria. When I stuck my hand into the envelope, there was a post-it saying "Queen Victoria!" (I once played that queen in a local Mary Poppins musical theatre production. The note came from there.) What a funny and great universe support sign! "You got this, queen!" It put me in good energy to write and send the letter!

(I actually left it in the envelope for good measure. Ha! Can you picture the face of a stuffy straight bureaucrat seeing it? Lol!)

✱ I mailed the letter at 4:44 by "accident" — it's not like I planned my whole day to make that happen. I just felt the nudge to "take out your phone and take a picture," so I did! It was 4:44 in the afternoon. (4:44 is a powerful angel number message that the universe has our back. Google it to see if "seeing angel numbers" also resonates for you as a fun way to get messages and signs!)

At the post office, with the glimpse at my phone screen: it was exactly 4:44 in the afternoon.

So what happened with that appeal?
Many months later, it actually did get denied.

But again, as with all challenges, if we are curious, I also got to find a gem here: I ended up choosing to let go of any attachment to "security" and more scarcity thoughts and replace them with TRUST.

Trust in myself, in me being supported by the universe, and in me creating my own wealth and abundance through ME.

So good.

singing and dancing in the rain!

(This is where you start stepping up and sparkle

— even when sh!t hits the fan!)

permission to
not care.

---

how this chapter helps:

This chapter is about giving yourself permission to say NO and still feel good. It's not about becoming a cold person who doesn't care — you'll always care, of course. This is claiming your own path and giving yourself permission to make choices that follow your heart. And -=— yes! — to be okay when others are not on board with it!

In fact, as you'll see, this is a powerful way to find your real soul tribe.

Yesterday was a sparkly universe day, where a whole inner growth storm opened into sunlit clarity and led me to a huge gem. And this chapter of the book. This is all about permission to not-care.

What do I mean by that?

I don't mean you trash the planet. Or stop caring about others. You keep your heart. Of course! I still like the idea that we all do things with the best intentions for everyone and the world in general.

AND you don't have to care about what others think.

How is that possible?

Let me share part of my story, beginning with a dream I had.

this was **my dream:**

I dreamed I was in a place where I had a lot of fun. I was playing, doing something exciting. Good energy. Good people. There were also children and babies. I don't remember more details.

(I gave myself permission to not write it up yesterday, as it didn't feel aligned. I trusted that in just the perfect time, I'd know when to write it, and I gave myself permission to wait. I trusted that the universe would help me remember just the necessary details.)

In that dream, one of my friends showed up. She had a lot of heaviness in her life. She was on my far left and didn't want to come to me. I invited her in the dream: "Come over here! Come play here!"

I felt a huge guilt energy flying my way from her, of "How can you be so insensitive! I just had an abortion! (That was the story in the dream.) How can you be so cold to invite me over just now to play?" With babies!

Wow. I felt the hit. I felt the huge guilt energy. And felt terrible.

When I woke up, I became curious.

decoding the dream:

What the heck was this about? Was I a bad person for not going over to her, for wanting to stay in the fun zone?

Was I a bad person for inviting her over to my side?
Did I need to take on any of that guilt as a real thing?

What do you think?

— I'm pausing to let you ponder —

Here's another story before I reveal what I found. Remember I said this was a magical-sparkle-universe day? Several similar stories came to me — all with the same message!! (Universe signs noted! This has to be in this book!)

story #2:

My dear soul-sister friend, coach Kavita, and I connected for a quick connection call, and she asked me for a favor. To help her decode something that was going on.

Get this. You'll snicker. It was like a parallel universe.

She said she had a dear friend tell her she was offended because Kavita didn't play with her like she played with me. (We had just done a Facebook Live the other day, having fun.)

She too stepped into curiosity:

She already knew this was not her story, and she didn't need to take it at face value. Yet, she noticed a kind of shadow in her energy. She felt it was coming from her intense childhood where she did a lot of hiding because she didn't feel safe.

So, to give you a bit of a side-story: Kavita and I play the sparkle game all the time. Growing our awareness and our inner game. So Kavita was already super aware about details and already in a great space.

However, since she started playing more and more full-out with visibility in her dream business and purpose work, this situation brought up a light dust, which she wanted to release.

Yay, we both loved this — this is always a reason to celebrate! An opportunity to release another spot of dust on her diamond!

Allowing her to claim more of her true power. Being her full magical sparkly self. I was so excited. And honored. To be there and hold space.

I intuitively asked her some coaching questions, feeling into that dust energy that she felt in her body... leaning into our curiosity.

Then I also felt inspired to share the dream that I just shared with you.

That already helped her release this dust energy.

It was just the nugget she needed to hear. To heal!

I continued, all sparkled up, finding even more parallel stories that day. I want to share these with you too before I share my conclusion.

Join me! Be curious for yourself. How do these stories inspire you?

story #3:

A few months ago, I self-graduated myself early out of a big business coaching program that I had joined to (as per the program's promise) "become unstoppable."

The day recently came where I felt I did just that. I had found my sparkle!! With their help, with additional coaches I found on my own, and a lot of inner game sparkle work I played with on my own... I felt I HAD, in fact, become unstoppable.

I started playing full-out. Owning my sparkle. Posting in the program without fears. Fully being me. All in positive intentions, with my play sparkle energy, sparkling up the place, inviting to play. Celebrating others. Also, sharing my truth, inspiring to think.

I wrote one post from deep passion, full truth, about a topic I deeply care about: that people shouldn't hard-hustle themselves into oblivion but claim their sparkle! Live their lives! Stop the hustle when they are burnt out! (There was a lot of hustle energy in that group. One person had actually posted that she worked so hard that she felt suicidal. That had inspired me to this post.) I asked challenging questions: How much more does it take for you to stop the hustle? How much more evidence do you need that something is not working?

A few days later, a lot of drama got flung my way.

I was asked by one of the leaders of the program to tone it down. They said I was playing too big. Too loud. They felt I was attempting to solicit business from others in the program by inviting them to play with me.

Ha!! Oh my gosh. Really?

When that accusation came, I felt a HUGE energy of heaviness. Then defensiveness. A program that was intended to allow everyone to become unstoppable (and also grow their business) asked me to tone it down when I finally felt free, and played full-out as me? Simply engaging others to also come out of their shells and play with me? I felt betrayed. I had invested a lot of money into the program. And just when I started to speak up and shine my light, they told me I was too bright?

I tried to craft a response.

Even though I kept pausing and reconnecting with my inner guidance, cleansing my energy, calming myself... I kept feeling off and defensive. I wasn't able to totally clear my energy (and my answer) to a peaceful one.

At the end of that weekend, I finally asked for help. I asked coach Jean Berry to be my mirror. Was this last message finally fit to send?

I told her my intention that I wanted to come from peace energy, speak my truth, yet end on a good note.

What she said, deeply inspired me.

> "Play where it matters. Play where you make a difference." – Jean Berry

I ended up writing a super short bye-bye message and left the program with blessings and peace.

It wasn't even worth writing long letters to them. Or any longer note. They were not in the energy of asking. (They were in the defense.)

Yet! All the processing I did that weekend was a sparkle rain of gems for me! I healed so much. Which helped me get here.

story #4:

Recently, I had a similar thing happen to me. I blew another circuit with my sparkle. And it was another odd place to have that happen:

In a women's empowerment group with the purpose of celebrating and empowering each other on our life journeys and in realizing our dreams.

There, too, I came from a place of best intentions for everyone and was being more and more my empowered and sparkly self and ... one day, BOOM. I was also asked to dim my light.

Apparently, I triggered the critters out of some of these people as well. Including the leader. One person started talking behind my back to others even WHILE we were having a supposedly sacred group call. She complained that I didn't make any sense, and she couldn't take it anymore. And the leader felt like I was taking away leadership from her and was engaging too much with others.

The leader and a co-leader called me up to ask me to play less big, less loud, and more in the background. Let the leader lead.

Um.... were we still using the same rulebook? Was this still about empowerment? About inspiring each other to become all our own most powerful leaders and play full-out?

Again, I felt heavy energy coming my way and guilt-energy floated up... What did I do wrong? I was in defense mode at first and confused (some of it rightly so, because I was getting very mixed messages!)

I allowed myself to calm down and go inward.

By the way: if you ever need a quick tool to calm down, here you go.

tool to calm down:

Breathe. Count three in, hold three, count three out.
(Or pick your own feel-good numbers.)
Repeat until you feel better.

This time, the whole process went a whole lot faster. I got a whole flashback and benefited from all the thinking and processing I had done earlier in the story about the other coaching program.

So now, I was asked to tone down my sparkle in a women's empowerment group. How ironic. What universe humor. I was being tested. Was I going to keep shining my light? Or dim it?

I looked into the sparkle mirror. Put on my facet glasses. Looked at all the angles. What could I learn here? What could I do differently?

So! What did YOU find here for yourself in this chapter?

play prompt

Think of a time in your life where you were told to dim your light.

What was the story? Did you stay? Did you leave? What did you do? How did you feel? What did you learn? What gems did you find? What was about you? What about them?

Where are you on the scale of not caring what others think? 1–10?

Here's my takeaway from my adventures so far:

It doesn't matter what others say or think. Play where it matters. Play full-out.

(After-note! Since I wrote this, I've found that in the tension and discomfort can actually often be great learnings. Even soul-lessons. So before just leaping, I've now started to pause. To be curious for gems. To use my facet glasses to look at all angles and to have compassion for others (and myself!) and our paths. We all choose our own adventure.)

All that being said, as we grow, some people WILL get triggered. That's a good sign. It means you SPARKLE. You're playing full-out.

If someone is not aligned with what you do, they'll either grow with you, or they'll fall away. There's no good or bad in all this. Things simply rearrange. More aligned people and situations will come into our lives once we say yes to our sparkle and act on what we want.

One time, my friend Laura Axelson said something really cool to me. I was wondering, "OMG, what if one day I turn into an eccentric and crazy old lady?"

(Notice the self-judgment and fear of judgment in that thought!)

Laura said this great thing: "I HOPE that you'll be an eccentric old lady one day! You do you, girl!" Take that from Laura. She's badass-flamingo-do-your-own-quirky cool.

"You do you, girl."
–my friend Laura Axelson

Here's a picture of me and Laura to shift your energy to play.
We're doing a hippie quirky cookoo happy dance for her doggies. Yay!

play prompt:

If you have dogs, try to get them to dance with you just by <u>showing</u> them how to dance. (Of course, this is silly and won't work. I think they were laughing more about us than we were about ourselves, haha! But the point is that you shift into fun! Dare to be ridiculous! Live curiously!)

(And yes! That's a "raise your frequency to SPARKLE" party right there!)

Here's how I see it, regarding not caring about what others think.

Being fully you and fully lit up and happy is your birthright. Don't allow anyone to dim your light.

You have the power to let someone dim your light or not. If you think you can't openly play full-out where you're at, you always have choices:

Like expressing yourself in truth, big, no matter what! Or find other spaces. Where you get to do that. Or see if you're complete with where you're at or feel called to stay there longer, and maybe learn to express yourself there in different ways, also staying true to who you are.

We always have choices. And, whatever we choose... let's choose to fully be ourselves. If you can't do that where you're at...

Play where you can be you.

I found priceless gifts when I did that:

It felt amazing to come from my heart + speak my truth. Like a breath of fresh, sunny air sweeping through my home!

Also, a curious thing happened: While some may have gotten triggered and pushed back, unexpected supporters showed up, people who LOVED me — my soul tribe!

Allow yourself to be the real you
so your real tribe can see you.

Mic drop. Ponder that!

If you're not a sparkly unicorn, how can your sparkle unicorn tribe see you? They won't just magically come find you in your closet. You have to step out into the sunlight. And shine all your colors!

You're meant to sparkle. You're meant to feel all warm and happy like on a gorgeous day full of sunshine. You're meant to BE the sunshine!

play prompt:

Ponder these:
Why is sparkling full-out important to YOU?
How may that change your life if you DO?
What may you win? What lose? What may you lose if you DON'T?

As I reflected on all those stories and angles yesterday with Kavita, and now, I am noticing that my journey to sparkle went (so far) like this:

1. Playing freely as a young child,

2. Getting put into boxes (limitations and rules by parents, friends / schools / society / culture...).

3. Inner growth, growing my intuition, reconnecting with my power, knowing myself. Waking up to realize who I really am, what works for me, what I like, what lights me up.

4. Bumping up against things that are scary! Growing pains. Doing things anyways. Baby steps + big steps.

5. Playing rebel. Giving myself "Permission To Sparkle" again! Blowing up boxes (like in my stories from earlier) as I fully sparkle. That's GOOD. That's a success sign. :)

6. Learning discernment. And to not care. (Not allowing myself to be held back by other people's opinions.)

7. Being (mostly) at peace, just being me. I.e., giving myself full "Permission To Sparkle!"

Depending where you're at on that journey, different play prompts will resonate for you. Some may take too much courage right now, and that's okay. Start small. But stretch your courage.

It's not about how big a mountain is, it's about taking ANY small step to climb it.

Any small step is a step toward conquering your challenge! :)

What's a small (even tiny!) inspired step you can take right now?

If you like a fun and gentle daredevil muscle stretch:

Here's a fun play prompt!

play prompt:

Take a water aerobics class!

I just did that, and it was hilarious. The teacher was like a drill sergeant. I was expecting dancing in the water, and here she was, doing something that didn't really light me up. One two three GO, GO, GO ha-YAH! Commando forward!

There's nothing wrong with that. There's no judgment. Ever.

The class was great. It just wasn't for me.

It was hilarious to me.

It was such a contrast to the playful, creative mood I was in!

I just couldn't do the military-like stuff to the music that she was doing! So I started to make it my own. Do different moves underwater. That really made me giggle! Here was, "Sparklegirl!" trying (and then not trying) to do this whole drill-sergeant thing to this happy music! What!

It felt so great to be a bit of a rebel and secretly do my own thing. Claiming my own power to express myself. Not taking it (and myself) so seriously.

First just under water. Then also, above: I even ended up doing my own kind of water ballet! Lol!

The instructor didn't even care. (Yes, it's not like my old boxes in childhood, like being in school... Who cares? I'm grown up. I can do what I want. Nothing will "happen" to me.) Releasing fears. Just doing things.

After the class, she asked, "How did you like it?"

And I shared, "It was good! Just not all for me. I ended up doing my own thing." (I spoke my truth.)

And again. She didn't care.

So this can happen too! That people don't care! And if someone did get upset... Then you simply get to play with that:

Either they have a point, and you get to learn and change how you act and respond to this. Or they got triggered by you because of their own story. And then it doesn't have to become yours.

We all have our own stories.

You do you. Sparkle. Express yourself!

Do what brings you joy!

but... what if you're too scared?

hot tip:

Look for role models / shows / stories / quotes that inspire you that you can do it too!

One of the current surefire things to inspire me is the show "60 Minutes!" They feature unlikely superheroes who achieve amazing things despite all perceived odds. Check it out!

What shows might inspire you to boldly express yourself? Find one. Then take one action for yourself to stretch your own comfort zone.

Here's more inspiration for you.

I just got inspired by two friends who are coming out of their cocoon and playing full-out online, despite what their mind says. One did an — amazing! — dance improvisation video, fully expressing her feelings:

Transformational coach Ruth Levin sharing a play-full-out dance video with the world.[m]

---

[m] Find out more about Ruth on www.embodiedinmotion.com

This is Ruth Levin, a soulful and powerful leadership coach who helps leaders access their full potential through coaching and dance. Ruth mentioned she caught her mind trying to hold her back with things like, "This is narcissistic," and then she did it anyways.

We all have inner voices that are trying to hold us back. It's a normal part of our inner growth. We can simply embrace them, then act <u>through</u> them as we choose to let them go.

Where are you currently holding yourself back from doing what you really want? Are you saying yes to what excites you?
Or letting fears hold you back? Where do you want to play more full-out?

_____

_____

Pick an area and do something that makes you a bit nervous (which can be seen as simply another word for "excitement!") right now.

The only true obstacle is us holding ourselves back. Once we say YES to ourselves and act based on that, we move forward!

Ruth ended up getting tons of comments and shares — the video literally lit up the world as soon as she made it live. Imagine if she hadn't shared. How many people wouldn't have gotten inspired? Her being brave inspired others to do the same. More importantly, imagine how she felt in the first place, just for herself, dancing, full-out?

Her video also inspired me to play with this, in my own way:

I decided to record a video, too. Dancing full-out, no script, just being myself, and just put it live. Challenged myself! Guess what happened.

Crickets. No reactions from anyone. AH!

And that's beside the point AND part of the point: It was UNCOMFORTABLE for me not to have instant responses. My inner voices gave me all kinds of crap. "This sucks! No one cares! ... "

And guess what. That simply meant that I found MORE limiting thoughts and fears to release.

In the discomfort zone, we find gems!

Watch what was going on for me, right after I released the video and felt this comfort-zone stretch: I observed my mind as I took a shower.

My mind-stories went wild! They said things like...

- ⭐ "You! What did you do? This is uncomfortable!" (My stomach also had a say about this.) I stayed curious. Just noticing stories.

- ⭐ "She is amazing and actually gifted at dancing. And then here YOU come. What a comparison. You were 'just' dancing." Again, I just listened.

- ⭐ "Your video is BO-RING." The mind continued (yawn...)

- ⭐ "What if my hubby or friends see this and shake their heads." Oy vey. So be it (I let that wash down, too.)

- ⭐ Now my chest feels tight... I wonder what that is?

I'll stop here with writing (though I'll stay open) — you get the point: I was uncomfortable. And guess what. That's AWESOME.

When we're uncomfortable, we're growing. We're stretching. Develop new superpowers. Find gems.

All the things that I heard my mind say are things I can now evaluate, catch, observe, look at from different angles, and then let go. Either with one of the tools in this book or (if the voices keep returning!) with some get-to-the-core deep release coaching.

Judgment brings us down on the sparkle-meter; letting it go brings us up.

Yet, as you see, it's totally GOOD to take a moment to really sit with judgment and all the thoughts you were telling yourself.

You get to see the stories, learn what's there to learn, then let them go. And focus back on what makes you SPARKLE. Brings you JOY!

But what if they keep coming back, again and again...?

Stay curious! Ask: What can you do differently?

Is there a reason you're holding ON to old stories? Sometimes it's less scary to keep doing the same thing (even if it sucks) than to embrace change. What are your stories as to why you think you can't sparkle? What's the WORST thing that could happen here?

Look THAT in the eye, then give yourself "Permission To Sparkle!"

permission to claim
pure freedom

how this chapter helps:

Just when you think you're all sparkly and smooth-sailing along, the universe can surprise you with a turbulent sea. Which then also turns out to be perfect. Because everything serves. Even (and often especially) big waves can help us grow and reach our next level of sparkle.

This chapter is a real-time account of me role-modeling how you can ride this big wave without drowning — and even while actually sparkling.

This is also a chapter about staying in curiosity. Allowing new big things to emerge. While you keep riding the wave and looking at everything without judgment.

What am I talking about? Get ready, buckle up. This story is a big one. But, this chapter is probably for you since you're here!

I'm guessing you're ready for something big!

So! Here I am, in another big life adventure. Again, you get to experience my story as it's happening in real-time. And I bet because of this, you'll get your own shift into miracles. And bravery!

So lean back, and lean in.

I'm on the upswell of a big wave for me here... I'm feeling it. I'm already getting a taste of fears and of all kinds of things that I'll get to choose to embrace, including challenging myself and really stretching my comfort zone.

That being said, what I'll say here may also trigger YOU.

You may read things in here that will make you go "What??? That's crazy! That's not something I'd <u>ever</u> do!" Or "Who is SHE to say <u>that</u>?" Or "Wow — she's THAT kind of person."

Or whatever judgment comes. I'm preparing you.

(A,nd of course, these are only assumptions from me of what you might think, and therefore simply some of my shadows. My fears. What WILL people say when I share this?)

It's actually impossible to really know what other people think. And not manageable, actually. And why would we have to? If we design our lives based on what others think, where does that leave us?

What DOES matter here is how I want to live and how I want to feel. And to create that life that I want, I have to take charge of what I think and what I want to believe.

All beliefs are something we choose. We always get to choose what we want to believe. And that influences how we get to live!

Only when we are okay with EVERY belief that we carry are we truly free. Ponder this for a second: Do you live according to beliefs from society that you wish you didn't "have to" live by?

Which ones?

Run your radar over areas in your life: dos and don'ts in your spiritual life, society norms, gender norms, family rules... What your community sees as cool and not cool... Your love life...

Did anything pop up that happens to stand out, that you'd love to not have to live by? What rules or beliefs would you love to live by instead?

Give yourself a moment. And know that you get to choose everything.

It can take bravery. Of course. But that's what it takes to be free.

Heroes make their own rules. Get ready to become the ruler of your own destiny.

Of course, there are some things we typically take into consideration. Like coming with good intentions. Not purposefully harming others. Common courtesy. Helping others. And so forth.

Even with basic rules of living with other humans, there is still an incredible amount of freedom available for us to be who we truly are.

Also: We don't have to KNOW what's to everyone's highest benefit in order to freely express our feelings. We don't know everything. It's enough to live with that intention. And to trust that as we follow our hearts and lovingly speak our truths, everyone around us gets to do the same, make their own choices, and find their own power and support.

I find that it's a universal law that ultimately, things balance out, whatever change speaking our truth brings about. Everyone around us has the opportunity to eventually be okay, and things always somehow work out.

We live in an age of pure possibility! No matter where you are and what your circumstances are. Yes, in any part of the world. Any situation. (Is that challenging your mind? Or are you with me so far?)

Get ready to expand your mind:

If we only carry a belief to comply with what society may suggest, or what apparent circumstances seem to suggest as a limitation, yet it's not something that feels true to ourselves, we are draining our energy. Not sparkling. We aren't flying free. We are fitting ourselves in.

If we shift into curiosity, regardless of what our situation is, we open our minds again to possibility.

Here's the pure magic: When we're getting upset by something someone says, we have the chance to look at those "how dare they say that or do that" things, throw them all in the air, and then be curious what we really want to believe for ourselves. And how we truly want to live! Chances are, when we're rattled by something, we may secretly actually also want something there that we so far thought impossible!

We can go even further. And create a whole new paradigm for our lives!

Every storm in our life is an opportunity
to re-evaluate and then uplevel our life.
To live fully, in sparkle, living all our desires!

The more we allow the storms in life to bring us to our truth and what really makes us happy, and the more we give ourselves permission to truly say yes to THAT, the more free and magical and truly sparkly we become.

So you have been warned.

And you're still here. Congrats!!! You're leaning in!

Already then, adventurer! Grab your pen, paper, and listen in.

One rule, as always, to really benefit in the sparkle game:

Catch the judgments and learn and release them!
That's you catching gems.
You get the idea.

So when things come up that make you go "Whaaaaaaaat???!!!", put on
your curiosity hat.

And then you get to choose what's your truth and what is crap.

You decide what you want things to mean for yourself. You get to choose
your own truth, and you get to create your own life.

The braver you are in breaking old rules you've been living by and
embracing your objections and fears, the more freedom you'll find.

Think of this like a spooky ride in an amusement park. Behind all fears
and limiting paradigms are freedom, popcorn, and a magical sparkle life.

Now! Let's begin! Back into my story!

Here's what's happening in my life as I am (was) writing this. Watch me
ride this wave and expand my mind. And potentially uproot and change
my life. (Yes, I'm bracing myself.)

story time.

So! At the time I'm writing this, I'm happily married! And, always
following my heart, I had a really beautiful story of how we fell in love. I
feel he's a soulmate.

We were pretty much (almost) ready to get married within two weeks. He
treats me like a queen, takes care of me, understands me, loves me, makes
me laugh, expands my being me... We have a really great independent,
strong relationship in which we allow each other to fully be ourselves —
he lives his freedom retirement life hiking, hunting, enjoying nature.... I

expand my passion business, dance, travel on my very creative spiritual expansion journey... All good!

And I'm not wanting, not feeling any desire to change a thing...

Yet, 30 minutes ago, I almost said I LOVE YOU to another man.

Whaaaaaat??

It gets better. (Or worse.)

I truly honestly feel I'm going to. And that I can actually love more than one man. Without — at this time –=— changing anything.

Whaaaat?

All kinds of conventions, vows, beliefs, societal norms are already flying. Yup, I'm with you.

To relieve you if you are concerned now where this is going, this will not be a drama story of cheating of any kind. I'm riding the top of the wave, following what feels soul-aligned.

And I'm bravely embracing a bigness here that is just starting to dawn — as I'm writing this, I haven't said anything to my husband yet (nor to the other man) — I'm following my mind expansion sparkle journey.

Sparkle. Bad taste in your mouth? Not mine.

We can find sparkles and goodness even within storms, when we choose to embrace the adventure and ride out the waves.

If we stay curious. And open to possibility. Knowing that we can choose our destiny. We can make magic wand wishes. And the universe aligns. We get to set course, and we'll sail.

I WANT to sail in my truth.

So I'm digging deeper. Beginning the real story.

By the way, as I'm writing this, I'm in my car, with this view:

Morning sunshine in Kodiak, at the Near Island plane dock.
How can the world go under with a view like this?

I see a sea otter cracking shells on its belly. Let me crack this story wide open. (I get it. Universe humor!)

Apart from this crazy development, I've actually been having a really good day. Lots of amazing things already happened just in the first few hours of my morning. Business magic with lots of (universe magic!) synchronicities. Wishes answered, great connections, great awareness, even a celebration call with my Alpha group for this book...

A typical magical day in my sparkle world.

Even that other man, and him popping up with a message, and a quick celebration ping... me on a roll. It actually all felt strangely good!

And then, the energy changed. Of course!

These are big things. My thoughts and feelings started taking a spin. Stomach turning. The storm begins.

What am I getting myself into?

I went from high flying to denial (?) (nothing happened, really... !?) to feeling all was falling apart, to guilt, to craving that other man...

All kinds of swirls.

In the name of self-care, I first took a nap.

Today's inspirational cards, by the way, for me were:

* CHAOS AND CONFLICT

* ROUND AND ROUND (both from the Wisdom of the Oracle card deck by Colette Baron-Reid)

* INDEPENDENCE and the Goddess Bast (from the Goddess deck by Doreen Virtue)

* and SHIELD YOURSELF – Bougainvilla Flower (from the Flower Therapy deck by Doreen Virtue)

CHAOS AND CONFLICT. No kidding!

The CHAOS AND CONFLICT card is saying all is being uprooted, and that it's actually a good thing. It allows us to see what serves and doesn't and choose our new true wants, allowing things to re-align.

The ROUND AND ROUND card, which I pulled when I asked to see the energy of the day, talks about situations we've been in that seem like repeating stories. Where we may get frustrated, thinking, "Not again!!" However, the card reminds us that we're always further ahead than before. We simply get to find new layers and play with different facets this time.

Yup, that also totally rang true!

With my eyes closed, I also pulled two cards to give me guidance as further support. Goddess Bast showed up suggesting I seek solitude and that "Independence is a foundation for my strength and success." — Nice!

And a card saying SHIELD YOURSELF, suggesting to ask for energy support and visualize the energy of a beautiful Bougainvillea, to shield from negative energy, and the potential of going down a rabbit hole.

Lovely support indeed! Thank you, universe! We're all so supported!

By the way, if you've never played with oracle cards and this freaks you out (it freaked me when I started out!), just see them as inspiration. Helping you hear your inner wisdom and get clear. You feel into what it inspires in you, and then you simply choose what feels right as next steps.

While you can access this wisdom also just by listening within (see chapter for "your magical game tools") — cards can be a helpful and fun tool for additional awareness. Don't think you need-need them. You deeply already know everything. (As you free more and more of your sparkle, you'll get better at hearing your inner knowing.)

For me, those cards were all spot on! Totally resonating!

What the heck was happening here? And how did I get here?

So, let me backtrack a little and give you a glimpse and essence:

A few days ago, I met a guy whom I clicked with so powerfully that it threw us into a magnetic storm of all kinds of attraction and fascination. Not just physically — but on a deep soul level.

It was a feeling of deep closeness, as if I'd always known him.

Not surprisingly, after meeting this person, the cards (both from the Wisdom of Oracle deck by Colette Baron-Reid) were:

★ SOULMATES !!

* And UNFINISHED SYMPHONY, which said, "You are meant to evolve and transform with the companionship of others. Certain people enter into your life in order to take you to the next level of healing, consciousness, and (...)" (There was more, but that's what really stood out to me as the perfect message for me.)

All essentially a beautiful thing!

Except I was married!
And now in this crazy-ass mind-storm!

Not so beautiful then, meeting a soulmate, right?

Nope. It's all good. Things happen for a reason. Even this mind-storm.

Because essentially, like the card says, through contrasting experiences (in other words, when SH!T falls apart), we can again find gems. Mind-storms stir things up so that we can choose what we want to keep and what to let go.

I'm talking about tangible physical things here too, but first and foremost, our inner game.

Our true feelings. Desires. How we want to live. Are we happy? What does it all mean! We get to discern. Who can we be, deep inside, when we are fully sparkly? What paradigms and beliefs do we want to live by?

What do we want? What feels right?
Is there something in our current reality that we can release?

Like... yeah holy sh!t, I'm married.

Time to put my facet glasses on (see "your magical game tools" chapter) and discern. Time for some introspection, solitude, and pondering.

When we give ourselves permission
to fully be ourselves and admit all our desires,
we access unlimited possibility.
Our pure sparkle.

So, where was I not fully being me? What was coming up here that I
could release? Or invite in? What beliefs? Things? People? Why was this
intense attraction happening to a supposed new soulmate when I was
supposedly happily married?

OMG. Yes, looking at all of it, riding the wave. Scary! But I'm game.

play prompts:

Ha. This almost feels a bit harsh. What? Playing? Yes. Especially now.
(Play lifts us out of rabbit holes and also gives us our best ideas. Also, it
makes us feel good. Instead of torturing ourselves. No judgment needed!)

When you're in a dark place, the energy of play
is even more of a superpower than in the light
because it helps you get out of the muck and
feel and see your real truth inside.

– Truth bomb from the universe!

I get it! It rings true! Play helps us navigate the big waves when our lives are uprooting in crazy ways, in whatever shape or form. It helps us find forward, true north, our clarity, and follow our hearts through the storm.

So I'll play! I'll take all the support I can get!

Here's what I've done so far, playing and getting support and otherwise:

* Staying curious and not taking any truth as truth, questioning everything, weighing how all feels... what does it mean to me?

* Trusting the universe like my hubby always says, "Everything always works out eventually." That served me well when we met, which was a storm of its own. And it's true. All is temporary. And the universe always re-arranges and creates new harmony based on our wishes and how we like to feel.

* Talking to my close-knit inner circle of supporters. I mean this from a place of power, first listening to myself, not just asking for advice, but sharing what's going on, knowing I don't have to go through things alone. We don't!

* Paying attention to my dreams — even in that before or after sleep phase when half-sleepy. I stayed curious. Took notes. Was there something I could learn from the dream?

* Journaling. Of course. My first go-to. Purging and noticing what my thoughts say, but also then focusing on what I WANT. How do I WANT to feel in my life? What is my heart-felt magic wand wish? What would I like to experience?

Suspending everything around what seems possible / how things "should" be done. (Discernment and my actual choices will come later.) I'm not letting old paradigms bind me down before even looking at them! Question is: What do I REALLY want? If anything was possible? (It always is.)

Note: If you're in a tight spot too as you read this and want more ideas on how to make yourself feel better in times of chaos and inner conflict, see the back of the book! There's an additional list.

We can always do many things. Listening to our heart (or just picking what feels fun!) will bring us forward. There can be answers in anything!

play prompt:

Play bibliomancy:

Ask this book any question — like "What would serve me right now?" — then scroll or pick a random page number.

What awareness did that section inspire?
And what are you inspired to do next?

Taking any small inspired action will set the universe in motion and then show you the next steps forward after that. (Note: it may be that your inspiration tells you to rest as the next step. Or take a bath. That can also be an inspired action. Listen to your heart.)

It's only when we don't take <u>any</u> inspired action and avoid the voice of our heart that we go DOWN into rabbit holes. (Otherwise, we go UP!)

So! If you just flipped to a page in this book... and got some awareness there... Did your heart give you an inspired action step?

Do it. Even if it's scary. (While being kind to yourself, of course.) If we KNOW something is the right step and delay, that only becomes more painful when we avoid it. Not easier.

I know this can take guts. AND it can also be easy. Sometimes our heart leads us to take action way out of our comfort zone, and sometimes not. Permission to sparkle means embracing the adventure.

Remember, you're always supported. (Yes, there is divine support! And helpers and resources will always show up.)

The universe has all kinds of signs and support in store when we make an ask, then let it go, and become curious.

Staying curious also helps you practice hearing your very own wisdom and universe guidance and growing your intuition. Which is where you get your personal best steps forward that are exactly what you need!

Growing your intuition and trusting your inner wisdom will bring you more and more inner power and sparkle.

P.S. Intuition can be subtle. It just feels "right." It feels like your truth. Even if it's not necessarily what you like to hear.

For instance: It can also be an "oh sh!t." Moment. A "that's my action? That makes no sense! / That's crazy / That's too hard / impossible... scary as sh!t...!!"

Yes. Intuition can also call for THAT. For actions that challenge us.

Again. The voices are the voices. Our heart knows what's best for us.

Not sure how to tell the difference between intuition or your voices?

Intuition always comes first. THEN the mind kicks in. So do the FIRST thing. Before you lose yourself in the thinking.

I know following our heart can take guts. And...

You gut(s) this ;-)

So let me role model on here. Back to my story and me finding gems!

I feel like this guy came into my life to allow me to evolve.

Like the soulmate card said: "Certain people enter your life to take you to the next level of healing, consciousness..."

His presence allowed me to experience what it feels like to be a queen. Me fully being sparkly. He connected with me on such a powerful level, fully seeing me, seeing my magic, wanting me to succeed in big ways. Also, we really had some magnetic sparks!

Of course! What did I ask for? The sparkle path!

He sparked me up and made me want o fully express myself. Something I had not really been doing.

He showed up like a soul-guide firecracker to help me blow UP and claim my sparkle crown and become the queen that I already am.

Why, thank you so very much, dear magical man!

What does that feel like, you ask?

Well! He made me feel like I'm PERFECT, just like I am. Sexy even. Goddess-like. Imagine someone totally adoring you. Wanting you. First sight, boom, hellooooooo there! Pure attraction.

Wanting to take you home at first sight. But then being a gentleman.

Being an amazing conversation partner. A magnet of sparkle that you also cannot help but be around. You both sensing the firecracker magic, and it's truly lighting you up. On all levels.

And you really feel it energetically huge! In your heart.

Yum! Doesn't that feel amazing!

My new soulmate friend wants me to always feel that way. Live a full life. Full-out. Be super abundant, super successful. Having fun. The whole spectrum! He said that to me. (Among other sexy things.) Blush!

I got to feel that in-person, like an energy-transmission of YOU ALREADY ARE THIS. I see you. You are a goddess.

It was ELECTRIFYING!! Exhilarating! Game-changing!

And that made me feel amazing! (Understatement. Are there words?) Beyond sparkle! Truly me. No judgment. Just magnetic unconditionally. Like being my inner queen.

If I were to ask you if you want a piece of that cookie?
I hope you'd say, "I want that whole cookie!"

Because you deserve that whole darn thing!

How are you feeling right now? What's coming up for you? Quick! Write it down. Embellish it. You're on to something. I sense it.

play prompt:

1. Imagine: someone is making you feel like your most magical you! Turn up the volume, and play with your imagination! Feel it! How does it feel? In three words? _____

_____ _____

2. Now give yourself a big hug and declare that you're now starting to love yourself just the same way.

Yay! You just gave yourself Permission to fully Sparkle!

3. Date night play prompt! While fully loving yourself, what could you do that feels like the date night of your dreams — with yourself? When do you declare to do it? Put it in your calendar! Then do it! Why not right now? And today!

How did this play prompt (or reading all this) inspire you?

What is CHANGING in your life for the better because of this? If nothing is better yet, did you do a play prompt or inspired action? Do it!

Then share your sparkle story, celebration, or what you did for your date night with a friend or in a group that supports you.

Back to my story.

On Saturday night, a magical dance had happened with that man, sending me over the moon. I felt my heart and mind unlocked, limitless. Feeling a taste of being my most free, most happy, fully expressed queen — in my full possibility, goddess-queen-sparkle me.

That was AMAZING!!! And it made me wonder:

What becomes possible when we operate from that love-goddess, full Permission-to-sparkle QUEEN (or king) energy?

Sunday night, still at that dance weekend where I had met that man, the connection to him really hit home, sparks flying, enjoying an experience akin to being in love. I really wanted to be around him at the potluck party the other dancers held right after that dance weekend. I was soaking up every moment I could to be next to him. By the way, all of this happened within the party crowd. We never even talked alone.

Goodbyes said, and back at my Airbnb, I noticed he had sent a friend request, and we instantly jumped into a curious full-out open and honest "wow. we really like each other" and "hello there! what's happening!" Sparkle conversation. I boldly mused that we had some deeper soul connection, like from another lifetime. Speaking my full truth.

We had known each other for less than 72 hours, yet we had a pure, honest, truth-bomb, heart-to-heart conversation.

Monday... conversation continued, an airplane ride away, and home...

I pulled oracle cards (you saw them earlier.) Remember, one actually said SOULMATE? Of course.

The sparks between us started to become brighter.

More conversations on chat. Over the following days, we mused about all the electrifying moments of the weekend and our powerful connection, reveling in the feeling. It was so magical. And all that had happened without a touch (except for that dance that blew me out of the goddess-sparkle ballpark.)

We both had a deep, powerful soul connection. Almost bigger than sex — (sex would just be the human expression because I suppose there's no stronger expression of feelings on earth.)

Then he shocked me by saying that if something HAD happened between us physically, his amazing girlfriend would have understood.

Um, what? Paradigms started to shift for me.

What?

At first, I said that I don't operate that way. That I would feel as if my whole inner being would shatter if I had an additional relation (or worse, if I cheated!) while being married.

Then I had a big epiphany that started to expand my mind:

If we really love ourselves on a deep, powerful level, then we (as in humans) can handle unsteady fluctuating relationship connections without pain because we don't depend on the love from another — it just emanates from ourselves.

That felt really big.

The next morning, I chose to give myself permission to be both happily married AND feel long-distance love for another man.

In hindsight, that seems small to me, but the simple act of declaring this was a big growth moment for me!

(I wasn't really doing anything, and I couldn't change my feelings, yet it was also a conscious decision to not take on any guilt but simply acknowledge my feelings.)

Tuesday...

(That was the morning in the sunshine by the dock, with the otter, where I almost sent this new man the L word, sharing my love.)

Later on that Tuesday, one of my close supporter mastermind friends sent me an article about relationships outside of norms. Of a married woman who chose to bring a boyfriend into her marriage as an additional relationship. I kept stretching my mind.

Following what feels right.
Redefining paradigms.

Wow. Mind expanding. That helped! This lady simply did what felt right, no matter the cultural norms or whatever personal limitations she may have had... she simply said yes! And allowed her life to change to that!

If she can do THAT, I can find peace too, doing my thing? Sigh! Support felt amazing for me in this challenging time! (Allow yourself to be supported too! I'm so glad you're here.)

I went on to do more "soul-journey"[n] introspection. This one was big, and deep, and uprooting. The storm was taking shape.

In the soul-journey visualization, I saw myself as a sad, lifeless, dead-faced princess in a shadowy cell, wearing a queen gown and waiting to have my heart unlocked to be free, which would make me queen.

Isn't our subconscious mind and the universe amazing! I got such powerful visuals and awareness when I simply allowed myself to be open!

I stayed curious. Percolating. Still in honeymoon-butterfly phase (with the new man, not my husband!!), yet realizing the winds were changing. I felt some big foundational things were shifting, and at some point, I would have to speak with my hubby.

---

n Jessica Paschke from intuitivebythesea.com teaches these as guided meditations.

Then I started feeling like a pinball machine.

I began running scenarios in my mind and heart of all kinds of extremes — from butterflies and love to leaving my husband to wondering where I would live (and slightly freaking out!) to just enjoying the sparkles of being long-distance adored... then to feeling lonely again. (There was this other man long distance that I could not be with, and something in my marriage was also off.)

Wednesday.

That morning, a helpful resource showed up again: An online group call with the purpose to open and heal old mind patterns. It hadn't felt aligned before, but now it felt right. As I entered the call, it turned out that the week's topic was SOULMATES. And love. And redefining paradigms while healing ourselves.

Talk about Divine timing! And being fully supported!

That was EXACTLY what I needed. Bring it. I was in.

Isn't it interesting! I had to have that weekend experience before joining. Now it was perfect for me. And it was okay that I hadn't been there from the beginning. All happens in perfect timing when we follow what feels right — not from pressure or logic but from the gut.

The universe supports us in the most magical ways when we follow our hearts.

Hello, there, universe synchronicities! Of course!

That session was amazing. There were a lot of tears from everyone. I was crying buckets. Full-out. I fully shared what was going on, letting my emotions flow, and so many of my limiting beliefs and limiting paradigms were cleared... it was so powerful![o]

I was allowing myself to be free! To fully say YES to my feelings. Yes to ME! Yes to what my heart wants. Free to be in my truth. No matter what!

Side note: In that group call, I almost turned off my camera because I was crying so hard (my mind said: "embarrassing! All that snot! Oh my gosh!"), but something inside of me (hello intuition, or universe nudge) said to keep the video on. It somehow felt cathartic to not hide. And simply live my feelings full-out.

Later, several in the group said they were so grateful that I kept the video on, and they were so proud of me. Seeing me cry and be me unapologetically somehow also "gave them permission" to also fully feel.

(Of course, we can always choose what we give ourselves permission to. But seeing someone do something first makes it then easier.)

After that session, everyone mostly stayed on camera for all the following calls. Even through occasional tears. And there were quite some, as we all continued to embrace our inner shadow stories, release them, and heal.

> When we play full-out, and dare to freely express our true selves, we give others permission to do the same.

(As a side-effect. Everyone wins.)

Afterward, I canceled my afternoon commitments, giving myself permission to simply do self-care and sleep. Allowing things to process. Being gentle with myself. It was big stuff.

---

[o] It was a program by Yola Mehmeti (instagram @yolabear17) and Kavita Singh (www.kavitasingh.today)

I was now giving myself permission to suspend all beliefs.

What other limitations were constricting my relationships? What societal norms?

Thursday. Valentine's Day. Nice timing, universe.

This day was huge. I went through all the emotions.

- From crying in the business call earlier in the morning, feeling like my whole world was falling apart and giving myself permission to just be in it and know it all works out.

- To having a rough patch with my hubby, feeling below-zero communication, and not seeing how to change any of it.

- To reconnecting with that feeling of absolute heart-freedom goddess-love energy I had experienced Sunday and since then, and making a powerful post about it, written all in flow.

- To a magical client session that was full of love from Kavita and our client and me — she was so grateful for us, she called us angels from heaven, and we all cried tears of gratitude.

- To a quick two-minute break between client calls where I got to catch my hubby coming home from an errand, wish him happy Valentine's Day, and we reconnected with love.

- To seeing a message from D (that man!) about "opening hearts." (He had seen my Facebook post and cheered me on for sharing it with the world and opening hearts.) Yes!! What an amazing cheerleader for me and my purpose work!!!

- To having another magical client session with Kavita where our next client too was moved to tears because her business had been six or nine years in the making, and she got such deep clarity about her brand and her business that her website suddenly

became so accessible, and off her shoulders, like an easy 1-2-3... P
She had a huge breakthrough of clarity and gratitude happening.
That made me so happy to be able to help facilitate!

★ To coming out of that session to find a really sweet Valentine's
gift from my hubby with a card that was SO ME! He did get me
more than I thought he did! Among all the sparkles, hearts, and
stars, he wrote that Valentine's Day with me is a jackpot... Aww!

★ To a very close-connection Valentine's Dinner with him, where I
was able to speak my truth about our relationship (just not
mentioning D yet), all from a positive place of celebration,
making magic wand wishes, and saying what I'd also like to see...
A romantic evening, thank you, that was so needed.

★ To knowing that all is still moving. More coming.

I know and feel that I'm in a big evolution and expansion.

I continue giving myself permission to question EVERYTHING.

What I really want in my love relationships. What relationships I want.
What life! What to let go. What paradigms to shift. What makes me really
feel like that queen.

Who is this true real sparkle person that's me?
Who is purely me, and in no way whatsoever just "fitting in?"

What IF I choose to have a boyfriend and a husband, like in that article?
How might that feel? (Not caring about society or others for the
moment. Just pondering. Suspending. Playing. Feeling. Curious.)

What IF I have no relationships AT ALL, and just be me, and give myself
permission to experience freely and without expectations when I make
amazing connections.

P If you look for brand magic like this for your own business, visit www.astridmueller.com

What if there are electrifying-amazing-queen-supporters and soulmates out there waiting for me, and I get to travel the world, fully savoring that and them as I'm inspired to, and be fully independent?

What if I can have several soulmates as partners at the same time?

Playing with paradigms. Stretching. Permission to choose.

We get to choose to be totally free and totally happy!

Daring to make "unorthodox" choices.

How do I want to feel? And live?

How can I ALWAYS feel

like that sparkle

queen, me?

play prompt:

Ready to look at your own paradigms? Free yourself of what doesn't feel right and create your own dream life?

You can start gently:

Think of a story or stories from your childhood where you did something that went against all the rules.

(To remember your paradigm shift superpowers! We all have them.)

_____

_____

No idea yet? Here's one from me:

One time my mum took me to the dentist to have a tooth pulled, and I was all prepped, my gums completely numbed. That syringe sting was already behind me. Yet, I did NOT want to have that tooth pulled.

I wouldn't have ANY of it. I was a clear NO!!

There was nothing they could do to convince me.

So my mum took me home. That was so awesome of her! I remember feeling stunned that she went along with it.

What? I was that powerful! She listened?!

Of course! Think about it:

When we stay firm in our truth, not giving in ... what else can others do, really?

Nothing. I got my wish.

Note that I'm not talking about fighting energy here. (That would have brought the same reaction back. Energy attracts energy. Fighting energy brings more fight.)

My power came from peace. Simply standing in my truth.

We have more power than we think! Simply by calmly speaking our truth and staying with it.

On that tooth-pulling-not-tooth-pulling day, I remember eating lunch afterward, my mouth all flavorless and numb, shocked at my own power and that I actually still had my tooth.

I had gotten what I wanted. Not with a tantrum. But with my own power of staying in my truth. And I was just a kid!

What are your stories where you felt your power in similar ways?

Where did you go against the grain, dare to speak up, and then get what you asked for, and maybe even also stunned yourself?

Notice how powerful you are.

And you can use this power to change any paradigm of your life. Right now.

Back to my story of February 2019.

I just found a new facet of the whole story, which again is allowing me to grow to a next level and find my power.

Get this.

I just realized that I am currently giving my power away. What?

This has to be its own chapter. It deserves a title! Even if the chapter will be short. I want this one to stand out. To get noticed.

So here we go, this is a new chapter!

where are you giving your **power** away?

how this chapter helps:

I intend this one to be short. Concise. The title says it all. Let's connect you to your power!

To continue the last chapter's story, I just realized that I gave my power away. To what or whom?

With all the excitement of this soulmate supporter who really sees me and wants to support me and these butterfly feelings of feeling in love, I suddenly found myself constantly checking my phone.

Ah! Was there a new message? When may I get the next sparkle dose? The next butterfly comment of how magical one of our connection moments was? When do I get to chat again and lean in, feel held and soothed in this friendship? When? When? When?

Refresh. Refresh. Hello, losing power!

I was also kind of losing myself.

Not a good feeling.

What book am I writing? Let's get back on this sparkle path!

play prompts:

I'm not saying you have to claim all the power there is.

This is not a power game. This is a game of EMpowerment.
This is your game of owning your Sparkle.

We always have the power of choice — no matter what is happening around us. If nothing else, we can always choose, even in the middle of crazy upheavals, how we WANT to think and how we WANT to feel! And claiming THAT will also change our reality.

So! Let's journal or give this a think!

What THINGS are you currently giving your power away to?
Even habits! Coffee? Chocolate? Do you sometimes say, "you just need _____ whenever you..... ?" Just notice and ponder!

_____

_____

In what SITUATIONS do you tend to give your power away?

_____

_____

What PEOPLE are you currently giving your power away to? When?

_____

_____

I'm not suggesting that we have to overpower others. I'm suggesting that we live from our own, centered place of power. Where we feel calm and strong within ourselves, no matter what is (or isn't) happening around us.

When we are calm and complete within ourselves, we shine our sparkle. We live from our power.

When you think of the situations or people that just came up for you, where you feel weaker somehow... What may those moments look like for you if you STAYED in your power and SPARKLE instead?

_____

_____

How may it make you FEEL to experience the situations that way?

_____

What would it take for you to try that next time, or right now?

In order to change such situations in your life to more sparkle, it is helpful to know what you want (and what you don't want.)

What are your new STANDARDS for the relationships in your life?

Again. You get to choose. Like me with my soulmate friend... I cannot choose how he or others want to show up for me, but I can choose what I'm okay with and set my standards for myself, and then I also say them. Like "this is how I want us to communicate." What's a yes. What's a no.

(Then that experience can unfold with that person or otherwise.)

_____

_____

In this whole unraveling story, I sometimes caught myself spiraling down a romantic lane with my thoughts, feeling like I was losing my power.

There's nothing wrong with being romantic. But I spotted a shadow side of it: I was making my own value dependent on responses from others. Instead of simply knowing that I'm awesome and that I can create my own sparkle life experiences, no matter what.

For example: Here, I noticed that I'd like to have more romantic experiences in my life. Now that I stated this desire, I can allow that to come into my life. This may happen with my hubby, this new partner, or even otherwise (the universe loves to surprise us)!

Give your wishes up to the universe, and then let it surprise you!

Did you notice something you want more of in your life?
In what way would you like your life to become more sparkly?

_____

_____

_____

There's another really great area you can look at regarding reclaiming your power: Energy leaks!

When you spot them and de-clutter in that life area, swoosh! You just claimed back more of your sparkle power!

For instance: Every time Kavita and I clear up our calendar and streamline it to feel really spacious, with space for client AND feel-good time, totally feeling expansive... new (and more aligned) clients show up!

What areas in your life may be energy leaks for you?

We can surround ourselves with positive energy or allow things to drain us. Scan your life and look around. Where might you be able to de-clutter to invite more magic in? Relationships / your home / your calendar / your closet / your computer / your desk... ?

_____

_____

What area do you feel inspired to tackle now and let some things go?

_____

_____

By the way: As soon as I reclaimed my own power, shining from my heart-center, loving myself (regardless of whether he had responded), the day continued in most amazing ways. And suddenly, D showed up again online. But now, simply as a cherry on top of my own sparkle experience.

When we are in our calm, centered, sparkle power, unattached to outcomes and how others respond, things start to flow to us. In ways better than we may have imagined.

(Otherwise, we're in a "crave energy." Which is a pretty effective sparkle repellent. People feel that!)

define your own
sparkle life,
set your own rules

how this chapter helps:

As I'm writing this chapter, I'm redefining my rules in my life. I'm making my own personal happy sparkle list for how I want to live. Setting the tone for my next steps in my life adventure. Calling the shots! This is for you when you're ready to bust your old paradigms and define your own dream life!

Again, I'm leading with story — join me to get inspired to set your own rules for your own life.

As I'm writing this, it's 1:28 am. After what felt like a melt-down evening (I actually posted on Facebook that I needed a hug, feeling utterly alone.) I went to bed early yesterday, at 7pm. And got no inquiry about my feelings or good night wishes from my husband.

This is not going to be about blame or drama — all feels well. Well? Not really. But — I'm okay. I'm sharing this as a glimpse into my life to show where I'm at: It feels like a defining moment in my life. A new beginning. (And as I'm rereading this in 2021, looking back: Yes, I was "okay" but heck NO, I wasn't SPARKLY! Heck YEAH, it was time for change!)

Time for new rules of what feels sparkly to me!

Oh, this is also happening just a week after I met my new soulmate, D. (See earlier story.) Can you believe it?

As you now know, I had quite a turbulent week. Huge excitement moments and underwater ones, huge celebrations and feeling fast flow forward, flying high in new paradigms, not knowing what's up or down... It was a big wave! And I'm still on it.

Quick one-paragraph summary:

(For the full story, see the chapter "Permission to Pure Freedom.") I met another soulmate (my husband already being one.) And I experienced thrilling and magical relationship aspects that I didn't currently have in my married life. (Side note: Without any actual physical things happening!)

This whirled my world to the stars, then dragged me underwater... I went through a lifetime of learning in a week, and now I'm ready to choose what I want to let go, what to keep. And to set new rules. New standards for how I want to live.

And for your benefit, I choose to do it in ALMOST real-time: I'm not writing this while in the middle of the storm. (That was a time to question everything and to just be curious.) Now feels the right time to catch my gems; it feels like it's all finally landing. So let me land it.

play prompt:

(This is me journaling in real-time. You may also use these as a springboard for your own journaling and musings!)

What's all the good (relationship*) stuff that I WANT in my life?

(*This is my topic right now — insert your own topic as you desire.)

★ Deep experiences of soul-connections, feeling love shining from and into my heart. Literally feeling connected to and from the stars. I loved dancing in this feeling and want more!

★ Magical soul love energy — it feels way bigger than butterflies or sex (which didn't even happen) — it feels like soul sex!

★ Feeling utterly adored, inside and out, like a queen, fully free!

★ Deep, inspiring, soulful growth conversations. Where I can say anything, and am understood. Cheered on! Especially when I do brave things, playing big, pursuing my dreams! Being celebrated!

★ Adventure. Feeling ALIVE. The promise of travel. The experience of big love and amazing people (soulmates, soul tribe + otherwise) who I visit when I want.

★ Seeing me in my power "you can do anything!" and holding me to that standard ... also from men.

★ Guilt-free relationships in which I follow and express my heart freely (while honoring everyone's wishes and feelings).

★ Loving all my soulmates (hubby and others) at the same time, emotionally, spiritually, maybe even physically — as feels aligned.

★ Pure freedom of choice, moment by moment, guilt-free choosing what feels so(ul) good. I don't even know yet if I want or could handle that (or how I'd handle that if my partner did that!), but I feel if we all fully love ourselves from the inside out, we can! Beyond fears. Beyond paradigms. If we're independent and strong in our own love, we are strong to experience anything — from storms to our wildest dreams!

Isn't it the same thing as with money abundance? If we let go of fear, all flows? I'm calling in free flow feel-good freedom and possibility (while respecting everyone involved + their wishes).

(Obviously, this is a big one for me, and I'm just dipping my toes in. Permission to be curious. To suspend beliefs. To dare. Embracing the adventure. "Permission To Sparkle!")

* Relationships that feel free and empowering (not constricting). I'm catching my thoughts: I can view marriage as a constricting thing, or I can see that I ALWAYS get to choose. Choosing to see my power and not stay in victim mode.

* To freely express my wishes, dreams, and desires. Noticing I still have some fears to overcome here! How can you experience your dreams if you can't speak them? Truth bomb!

* To feel fully supported in my relationships. I love the freedom of having my own experiences AND I want to feel like my partner is a best friend, caring and curious, even if I don't feel yet like sharing. (And I do the same for him.)

* To have IN LOVE relationship(s) with butterflies. I'm letting go of the paradigm that we have to accept that butterflies happen only at the beginning. I want ebb + flow of excitement. Abstinence, butterflies, surprises, again, and again!

* To invite the freedom to play and follow my heart. What if one day I feel drawn to be with more than one person at a time? I'm expanding my comfort zone, being curious. Asking the universe for freedom-feeling and power to choose.

And now I want to ask myself, beginning with ME!

How can I create THE FEELINGS of all of the above for myself? Independent of what relationships I'm in? Curious!

(I don't need to know the HOW at this time. How this all plays out will be seen. I'm taking my hands off the steering wheel. Allowing the universe to orchestrate the details.)

Why that question?

It's one of the big things that kept coming back to me: While being adored is magical...

If we don't fully FEEL our worth and own magic, inside out, no amount of hugs or soulmates can fill our cup.

To become our fully sparkly selves, we need to love ourselves as our very own soulmate.

And... even bigger: Our true sparkle and possibility starts showing up when we realize that...

We are all magical, and we are all Divine.

We can all find and feel the Divine love within ourselves. We are universe-made!

And when we do and see the same Divine magic in all other beings...

- ☆ We have no limits.

- ☆ Our hearts are free.

- ☆ We fully express ourselves.

- ☆ Our minds are limitless.

- ☆ Anything is possible!

I also journaled the following question: What reality can I create when I'm in my goddess-love energy? In other words: What might my life look like when I truly, fully feel the magic of me and fully love myself?

_____

_____

Lanie Smith, abundance coach⁹, business consultant, and one of my play-full-out Alpha players in the makings of this book, just said so beautifully on Facebook also on Valentine's Day, 2019:

"Hope you are using today and ALL the days to romance YOURSELF...your power lies in how you love + treat yourself moment by moment."
– Lanie Smith

Yes, yes, yes! So well said, Lanie. Let's! I love how Lanie (who was in a super-parallel life experience as I was writing all this — universe synchronicities!) continued to say:

"From here, there is little space for disappointment because there is not expectation for someone else to make you happy if you are capable of that for yourself. All external gestures become a cherry on top. I get to choose clinging to outcome or — being open to possibility.

I choose the latter, and it's exhilarating to live in the present...open to receive. This is being in the flow of life... freedom to evolve."

_____

⁹ Learn more about Lanie Smith on www.LanieSmithCoaching.com

step into your full
sparkle & possibility

how this chapter helps:

In previous chapters, I made new rules. I made wishes. This is the chapter where I step through the portal of possibility.

This is the chapter where I allowed my dream life to start happening. On a next level. And not just wish it, but also EXPERIENCE IT.

Again. This is a real-time account. As it's happening for me. And see how it inspires you to step through your own portal of possibility!

As I'm writing this, I'm sitting in a sunny, cozy spot at our tiny Kodiak Alaska airport café, with a Bob Marley Mocha, in a new space of pure possibility. A new life. The world is my oyster.

I'm feeling totally free.

I'm not even fully registering how free I am, but it's like I stepped through the possibility portal, and now here I am! A place in the sun! No more limitations! A total fresh new beginning!

What?

Got some tissues? There's a lot of magic coming. And probably a few tears.

After that wild, parallel-universe Valentine's Day (see chapter "Permission to Pure Freedom"), I realized I needed to clear things up and talk openly with my hubby. And for that, I needed some additional outside clarity.

Kavita suggested I book a session with someone to find out if my soul contract with my husband may be complete. To get clear on all my soul contracts and my situation. And so I did.

Boy, that session was big.

It was a session with intuitive medium and artist Lois Warnock. I love her, by the way. If you ever want a magical spirit guide drawing, painting, and or clarity from your universe support team, she's amazing and offers universe guidance sessions and coaching.[r]

A LOT happened in that session with Lois. And I got EXACTLY the clarity I needed.

And here's the clarity that came through:

- ☆ To be patient — ha! Always a good one for me!

- ☆ To admit my vulnerabilities — this one was advising me to be mindful of balance. And self-care.

- ☆ To keep commitments — this one was especially referring to commitments TO MYSELF, Lois said. (Spirit guide Merlin was giving her input for me.) This meant to really listen to what makes ME feel good and to stay true to my passion path, purpose path, and what I want to do in life. In particular, wanting to change lives all over the world and do big things — THAT!

- ☆ To break free — this one was about my mind. This one was from my dad, who also showed up as a guide. Awwww! Not to make big decisions while my mind is spinning or emotions are twirling. It was a message of Zen. And to stay free of distractions so I could hear my heart speak + make decisions from there.

---

[r] Learn more about her on www.LoisWarnock.com

* A party card! Also, from my dad. An invitation to celebrate myself. Amidst everything. And how far I've come. I'm doing good! Being kind to myself. Awww again!

* To embrace my fears. To be brave. Awww! I love the quote on the card: "When you feel fear, do it anyway!" Boom!

* Not to repeat mistakes — hmmm, that one got me curious. Good to be aware of! Yes, making wise choices! I felt in earlier stories I had given my power away, stayed in relationships because of guilt, not trusting or listening to my heart.

* More cards about embracing fears! This was so big. Big support to be brave!

* "Commander Ashtar." He's a spirit guide/Ascended Master who helps world-changers create peace. It was a support card to dare to move forward with the big things I want to create.

Summary:

As you see, I got a LOT of encouragement. To embrace my fears. To follow my truth, and to dare to follow my destiny.

And what did that all mean for me and my hubby? And my soulmate? I became aware in the session that it was very important for me to allow myself to be fully supported.

I realized that while hubby is a huge supporter for me and wants me to be happy, he is also on a totally different life trajectory. He's retired, independent, does his thing... He lets me do my thing, and is happy for me, yet doesn't fully vibe with my work or know much about it.

I realized and experienced, as a comparison, that with my new soulmate D — OMG — that energy connection was SO DIFFERENT!

He got ALL OF ME. He understood my big world-changer destiny. All the little and big things. Totally sees me. Celebrates me as queen, change-maker, and entrepreneur. As visionary. Inspires me on so many levels. And I got all that clarity by just being in his presence and how we interacted, but mostly feeling it.

I feel totally LIT UP just having met and knowing him.

Lois said that THAT'S the kind of support and partner I need right now. She said that

"I need to be very careful of energy. And not make myself small."

She was literally calling me out to dare to sparkle.

It dawned on me, slowly, that this rang so true.

I had indeed been allowing myself to be small! To fit in! To just chill, relax, live in this small-town environment, with the couch-potato TV shows and beer... Hubby and I only really connected with friends on Friday in the local brewery and otherwise did our own independent thing.

In the extreme moments, it was him watching war movies in the living room and me in my room doing sparkle stuff and meditating.

And while it was "okay," and it was easy...

It wasn't ME anymore. And it wasn't serving me anymore.

It wasn't serving my big dreams.

I asked Lois: Can't I have both? Or ALL? I still love my hubby. Can't I stay with him AND change the world? And love other soulmates long-distance? (That was still muddy and a tentative wish for me.)

Lois relayed from the guides, and herself, that we always have choices. They never tell us what we have to do. And there's no right or wrong. We can always pick a path and then adjust if something doesn't work for us.

She said, yes, I COULD stay, but if I want to change the world in big ways, I'd have to be very mindful of my energy and how I manage it.

If I want to play big, I need to give myself permission to be in big energy.

And then she said something that really was the mic drop for me:

What if my hubby decided to suddenly support me more and traveled the world with me, joining me as I lead retreats and do big things?
How would that feel?

And then it sank in.

That did NOT feel sparkly.

It actually felt kind of heavy.

That's when I knew for sure what my heart was saying. I had to leave him. Ah!!! That was so big! Just within a few days, this had emerged!!!

I needed to breathe.

There was more in the session. Some special numbers I should look out for. And a huge blessing card from Christ Consciousness, reaffirming my big destiny. And that I'm up to big things. And that the universe is fully supporting me.

OMG, it was so big. Kind of overwhelming!

Thankfully, a friend had suggested (a few days BEFORE this session, without even knowing about what was happening in my life!) that I come over to her house if I ever needed space. She was traveling.

Perfect. So I did.

And I intended to CLEAR CLEAR CLEAR space.

To BE. Meditate. Listen within.

Ah!

I did lots of self-care that night. Took a long shower. Meditated. Prayed. Pulled cards. Journaled. Breathed.

Not freaking out but just giving myself space.

I was okay. One step at a time. Baby steps. Breathe.

I cleared my calendar of anything that I didn't really need.

Alerted my inner support circle of the situation (see, I also asked for support — please do that, too! You never have to feel alone or be alone. Okay?) I asked them to be aware and please hold space.

I kept client sessions and my calendar for the most part — I know I can operate without problem, with universe support. AND I always have a choice. This is one of the big magical things when you're co-creating with the universe: The world can fall apart, AND you can fully function in the middle of it all IF you do everything while you're heart-aligned, take care of yourself, and ask the universe for support.

By the way, this was way different from how I operated back in New York. Did you notice? Back then, in that burnout time when I wasn't connected, neither to myself or universe support nor any other support system... I just plowed through. Totally ignoring my body, my heart, my soul. Not giving myself ANY appropriate nourishing or support.

Now I do all that. So now I can fully function in the middle of storms.

And magic can happen. Because I always allow and trust the universe to fully support me and know that all is playing out in perfect synchronicity.

I allow myself to experience beauty in everything. And I allow myself to show up for clients and others if I feel it's aligned, knowing that magic can come from it – no matter what is going on in my life.

While always checking in with myself if that feels good. And if not, I always give myself permission to choose otherwise.

So the next day was HUGE. A day that would have thrown me overboard before I had this universe connection and access to my inner-sparkle strength.

Let me share all the different "mountains" I climbed that day, while being okay, surfing the life-adventure wave, AND doing self-care.

Again, I share this to show what's possible for YOU.

* 7 am: A change-maker connection + synergy call with inner-circle coaches and an author we all loved.

* 8 am: A BUSINESS meet & greet call with Kavita + Jean and my soulmate D — yes, we also have big business synchronicities and ways we can help each other grow on that level. And yes. I had to switch gears and put my business hat on! Amidst all my emotional life changes! And I did. And it was okay. Even great! Because I set the intention, and gave myself permission, and trusted that I got this. And I did.

* Self-care, self-care... canceling almost everything else. Spending time with the dog I was sitting. Enjoying that sunny apartment. Taking a hot shower. Being. Being okay with my life being lifted out of its hinges.

★ 11:30 am: A call with my podcast writer. While this wasn't urgent, it felt right to be on the call, and I trusted it. And it was! Big synchronicity — she actually had a recent life relationship story that felt super supportive to me in my situation. Gratitude!

★ Self-care. Pause. More sunlight. Outside time.

★ 1 pm: A call with another Alpha group participant to talk about this book. Also felt heart-aligned to be there and connect. And again, there were more synchronicities — she was going through very similar life changes, and we were able to support each other just by listening to each other and sharing stories. See how support showed up left and right as I followed my heart and what felt right?

★ 3 pm: An online class with Jessica Paschke, where I learned more intuitive tools like the soul journeying I mentioned earlier in the book. And, again, that felt just perfect. And I got just the right insights.

★ Somewhere in those conversations, Kavita had also given me a priceless support tip: To decide how I'd like my conversation with my hubby to go and feel. I could decide that it would go super smooth and easier than I'd ever imagined, she said. So I made my wish here, then did my best to trust it.

After all this, I took a nap, meditated just a bit more, even prayed...

And then I decided it was time to talk to my husband.

My heart had been clear this whole time about what I needed to do: I had waited to Zen myself, to be sure it wasn't just a momentary thing — thanks, Dad, for coming through in the Lois Warnock reading!

Now I felt it was time to speak my truth.

And then the most amazing thing happened:

I had the most magical breakup on the planet.

I spoke the full truth from my heart, crying buckets. Letting it all out. He simply said, "Okay! You gotta do what you gotta do. You have to follow your happy. I'm okay. Eat something before you go. Don't hit the road like that (crying.) Mellow out. It's okay."

And then he gave me a hug.

And that was that.

(What?????)

And the next day, he asked when I'd bring the divorce papers, so he could get a new passport.

(What????? He was going even faster than I was. I needed to catch my breath!)

Point was, we had a super-quick and super-amicable separation.

And in less than three months, our marriage was dissolved.

Of course, it took him and us longer than that to process it all, and later, he admitted that he never REALLY wanted to let me go. But he also didn't want to hold me back. He wanted and wants me to be happy. And I wish him the same.

He supported me through the whole breakup, and we remained friends.

Truth reigns. Love reigns. Friendship might even remain!

soulmate love

for all your life areas

how this chapter helps:

This chapter helps you quantum-connect to your highest love within yourself, attract your dream relationships or even soulmates (yes, more than one can come into your life!), and bring a feeling of more love (more sparkle!) into ALL your life areas.

I could begin by following my mind, giving in to objections like "Who am I to write this chapter?" or "I'm no relationship expert!" or … (Insert whatever I'm not giving voice to. Make it up. It's just as good.)

However. I woke up at 4:24 am with beautiful dreams that made my soul sing and lit me up from the inside, ringing with sparkle soul love for myself AND for relationships I have… and was inspired to write this chapter.

Without knowing what will come out.

I just realized something. While I can grow my love for myself and do inner-growth work, be independent and self-reliant and all of that, and not really need a relationship to feel complete… I get now that someone else can also ignite your bigger self-love cylinders.

This is what happened for me with D, without ever having sex (or even kissing!!!) and only having met for that one weekend, that one amazing dance, and a few conversations and long-distance chats.

What am I trying to say?

(Feel into this as you're reading.)

I'm trying to relay the magic of this feeling, and how I'm feeling this is much bigger than any random butterfly fling or any just-physical-attraction thing (not to play them down, everything has its own magic.)

What I'm trying to express, and words do little justice, is that my soul is lit up from the inside and connected to the whole love of the universe.

Wow.

(I'll have what she's having. Ever see "When Harry Met Sally"? Ha-ha!)

I'm letting my heart write so that you might vicariously feel this feeling:

I feel an oven glowing in my heart chakra, and I know it's about more than "just" feeling attracted to another human. I feel I got plugged into a love paradigm of the universe. Connected to soul love clusters. If that even means anything. Connected to others who shine so strongly with love for themselves. Floating in quantum space, connected, glowing, like little suns in the universe. Our own soul-love-expansion-milky-way.

Wow. Maybe that's what it feels like to start lighting up the planet and shift the whole consciousness energy?

I'm writing with my eyes closed, just allowing words to land. Feeling my heart further expand.

Breathe.

play prompt:

(Read this first, then picture this in your mind.)

Close your eyes for a moment and imagine being in this love-sun-soul-love-cluster of bliss. Can you feel it in your chest? If not there, where in your body do you feel it? You can also just imagine it. Know this quantum field is always here.

Give yourself permission to be this lit up. To be this shining being, soul-nourished with love. From inside of yourself, from the universe, and connected to others who are also tapped into this field of sparkle, soul clusters of galaxies of love.

Wow. This is so big. Just meditate on it.

And feel it.

How is that?

Give yourself permission to breathe out all reality, all thoughts, and just be in this. Float. Feel. Fill your cup. Feel my virtual hug. Give yourself a real hug. Then open your eyes, and notice how you feel.

This is you, feeling your very own quantum dream universe sparkle love. This is you, filling your heart. This is you lighting up your heart. Inside out. From here, anything is possible.

play prompt:

(Here come make-a-wish + journaling prompts!)

Imagine you have no relationships with others; it's just you. Yet, you're feeling fully fulfilled and in love with you. Beaming with love. As if your lover(s) or partner(s) are with you, and yet you don't need them. Feel fulfilled simply by loving yourself and feeling filled with all the love of the universe.

Feel this powerfully in your heart.

How do you feel in this? How is your life different?

_____

_____

What might you have to let go to BECOME this fully sparkling you?

_____

_____

What might you do differently?

_____

_____

In which life areas would you like to feel more love? And in what way?

CREATIVITY / HEALTH / CAREER / MONEY / RELATIONSHIPS...

_____

_____

play prompt:

(This is a play-journey for your heart and mind, a visualization to access your inner wisdom, inner wishes, and also call in what you wish!)

This one is inspired by a garden visualization[s] that I experienced in a class with Jessica Paschke from IntuitiveByTheSea.com:

To do this by yourself, I suggest you first read it, immerse yourself in it, and then grab a pen and paper to journal. You can journal after you do the visualization or while you do it, with your eyes closed.

Instructions to this garden visualization:

Close your eyes and imagine getting invited to a garden that represents all your areas of life: Financial / Family + Friends / Recreation / Love relationships. In your mind's eye, enter the garden, and notice what gates you see there for your different life areas. Choose ONE.

What life area garden did you pick?

Go to that gate, walk through, and imagine meeting your guide for this garden area. (If you don't see one, just enter.)

What do the guide and garden look like? There is no right or wrong. Just journal what you see / hear / smell / know / in that garden area. What is the experience like there? How does it make you feel?

---

[s] (The visualization is loosely based on a Colette Baron Reid exercise)

What was the experience like for you? For instance, maybe it felt crowded. Or perhaps colors seemed dull. Or you want more sunshine.

_____

_____

Now, turn to your guide and say what you want to change in that garden. Speak your wishes. If there's no guide, speak it to yourself. Maybe more of certain flowers, a different feeling, taller trees, a more-winding path, or smoother flow...? Just allow your mind's eye to float.

What were you wishing for?

_____

Does your guide or garden have any messages or wishes for you?

_____

_____

Then say thanks, and leave that garden area, then the garden, and open your eyes. And your journal. (If you haven't yet.)

Journal your experience, and simply note down anything else you remember. Then, when you feel complete, ask yourself what it all means to you for that life area you picked. What awareness did you get? Do you realize anything you'd like to do or change in that life area?

_____

_____

Jessica had us do this exercise once a day, with a different life-area every day, for a week. Letting each life area go after the exercise, without thinking about what to do next. Simply going about our daily lives.

And then she suggested we'd come back after a week to the first life-area we began with and see how that garden may have changed in the meantime. And how our life may have changed. And we'd make new wishes, get new messages for that life area garden, and then journal again.

This is a beautiful, very creative, yet easy way to redesign your life, including your love life. Without getting stuck in the HOW. You play with your subconscious and also the universe.

You make your (abstract) wishes, then allow them to come true.

How does this work?

This works because you don't just speak from your logical mind (language and words) and get in your own way with the HOW to do things... but you come from your heart and subconscious (images, feeling) and make your universe wishes from there.

And then you let the universe work in the background. While you take inspired actions as they come up. Following your heart. Step by step.

When you check back in with your garden meditation after a few days (or even earlier), you'll notice that your garden has changed more to your liking, and also, your desires have started to manifest! Maybe even better than you may have imagined! So fun!

If that's too fuzzy for you, you can also make rational heart-wishes. Speak your mind. Ask for what you wish!

And then leave room for the universe to bring things to you. (Don't nail down all the details.) You can conclude your wish with "This or something better. To everyone's highest benefit. And so it is."

Of course, in this exercise, you also get to see things that you don't want anymore. And inner mind-stories that no longer serve. Limiting beliefs, fears, doubts, all that stuff. Yay to finding more gems! Realizing what you DO want and what you no longer need!

That's how you discover and free more and more of your inner diamond. And sparkle more and more, from the inside!

Make sense?

Why do you think I met a new soulmate? Because I've been releasing such old stories, again and again, and growing more and more into my natural sparkly self. He showed up because I was ready to step into a next phase in my life. He made me realize what I was and wasn't aligned with anymore and what I needed to let go to move forward.

As we keep releasing old stories and claiming more and more of our sparkly self, the universe brings us resources, gifts, and helpers to step into next phases of our life!

Play with the book or the game every day. See what happens!

Not that excited about releasing old stories and things in your life? Sound like hard work? Or scary? (These are just mind-stories, by the way!)

Here's another great example of how playing the "Permission To Sparkle" game (or playing with this book) can better your life:

Before I started this game of inner growth and awareness, I was in a different frequency. Things were harder. It took me longer to get through stuff. I didn't really know myself. Or know what I truly wanted! I wasn't really happy! Things were less sparkly and more hard!

I'm so glad you're here. We've established that you're also ready for more sparkle! Let's help you make that happen!

play prompt:

How are you feeling right now? Do you have any pain or responses in your body, emotions happening, or mind-stories? ("not me" ...) Observe:

_____

_____

_____

If this feels hard — I know it can be! — simply embrace your emotions (and yourself) for a moment, with love and compassion. It's okay. Feel the feels. Allow them to process. I know! You might have bottled them up or used those old stories for years!!

Keep listening to your heart. In what life areas are you not giving yourself permission to experience what you truly want?

_____

_____

What are your true desires? What sparkle life do you want?

_____

_____

Now comes a great one:

play prompt:

Going deeper, with love... Desire check!

Are your desires pure? Are they deep down what you REALLY want, or did you limit or taint your desires in a way? Maybe you stopped at taboos? Or limited yourself by what you think is possible? Or by what you think you deserve? Or maybe there is a sense of obligation toward others? Or... a fear of what others may say...?

Catch those voices. Then, if needed, state your true desires again.

_____

_____

And here's another gem-finder pit-stop!

Do you 100% unshakably KNOW that your desires are as good as done? Or are there any voices or feelings in your body that say otherwise?

_____

_____

If you're 100% free of resistance, and there is nothing, if you simply feel like "of course!" AWESOME! Then you can easily manifest it! Yay! (Otherwise, catch your mind-stories! And release them to the universe.)

Sensing resistance but aren't fully clear on what's going on? Been trying to uplevel your love life or another area in your life, attract more abundance, but it just hasn't worked out? Great! You're on to something!

You discovered a repeating pattern in an area!

Now all you have to do is allow yourself to accept resources or help. And play with doing things differently. Perhaps all you need to do is let go of trying so hard. That was often the big thing for me!

Take your hands off the steering wheel. (If you're in control mode, that's the wrong energy to manifest miracles. You have to give the universe trust and pure KNOWING and space.)

Not feeling it yet? Feeling heavy? Discouraged? Or just not clear?

Great! You're on to something.

When we feel heavy, it simply means we're in shadow land, and we can find some gems! Something we can release to become more sparkly!

Lean into this. Shift into being curious.

Walk steady and with love. You'll come out all the more magical and sparkly on the other side!

manifest all your desires!

how this chapter helps:

This chapter helps you if the BE - PLAY - DO manifesting formula (see separate chapter) hasn't been working for you yet. Maybe you've been procrastinating. Or you've been doing "all the things" but hitting a glass ceiling. Likely, you're not feeling great, maybe even traumatized by hard work, or even overwhelmed.

This chapter is a DEEP DIVE. Again, you get to watch me dive.

This is not the chapter for you if you just want to dip your toes in. Or "see what this does." Or simply get the shiny things you want.

You have to be ready to suspend EVERYTHING you've been believing so far. To look at your inner demons. To take action despite and through all your inner objections and fears.

You have to be ready to see beyond the matrix of what you believe is real. And willing to see and act through what you think is possible.

All, of course, with compassion toward yourself and love. You're doing great. You're already here, so yay! Brace yourself for the next part of the adventure, but know that you'll be okay. Sparkle IS always waiting around the bend. By embracing this adventure, you'll get to discover it!

Are you ready?

Then here's the first secret that I found:

Manifesting isn't really about manifesting. It's all about our inner game. Manifesting happens as a side-effect.

And how I see it and am learning for myself, in this new era of spiritual awakening that we're in — the old kind of hard work wealth manifesting doesn't work anymore like it used to.

Not in lasting ways. Not beyond some glass ceiling.

Because if we don't do our inner work now and release those inner shadows, they'll keep gnawing at us. And keep pulling us down again.

To create true expansive wealth that keeps on building, without us grinding ourselves up on the grindstone (hard hustling), or spinning our wheels in other inner non-sparkly mind games, requires us to catch our learning gems, cast out our inner demons and shadows, and find our sparkly, pure empowered way of being.

We have to not only have the right money mindset but also uplevel our beliefs and our inner way of operating. And as we do that, we start to powerfully manifest our desires. As a side-effect.

In lasting ways. As fully nourished, empowered, self-expressed, and fully "sparkling" beings. Because we did all the inner work to be happy!

(And yes, I'm also on that adventure to get there, as I'm writing this.)

I believe that we live in an amazing time where we no longer need to sacrifice ourselves and simply be of service or be hard-asses who are only about working hard and making money. (And then be starved on the inside.)

Those are all stereotypes and old society conditioning.

In this age, I believe that we get to have ALL we truly want. Live how we truly want. Manifest all our soul's desires. No matter where we live or what's happening in our world. I believe that if we believe that, we will always find next steps and get access to solutions and resources.

We are MEANT to experience AMAZING.
We are meant to fully express and enjoy
ourselves in all our SPARKLE
and our brilliance.

And of course, for this to happen, THAT's where the bravery comes in.

Because we have to truly embrace this new possibility and face all limiting beliefs, old energies, and stereotypes we have been living by. Spot them, see through them, step through them, and then step through to the other side.

Which means we have to see and embrace all the places where we have been fencing ourselves in.

Do you already fully and deeply believe that any and all things that you desire are possible? That you can manifest anything that you want?

Whatever objections you hear as I say that, you have to release.

And that's where the inner journey OFF the sparkle path begins.

Are you ready for the deep dive? Great!

First, a quick recap of the BE PLAY DO formula (see separate chapter):

- ★ BE (Pause. Simply BE. Listen to my heart and my desires.)

- ★ PLAY (I do something playful. Enjoy. Get out of my head.)

- ★ DO (I take action, as inspired.)

So what DO you do when it's not working? And where is the hole in the whole manifesting concept for you to "fix"?

What have you NOT been doing/seeing?

cracking the code

You look for the shadows.

If your manifesting isn't working, you have shadows in your manifesting gears. Meaning — conscious or subconscious inner voices, old stories, emotions, or energies are somehow holding you back.

For example. Take an Olympic athlete that has doubts about winning. Guess what. With any doubts in their system, they won't win.

That's an example of grains in your system.

Now, you might say... well, I'm not an Olympic athlete. I don't have to play that hard. So it's not THAT relevant.

Well. Do you want to manifest your pure desires?

Or are you saying it's not that relevant?

You are being tested, you see.

Are you ready to say yes to yourself and get to your next level of inner sparkle and empowerment?

Then keep reading.

Now, if you're like I was (up until very recently), you might get pissed now. "Sounds like a lot of work," might be one of your voices.

Or you may think, "crap, all that stuff is so NOT serving me..! Let's just get RID of them!" NOW! (I, for instance, went into A-student hustle mode. Which is also shadow. That's us bullying ourselves.)

There actually IS ALL the benefit, right here:

When we discover shadows, we grow. We find awareness gems. And then — as a side-effect — we manifest our desires. Our dream lives! The more we release old mind-stories (or simply act through them and live by new, empowering stories), the more we start living in full SPARKLE!

Quick story, with a before and after:

Once, while still living in Switzerland, I was single for about four years and quite frustrated with it. I went out, but I was jealous of others who seemed to have love, and I didn't.

Once I focused on what made me happy (which was going to the U.S. for a sabbatical, and studying art, and enjoying Alaska outdoor adventures...) suddenly I had three men interested in me. Just as I was about to leave.

What changed? Where do you see I had shadows?

I'll tell you: I dropped the "trying hard" and jealousy and being so attached to my desires — all shadows! — and instead focused on what made ME happy. Ironically, NOT trying to find a partner made me magnetic to potential partners. Suddenly I had all. Men, feeling more free, and living fully. AND my learning gems were plenty!

So! Ready to catch some shadows in your own manifesting gears?

Go where your heart leads.

play prompts:

state your current desires

What do you want? Make it specific without worrying about "how."

_____

_____

_____

a "why" shadow check

Imagine your genie wish WILL happen. No risk, no downsides. Your order to the universe got delivered. Exactly as posted. That Italian Romeo you wished for (or whatever it was) landed.

Is it really what you want? Why?

_____

Sometimes, if we're on auto-pilot or don't pause, we THINK we want something, but really, from the bottom of our heart, it's not true. If our desire isn't ours, our subconscious will rally against it and sabotage us.

Also, you don't want to go after something and do all the work only to realize it isn't even what you wanted, right?

Shadow example 1: Do you want this "so that you can" have something else / feel a certain way? Like... "I want to make 100K a year so that I feel I made it." Doing something to prove your worth isn't a pure desire.

In general, desires that continue with "so that _____" desires aren't pure. Because there's some condition. An attachment to the outcome. So what if it doesn't happen? What would you make it mean about you?

Shadow example 2: Do you want this desire because of others? Also unnecessary pressure. And why would you live other people's desires?

Shadow example 3: Is your desire as big or as small as you truly want it? Or were there voices that made you make it smaller?

Sniff for shadows. Does your desire feel yours, pure, and what you truly want? If not, find what's truly juicy and exciting and yours.

"oh sh!t" shadow catch

Imagine for a moment that your wish is fulfilled. RIGHT NOW. What comes up for you as you hear that? Some freak-out? Catch the voices.

Tip to help forward from here: A little nervousness is normal when we pursue new desires. To overcome it, try seeing it simply as an experiment! Then you're in curious mode again! Like an inventor! "I wonder what'll happen if... !!" That's the energy for sparkle, magic, and growth.

If the "oh sh!t" is more like a freak-out, and you believe you can't do it / this is terrible / your body freezes / Full stop! No time! Impossible! ... Those are all shadows.

What "oh sh!t's" (if any) are you noticing?

Write them on a sheet of paper, then toss it away.

As you're running these thoughts and emotions through your system, it can also be useful to get up and stay in the question. Do something else. You'll notice more voices. They'll just pop in your head.

Or talk out loud. Write. Scribble. Talk into a mirror. Blab them out.

Don't believe any of the voices!

Try saying "So what!" to each voice. And then "So what!" to the next one.

Just notice them. See through them. Embrace them. Until they leave.

self-sabotage x-ray

Back to your desire that you stated. Maybe you're in the great place of thinking, yeah, that's not you. You got this. You're on a roll. I was in that place. Playing all day long. Feeling in flow.

Well, let me ask you this:

Why do you think <u>you don't already have your desire in your life right now</u>? Pause. And sit with that for a moment. Be honest with yourself.

How may you have been holding yourself back?

What have you been telling yourself, or how have you been avoiding taking action? Where do you keep dropping the ball from taking your inspired actions?

Why? Now catch THOSE stories!

shake the shadows up and out!

See if you'll shake out some shadows with this statement from me:

<u>All</u> the voices that tell you that you canNOT
have all that you desire are not true.
You CAN have ALL that you want.

And you can have it now.

What inner objections come up for you as you hear THAT?
But... but.... all shadows.

Do you <u>want</u> all these objections to <u>remain</u> true?
As the captain of your boat, you have the say.

Are you ready to believe in miracles?
Try that. And take your heart-inspired actions from there.

In the moment that you believe
something outrageous is possible,
outrageous things become possible.

This is the alternative:

If you believe that only what <u>has</u> been is possible, you'll keep only getting what you've been getting so far.

See how that's simply a switch in your mind?

It's all about believing big. Limitlessly. And then taking step by step. Without knowing all the details (that's where the universe comes in).

So, what do you decide to believe around the possibilities of your desire?

facet glasses on!

Put on your "facet glasses" for a moment (looking at all angles and seeing any obstacles as totally feasible), and get curious.

For the sake of this "Permission To Sparkle" adventure, let's just assume you SEE them all as SEE-through. Suddenly you're super(wo)man!

How do you think it will affect your life if you drop ALL the limiting shadow voices that you found? What if you start to believe that ANYTHING is possible from here forward?

What different actions might you take now?

_____

_____

_____

What would fall away?

sparking your superhero!

What superhero qualities do you want to awaken in yourself to live in full sparkle, act freely and boldly, and start manifesting miracles right now?

_____

_____

_____

That being said, here's a next play prompt for you to get the courage and right energy to get going:

superhero pose!

Imagine that you ALREADY HAVE these qualities in your body right now and strike a superhero pose! Really embody that, for at least 30 seconds. If you want, move around in the room, BEING that superhero. Own it!

If you want, pick a theme song! Pose! Walk! Strut! The whole song! Dare to be silly. DANCE and POSE IT OUT! Allow yourself to be ridiculous!

How did that make you feel?

What action does your heart want you to take now toward your desires?

_____

_____

superhero action!

While you're in the energy right after this dance play prompt: Take at least one of your inspired actions right now. It can be a small one!

It doesn't matter how big an inspired action is. Any action is movement.

And here's a corny quotable for you, haha!

Even a baby step a day can bring your miracle your way!

So what else do you do with all those shadow voices that you caught?

Most often, you'll realize that you can simply let them go.

You might notice that the voices and stories were not even YOUR stories! Society ideas! Or something your parents used to say or do. Or something you no longer want to believe in! And then change course.

Then there are other shadows that may feel like tougher nuggets. Harder to notice. Perhaps you simply catch that every time something happens, you feel like sh!t! Once you spot what's going on and realize what stories you're telling yourself (and what you can let go), some shadows may also be harder to let go. Especially if you've been so used to living with them.

No matter. We can always change and move forward.

Before you let the old stories go, though, it's worth pausing!

finding treasures & gems

Sometimes there's a deeper learning waiting for us! Even soul lessons!

As you look at the shadows and voices and even the hard feelings you found in this chapter, what awareness gems did you find? Like... did you learn a deeper aspect of compassion? Of relationships? Of love? Perhaps you were able to heal an old story and were able to offer forgiveness.

What do you see? What do you maybe want to ponder more?
What do you want to celebrate?

When you feel complete, here's the forward action:

dropping beliefs

What old beliefs do you decide to drop, which new ones to live by?

_____

_____

_____

energy scan.

Here's a way to catch more shadows. Ask yourself:

Do you feel any icky energy when you think about your desire?

(You can play with the Sparkle Mirror Tool here! See chapter "Your magical game tools for every day".)

Everything is energy. We manifest what we put out there.

For example. Picture someone going on a date. If they are in a "there's something wrong with me" energy, their date will sense it and probably skip dessert. Or they might be too eager. Which can feel like "too much, too fast!" Same thing. Not very attractive.

Shadows can feel icky. And people will feel that. To stick with that example: Who wants an icky feeling date?

And as long as we keep such shadows, we keep recreating similar stories and scenarios.

Another example: Think of an A-student. If someone is in an "I have to prove myself" energy, that person will likely keep creating — even actively look for! — opportunities to prove themselves. First the A grades. Then competitions. Degrees. Diplomas. Whole walls full.

Until they catch their inner "I have to be an A-student so that _____ (whatever their inner story is)" game.

Ask yourself: What energy do you think you're exuding right now if you think about your desire? Is it an empowered energy and story? Or an icky one? If it's an icky one, what do you think is behind your story? How might that story have been sabotaging your efforts?

(if there's something lurking, you'll get to catch a big awareness gem!)

_____

_____

_____

What energy would you like to exude instead? Notice the difference.

_____

_____

_____

What in your life do you choose to do differently now to start embodying this new energy and live in this more sparkly way now?

feel stuck?

It can be tricky to decode our stories if our mind is spinning, and we're just trying to figure things out from our (perhaps even frustrated!) head.

State your desire to the universe (and yourself) that you want more clarity on whatever is spinning in your head... and then do something to get out of your head!

Allow yourself to play!

That will not only bring you peace of mind but also get you out of your head!

Play! First, you'll feel awesome again. Then, you'll find your perfect next steps!

What could you do, right now, for play? Go for a walk? Pick up some colors and express yourself? Put on a great song and DANCE?

Look around yourself, and pick something.

(This can take less than a minute!)

how to **sparkle** without dependence

how this chapter helps:

In this chapter, you'll discover how to claim full sparkle, no matter who or what is in your life at this moment, or not. This is the chapter to find your feel-good sparkle independent of what you have and independent of others.

Now. Before I start with my real-time journaling, let me be clear:

I'm not saying you have to sparkle independently and never ever connect with anyone again. Or be lonely.

What I'm going for here, and discovering for myself, is that you find your true power when — whatever happens in your life — you're like an island in the storm. Not drowning. Strong. Staying on your course of your own sparkly desires. Even if no one is on board. You for yourself.

And that all the things and people around you are a beautiful cherry-on-top garnish, but you are not depending on them.

I did have a not-so-independent moment yesterday. But I just caught this as a pattern that I want to let go. I'm the observer now, hooray!! Yay to putting on those facet glasses and catching gems!

I saw myself doing all that mind wobble, and now that I have clarity about it, you get this magical chapter — and I'll declare I'm done.

So, what happened?

First of all, quick backtrack, to fill you in: I've been un-married for a month as I'm writing this.

I was blessed with the most amicable break-up ever.

All went so smoothly, yes some cry moments, but most of all, no drama, just purely fully supported. Still caring for each other deeply. Even still seeing each other — kind of — whenever we feel called to. Just no labels. No promises. Just choosing from the moment. Still hanging out as friends. Still soulmates. (Of course! That stays!)

No normal rules. Just authentic, moment-by-moment choices.

It's what I wished for! Total freedom! To be me. To do what I love. Live and travel where I want to. To be who I want to be with. When I choose to. That's where we are! And we have the best relationship ever now, more authentic, more deep, no prisons, just freedom.

And I did all this with pure honesty of my wishes and wants, every step of the way. He got to always say yes, or no. No secrets.

So what just happened now?

Yesterday was Friday. I was full of gratitude and living my freedom lifestyle that I wanted... And in addition to just leaving my marriage, my new living model and biz side-gig of house-sitting for dog owners is starting to take off (which I had no idea about when I left my marriage. That was a total leap of faith!)...

AND this last week, I also found an amazing studio rent opportunity — for in-between house sits. Super cozy, and a total win-win-win.

It all feels like I'm on vacation every day, and I'm so grateful. (I also thrift-store magic-shopped such fun-goodie design elements that the whole studio space feel like a Pippi Longstocking home-base of awesome. I love EVERYthing there!)

It's a big universe gift — a man showed up as landlord who's not in it for the money but had this ample space, and he's letting me live there for a super fair price.

Oh, and there's a Jacuzzi. And a porch. With sea view. And, and, and.

And food! He happens to love cooking and always cooks way too much. Actually grateful if I help eating...

Seriously! How blessed can I be?

Also, I'm surrounded with doggies every day now, just how I like it, getting outside, after a few hours of client and business playtime... then replenishing (and also catching gems and hatching business things while walking on beaches and in forests).

I manifested my new dream life. Me living in sparkle!

I also feel good about my marriage dissolution. I took some soulful time to process. While all went super-fast (In February, I realized I needed to leave, and on May 2, we signed the papers... !!! O. M. G.)

With all that, I'm okay. And grateful for EVERYthing.

Yes, and then the universe brought me another gem yesterday: I found a big shadow pattern that I'd been running pretty much all my life. Affecting all areas of life — even business! So grateful to have found it.

The tears were worth it!

So what happened?

Last evening, Friday night, I went to the brewery and joined my old (married) life friends when I spotted them there. Including my now ex-hubby. We actually all had a good time. No hard feelings from anyone, everyone said hi, we joked around...

Yet something was brewing for me. Other than beer.

I noticed backs turning towards me. My ex-hubby's, specifically. I saw friends disappearing without saying anything. G (my ex) interacted with me, but when I asked how he's doing, really caring, I felt all I got was the weather report.

I felt disconnected and left out.

And it started to hurt.

At some point, almost everyone had left to some other place (we used to all go have dinner together, but this time, everyone just kind of disappeared)... then, with a gesture of "I'm out" and a wave, G, too, was gone.

The night was early. I wasn't hungry, but I was sad not to have my usual gang of friends and not to have dinner plans. Especially the connection with G — I was missing it. (That had actually also been part of my reason to leave my marriage: the shrinking of our connection. That had already hurt me for a while, yet I had not asked for a change.)

So! Here I was. Somewhat butt-hurt and feeling lonely. I was being human. Not Zen. I was considering stopping by G's home to speak my truth and just really see how he's doing and somehow elicit a deeper connection — with the craving to get my own heart filled.

(If you didn't read earlier chapters, we still have a deep connection. And he's one of my soulmates. And still a friend.)

But as I was leaving the brewery, I happened to (thank you, universe!) JUST see his truck heading to town — not homeward — so I knew he was going to eat somewhere else.

So, I hadn't been invited — again.

More sadness came.

I got lots of puppy love in the car — I happened to have a puppy with me:

This is Winnie!

(Thank you, again, universe! For bringing me this super spontaneous three-day weekend puppy sit gig of an absolutely adorable love and solace giver. Just look at her!)

So what did I do?

(This is also showing how I process no-sparkle-path moments. I'll make a bullet list for you. Here's what I did to take care of myself.)

- ✩ I let my emotions all out. Cried. Talked to myself. Processing. Letting go!

- ✩ I shared it with a trusted circle / friends (in my case, a sacred small circle online support and inner-growth program I'm in).

- ✩ I allowed myself to receive love (the puppy licking my tears)!

★ I calmed myself enough to safely drive myself + the puppy home.

★ On the way, I decided to get more closure from G, and went by his place to take more of my last remaining boxes from the shed. I allowed myself to keep crying as I loaded my car in the pouring rain. It was like the universe even orchestrated the weather. All this helped me process and was part of my healing.

★ Arrived at the puppy's home, I decided to take a bath after taking care of the puppy. Turned out that I had just the right things with me: Earlier, I had bought a few travel items to put myself in a positive vacation feeling energy. Like a FUN unicorn bath bomb, a purifying mask... Little did I know (thank you, universe again) — that I'd use these things not to just love up my vacation lifestyle, but to help with my healing, and step into my unicorn sparkle self.

★ Crying, and taking care of myself through all the sadness with that bath, I suddenly noticed a text message a friend had sent earlier. She was "just checking in" and said, "Astrid, you're evolving into your brilliant self." Aw!! Just when it really soul-nourished me!

Can you see how amazingly supported I was by the universe, all through this crying and snot-blowing moment? We all are! When we're open to seeing signs and being fully supported and SAY YES to that support, it shows up everywhere. Always.

★ In the bathtub, I started catching awareness gems, and slowly began to feel better. Nourishing and feeding my soul. Remembering that it had been ME who chose my independence. And now I was choosing it again. I was not a victim here. They didn't invite me. So be it. Whoever <u>wants</u> me around can have me. (If I want to be there.) I don't have to make myself dependent on anyone. Slowly, I felt my magic emerging again.

★ I smoothed on the purifying clay mask. More feel-good.

★ I got inspired to rewatch *A Star Is Born*... and about three minutes in, I got inspired to sing. Despite my tears. (Another great way to release pain and process it.) Letting it out. Random. All of it.

These words came to me, as I sang to myself, free-style expressing myself:

You're like a butterfly, lying in a cocoon
The sun is coming, even if you feel alone

You feel so vulnerable. Yet, All you do is unfold.

The sun is rising, shining high,
on all the colors of your wings,
as you keep unfolding,
leveraging, your brilliant being.

There's no time lost, ever.
You had to be in the cocoon.
To unfold your wings,
you had to be alone.

Now you get to celebrate all the darkness and also the colors
They're already there, even if you don't see them yet...

play prompt

What does this chapter or the butterfly song inspire you to, so far? Did it make you feel better somehow about where you're at? Or worse? What are you realizing for yourself? Take a moment to reflect and hug yourself!

_____

_____

And then, what happened next? At 10 pm, when I had made peace with all there was and was just taking care of myself?

G called.

And invited me over. To watch the season's follow-up movie *Deadwood*. A saga we had watched more than once while married.

"You never look at your texts, so I'm calling! What are you doing?" he said.

"I'm in the bathtub. Just finished a cry-my-eyes-out session..." I always speak my full truth with him now — it feels so GOOD! (Before, I had been hiding some of my inner stories, assuming he wouldn't understand.)

And he said, "Well, quit your crying, get your mask off, and come on over. Let's watch a movie." Just like that.

Suddenly, everything felt so easy, I thought, as I rinsed off. And how curious! Just as I had let go of my craving to reconnect with him, there he was.

And we had a beautiful soulmate reconnection yet again.

While not all the words were spoken in the depth that I live these days (and wish for in my next partnership and soul tribe), we connected heart to heart, where not everything needed to be said, and I felt deeply seen and heard.

One by one, the stories I had made up in my mind, about what others thought, what he may have thought, and why I wasn't invited... didn't seem true in the first place, didn't matter anymore, and melted away.

However. With all the goodness and reconnecting and melting...

The next day I realized a bunch of things.

This was a familiar pattern I had been running here.

I had made my sparkle dependent on what others did or said.

And I chose, in that moment, not to repeat this story and to step into a different reality. And from now on, to save myself this whole tailspin.

I'm curious! What could it have looked like if I had not gone into this deep sadness and cry-in-bathtub misery but just been okay, knowing I'm complete?

What if I didn't need any invitations or validations to feel loved, whole, and seen?

I realized this was a total parallel to a perception I was running in my business. (This is often the case, by the way! When we run one pattern, one theme of how we react in one area of our lives, chances are, we also run it everywhere else, like in our business!)

In my case, I know that it has been a touchy area for me that when not many clients show up when I do something, or no new ones (or whatever my mind judges as not enough), I don't feel seen, assume I don't matter... feel somewhat deflated, sad... ah rejection!

That, of course, is NOT the sparkle frequency from where all magic happens and from where my true happy springs.

(And not, of course, how I create a magnetic, magical business!)

What if all these "not-enough, not-seen, not-loved" stories are just something my mind made up?

What if I can drop all these stories and feel complete?

How would I show up for myself in my life, if I fully knew and felt that I'm always whole, complete, and magical just as I am, me being me?

How might my business and life look different if I stopped buying ANY of my mind-stories about what others may say/think about me?

What if I don't NEED to know where I make a difference and how my work affects anyone (or myself?)

What if I DECIDE that what I do — and even simply WHO I AM — ALWAYS matters and is ALWAYS magical. No matter who shows up or invites me in? What may my life look like then?

Are you noticing there are some powerful journaling prompts here?

play prompt:

Journal these last questions and whatever else comes to you, as you're pondering all this for yourself! (Best take your own actual journal!)

When I went over to see G, he said some brilliant things. I felt humbled because here I was, making all this up — that I'm on this spirit-evolution and inner-growth-sparkle path, and he's "just retired," a "mountain man," and doesn't get what I'm talking about...

Talk about judgment, right? Allow yourself to be surprised. Assume you have no idea what others know or think.

Here are a few very pointed things he said:

"Things change. People change."

I feel that was referring to me and also to my old friends. And admittedly, while I still really like all my old friends, I also recently noticed I'm not quite as aligned anymore to hang out with them.

While married, I had enjoyed my hubby's and our old friends' topics, which were always very grounded, solid, mountain-man-like (typically revolving around hunting, fishing, beer jokes, etc.) A solid, fun, male protection energy of fixing the world and taking care of things.

It had served me for quite a while. I had enjoyed this energy as an energy of grounding. And had been happy to make myself blend in.

For a while, I had actually found it kind of funny. We were quite the contrast! Me and all my creative businesses... including a jewelry line where I had been an emerging designer at Phoenix Fashionweek...! That had, in fact, been the time where "mountain man G" and I had fallen in love, deep!

But then, I grew more into my sparkly new being... discovering the coaching world. My intuitive ways. Started to become more spiritual. More sensitive to energies. No longer into war movies... These days, I'm feeling more aligned to talk spirit sparkle + have deep and inspiring conversation. Hunting talk and beer and such just isn't enough anymore!

Also, I'm no longer satisfied with just assuming emotions. But want to talk about feelings. Free sparkle is more and more on the menu for me!

A big gem here for me was to realize that I had indeed simply changed!

And I'm ready to come out of my cocoon and SPEAK about my new me!

G continued to add another beautifully grounded life-wisdom piece:

He said he learned a long time ago not to worry about what others think.

"You can't guess what people think. It's never true. You just have to be you."

— my former hubby, G

And then he said…

"Just because I don't ask how you're doing doesn't mean I don't care.
I'll always care about you. Even if I don't always ask."

He admitted that he misses me too, like I miss him.
And "We'll always be friends."

He's giving me such a gift! To fully support me in my choice to leave
because I felt I had to. He's giving me space while still fully supporting
me. I so appreciate him.

To get back to my story here, the point here — and another gem — is:

I'm starting to make myself independent from validation.

I'm starting to spread my wings like that butterfly. Starting to taste what it
feels like. This new sparkle freedom.

Which includes sparkling free, without dependence, and filling myself
from within.

How am I getting there and solidifying this?

By staying curious.

By nourishing my soul with what my heart needs.

By giving myself time to allow a new friend circle to form, and new
experiences.

By trusting all is well and not buying into what ANYthing means about
me. Dropping fears and old stories.

By recognizing next time I'm sad, or feel unseen... Catching you, pattern!
I see you! AND I'm not buying into it anymore. I may still have sad

moments, but I won't go down the rabbit hole of feeling so darn-gone lonely because I made myself dependent on the validation of others.

I choose a new path. My more sparkly independent path.

That's what I'm declaring now to the universe and to you.

With permission to mess up, and that's okay too.

Sparkle forward! With more and more ease, and less and less baggage — letting go of a few more ropes that have been holding me back.

See if you're inspired with the following for your life too:

play prompt:

Journal or ponder these additional questions. Pick whichever ones stand out, or have a journaling fest! Whatever feels good is perfect!

⭐ Where in your life are you making your sparkle dependent on what others think? What situations? What people?

⭐ What story are you telling yourself there? What are you making it mean about yourself?

⭐ What is the worst thing about this?

⭐ And what's even worse than that? Stay curious. Keep asking, "what's worse than THAT?" until you hit the bottom. You'll find surprising, deep fears or thoughts that, once you see them, may seem ridiculous. Then you can embrace them and dissolve them with love.

★ Sparkle forward: How might your life look in those
situations if you fully sparkle instead? Independent of what
others think?

★ What are you inspired to declare for yourself, as a new way of
being? What do you choose to do differently?

★ Self-care forward: How will you fill your cup next time a
validation-dependency craving shows up? Independently,
you-for-yourself, no matter what others do or say?

This brings me to a powerful thing I once heard Kavita say: (I saved it! I
knew I had to share it here somewhere!)

"The best tool I have in my toolkit is the power
of choice. When I use it, I'm not a victim to any
situation or story that plays out."
– Kavita Singh

Take a moment to let this sink in. Catch your awareness gems.

Here's one more wrap-up to this chapter. A mic-drop. Are you ready?

I shared my weekend journey with my small circle mastermind on
Monday morning. How I went from having a technicolor day to going
down the rabbit hole at the brewery, took a deep-dive into sadness as I
left there, then wriggled myself up within a few hours, to full circle, and
feel-good again. Even before G called.

What did they say?

They gave me smiles of compassion, and then I received two huge
epiphanies from their mirroring to me. Before I share them:

Carrying on in my story:

Kavita said that what I'm judging for myself as breakdowns, etc., I'm already rocking from other people's view. For instance, we (at the time I wrote this) have clients who stay in that low space for much longer, not even seeing the possibility. Right! Heck, it used to also take me months, or even years, to get over stuff! Or to even see clear!

Kavita continued: they're not touching the lightness. Not owning their sparkle yet. Not even able to remotely understand how someone can feel so playful all the time and also run a business.

Kavita added that her kids often say things like, "Astrid would rock this and do this so playfully..." Apparently, I totally changed their world when I visited Kavita last year, just by being me. Wow! That was so touching! And put it all into a feel-good perspective for me. (Yay for inner support circles!)

(And of course, to fully own my sparkle, I fully have to feel that also for myself, seeing all that magic in myself. Yup the LOVE chapter is calling me to do that, as I'm editing this!)

Kavita went on to say that, just a year ago, it would have taken me weeks or months to process this. And I'm realizing, yes, the more I go back in time (not even too far!), I see I had NO CLUE about how to wriggle myself out of dark places.

Now I re-booted myself to feel good and have so much awareness within an evening, processing everything, and coming out on the other end.

Holy crap! How far have I come!

Then Jean Berry dropped in with something that totally landed it with me. (Words have so much magic, right? You can hear something in so many ways, not really receiving it, and then suddenly someone says something in just the right words, and it hits you like, "Heck, yes!")

Jean said my breakdowns are now "exponentially insignificant."

That was hilarious! And so awesome too. And really showed me how far I've come!

And all the magic is accessible here to you in this book to do that as well. Are you ready to claim more of this sparkle for yourself?

play prompt:

Be curious: What serves you best to see here for yourself right now? In what ways does my story inspire you for your own life?

This is us in the "Permission To Sparkle" adventure, walking on and off the sparkle path, staying curious, and collecting gems. Gems of knowing, and gems of releasing, cleansing, letting things go.

Such an adventure, this "Permission To Sparkle" game! All this inner growing business!

And no matter how challenging it gets at times... it can also be FUN. Even when something feels rough — especially then!

Humor helps us process, makes us brave! Also: smiles can be disarming!

(Try it! Monsters may lose their power if you smile instead of cower!)
(That goes for inner shadow monsters as well as others!)

I admit. I've had many moments where I got frustrated. "Does all this shadow hunting and learning this never end?!" (Yes, those were also shadow stories. I put myself under pressure! Impatience! Judgment!)

Thing is, there's always something to learn. That doesn't mean we're broken. And it doesn't mean we cannot manifest magic WHILE we're learning and growing. It just means that:

As we play the "Permission To Sparkle" adventure for ourselves, we grow more and more into our free, sparkly selves.

Living more and more of our true desires, being more and more of ourselves. We rediscover our sparkle. We de-dust our inner diamond. We claim our magic. Our own brilliance.

And as we move forward, we also learn, more and more, to see that humor in the darker moments. Which actually helps us accelerate!

Because... humor brings lightness!

Kavita and Jean also said something very big that felt like a big CLUNK nugget drop for me:

They said that it was actually a universe gift that I wasn't invited to dinner with my old friends.

Because in those circles, I'm dimming my light.

I was <u>meant</u> to move on. I am meant to find my own light.

DUH! Of course! I wasn't fully aligned to be there at this time! I kind of sensed there was this universe gift. But hearing it from them really brought this home to me!

I can always ask myself: Where am I ENHANCING my sparkle? Where am I dimming my light?

How many times I've been here. We often get similar life circumstances with the same kind of story. Again and again. That's just so that we get to learn from it, find those gems. And once we get all facets of it, released all that's not serving, those scenarios will stop.

Mic drop. This chapter is done.

(And the next time I make my sparkle dependent on validation from others, I'll have a yet lighter view on it, and then lighter and lighter, until I'm fully free and owning my power from inside of me.)

Even if I'm not fully there yet, this was a big shift and awareness for me.

How about you?

What's your biggest take-away from all this for you?

_____

_____

sparkle love:
manifest your dream relationships

how this chapter helps:

This feels like one of my bravest and most vulnerable chapters as of yet:
I'm defining my new rules for relationships and sexual freedom. I'm
hugely challenging myself here. And that's great.

For one, because as I'm facing and embracing my deepest desires, I will,
of course, find more sparkle, and two: because by sharing my journey
here with you, I intend to also inspire you to dare to carve your own
sparkle freedom paradigm.

(This, of course, doesn't just have to be in the area of relationships, but
any life area where you can use some courage to bring in more sparkle!)

It's been two months since I've dissolved my marriage — and freed all
kinds of inner limitations, making universe wishes regarding a new
relationship paradigm. And now, today, I have the opportunity to say yes
to the universe. And receive it.

Am I ready?

Heck, no!

This is why I'm here. I'm tuning inward and here to get clarity and catch
gems. (This is, of course, also a prompt for you to do, whenever you feel
an inner pressure build-up, or fears: play "Permission To Sparkle." Use
this book. Journal, stay curious... you know the game.

So what's happening in my world?

Just a few weeks ago, I made universe wishes to meet more men who are conversationalists. The soulmate material, kind of (though I'm not fully ready for it.)

That's exactly what came into my life, pretty much instantly. No new soulmates, but lots of new men! And they were conversationalists!

Haha, that's a great example of how we get what we wish for! I didn't clearly ask for my next soulmate because I felt I wasn't ready, so that's what I got! Soulmate MATERIAL, but not the "real" thing. ;-)

So! I'm super pampered these days with amazing men around me, great friends to have amazing experiences with. So, so blessed! I don't think I've ever had it like this in my life! (All that inner sparkle play work on myself is paying off! I'm evidently radiant!)

I have awesome men buy me dinner and take me camping, dancing, kayaking, on road trips... We have amazing conversations... they cook for me. It's ridiculous! They really all treat me like a queen!

Awwwwwwww. Receiving.

(By the way, that's also a thing I really had to release — resistance to receiving. That's part of having abundance show up more — are you ready to receive? Fully?)

It's really working, this free-your-sparkle and claim-your-queen thing!

So today, now, comes the next level that I asked for.

Total freedom, right?

I was curious (and still am): What if I give myself permission to have EVERYTHING I WANT? Also in the relationship realm?

play prompt:

Are you giving yourself permission to have the total DREAM
RELATIONSHIP(S) you want? If not, where are you holding back?

_____

_____

What I'm exploring here might not be the most revolutionary thing on
the planet anymore (at least in the Western world). In fact, I wonder if it's
actually more common than not to have open relationships or more than
one intimate relationship at the same time.

What if? Right? What if I give myself permission to do something like
that?

Do I even want that? I'm not sure yet! It feels super scary! And that's
perfect. I'm having an inner mind-sh!t-storm, a good one, with all kinds
of thoughts and feelings flying. I'm torn in different directions. I'm
getting ready to find the next awareness gems (and discover beliefs I can
release, for sure! I'm feeling it!).

It's time to free myself of more limiting thoughts like old society
conditioning or things my parents used to live by. I want to dare to freely
live my true desires and create my new relationship sparkle paradigm!

And to be okay with it.

Wait! Even THRIVE with it!

play prompt:

I'm ready to do some journaling! Join me, pick any of these prompts, and get curious!

Brain dump. What all is going on in your mind right now in terms of sparkle love? What are your hidden desires?

_____

_____

_____

Here's mine:

Holy crap! Sex — or any kind of fun short of that — with another man, while still occasionally being physically intimate with (albeit divorced from) my former hubby? To me, right now, feels like cheating!

Then here's the other voice inside of me:

I'm divorced. Come on, I can do what I want. I feel a conversation is necessary before I see G again.

Full transparency — one of my key values in this new paradigm. Noted!

(P.S. knowing our values helps us get clear on what we want. And say no to what we don't want. Took me a while to even think about that!)

Back to my thoughts:

Do I even WANT to be with the new love interest that started showing up? It feels exciting! But in a different way. It feels more like fun — not necessarily relationship material. Not at this time anyways.

I don't want to be locked down. (I'm noticing my truth in this moment.)

And how about the fact that I live in a SMALL TOWN? How would I even have more than one relationship at the same time?

(Shadow alert! Fear of judgment!) (That's a gem I just found! A shadow voice I can now look at and keep living by or let go!)

"But how?" my mind asks... would I have to keep names secret and go undercover when in public? Is that aligned with my values? Everyone knows everyone here... how could I handle this and be in integrity?

I'm noticing, as I journal, my heart is really excited about the possibility of saying yes to having fun. Of course! Giving myself permission to do what I want! And then do ONLY what feels fun. Permission to say no, any time too (I'm noticing subtle inner fears.) Permission to change my mind too. Sparkle freedom...! My mind is stretching like bubble gum. SO uncomfortable! Yet, I'm staying curious. Really feeling into what I want.

What are my true heart's desires?

I'm realizing I WANT that freedom. I want to play. I also want to be queenly (in my power) and in integrity. To move around this town while feeling good but not leaving destruction in the wake.

I realize I need to step up and ask for what I want.
And communicate it super clearly.

That, by the way, is also a huge recipe for powerfully manifesting what we want. Sounds logical, right? Yet, how often do we state and communicate our true desires freely and clearly? I know I am stretching my comfort zone here!

For example, if I want to have a physical connection with this new man while seeing my ex-husband in some way, I need to have a full-disclosure conversation with my ex-hubby about that new multi-relationship paradigm I'm considering. And he would need to fully be on board.

And what about sharing names? In a small town? If they know each other (which in this case, I know for certain they do), would it feel right when I share the name of the other man with G? Or would we all want to agree to keep names out of the equation? Does it matter? Would that be super hurtful and better kept secret? Or all out in the open?

Questions, questions. To get clear, time to define values!

What are your relationship sparkle-freedom-paradigm VALUES?

_____

_____

_____

Here are mine:

* Say what I want. That, of course, takes bravery — it's speaking my innermost desires and setting them free. Ahhh, the stretch to become a queen!!!

* Do what I want. Say YES to what feels good! And say NO to what does not! And then give myself permission to do it. Simple as that! (And that, of course, brings up all kinds of limiting beliefs and thoughts I now get to release!)

★ Clear boundaries. When someone says NO, it's no. No matter where in the game. There is no accommodating or bending this rule. I'm permitted to say NO at ANY time. (Of course! I'm noticing limiting fears here again. The idea of an open relationship seems fuzzy and scary!)

★ Full transparency. (With the exception of names at the time I'm writing this.) Honoring each other's privacy — yet otherwise fully disclosing. That gives others permission to choose to be part of that or not. This also means that I bravely do and ask for clear and constant communication. No assumptions. Open communication.

If this topic also pertains to you right now... What are your deep relationship desires right now? If you give yourself permission to suspend any and all existing society "rules?" What resistance/ objections to your true desires are coming up for you? What are your new rules?

_____

_____

_____

_____

_____

_____

Here is the resistance and thoughts sh!t-storm in my mind:

What will they say? Slut/cheap/she gets around... I can let that go. Catching that fear of judgment, and deciding not to let it confine me, is a huge gem! This is me claiming my queen and letting go even more of what others think. Stretching into that sparkle freedom!

What if I hurt G? He keeps telling me not to ever worry about him. If I suggest to him, in full honesty, that my desire is to be fully transparent (yet keep names confidential), he'll get to choose if he still wants to be physically in a relationship with me or not. My gem here is that I decide to be very clear in my communication and in stating my desires, and then not to take on responsibility for other people's possible reactions.

Trust that they have their own reactions and choices under their own control. And that whatever they'll choose, they'll ultimately be okay! And that even if they're temporarily not (yes, all is temporary), they can also find learnings and strengths through all their experiences. Allowing them to live and experience their own story. Journaling this just set me free!

Will I be able to look in the mirror and like — even LOVE — myself if I do this? I've judged myself before as being cheap and dirty for having had "too many boyfriends" in a certain time sequence. Lost respect for myself before. Thinking back, that had to do with NOT being in integrity with my values. And with overstepping my own boundaries. I was giving my power away instead of claiming own power.

Also, I didn't love myself yet. I was chasing love. Always feeling depleted! Because that just doesn't work!

I'm in a much stronger space now. Speaking my truth, my wants, aware of my values, and choosing to stand up for myself and my boundaries. Moment by moment. So then I should be okay! I should actually really be PROUD OF ME. And LIT UP. Because the idea is that I give myself permission to do and ask and live my innermost desires and wants!

How awesome is THAT!

Daring to fully ask for what I want, fully speak my truth, will — as scary as it seems — lead me to fully sparkle!

What comes up for you after reading the last few pages?

_____

_____

_____

What are you asking for? What's your truth? What do YOU want?

_____

_____

In order to GET that, what inner voices do you need to face & let go? In what new ways will you have to show up for yourself in the world?

_____

_____

I have one more journaling prompt for you. A question that was missing for me. There was something I had to do first:

Is there something you need to DO for yourself, <u>or for people in your life,</u> before you step into your new paradigm? What things?

_____

_____

(Drop into your heart as you ask yourself this. Close your eyes.)

Here's what came up for me (and I realized it after asking my inner circle for support, sharing my situation, and my curiosity about how I felt).

Kavita spotted this for me, and it was brilliant! And so important.

This goes to show, again, that you don't have to figure everything out on your own. Allow yourself to share and speak with a safe, empowering inner circle or friend, and then discern what feels like your personal aligned wisdom and next heart-action step. Not giving your power away, but sharing, then choosing what's true to you and what you want.

For me, what showed up was that I needed to speak with my former hubby G. And say that there's a chance I will step into new relationships/connections in the near future. So he wouldn't find out after the fact or as a surprise or hear it from others.

This wasn't an obligation but a feel-good choice.

It helped me also embrace my new chosen way of living by speaking my truth and daring to say it!

And guess what happened?

Again. I was fully supported by the universe.

He said, "Of course!" He was already expecting that. AND, as it played out better than I could have imagined... he showed me that he'd still care for me. And that he still would love me to stay connected. And to come see him. Whenever I felt like it.

Basically — get this! — my former hubby pretty much said that he is okay with the concept of an open relationship.

WHAT?

Not in my wildest dreams would I have imagined.

And then we had a most exciting, sensual, thrilling physical connection that evening. Since, like ever.

This or something better.
(The universe brings better things than we can imagine!)

So! What is your wish? What do you want?
What is your dream relationship paradigm?

Now. Of course, there are no guarantees. In fact, just a little bit later, I realized that the open-relationship thing was actually NOT his thing.

And for me, it turned out to be an exploration for a little while, while I was transitioning, but then what felt right was again a new, one-person-focused, magical new connection with another man.

However, it doesn't matter. Point is, I stayed in my truth, in what felt good to me at the time, and moment by moment. I dared to ask for it. I dared to speak my truth. No matter how scary it felt.

And that kept leading me to my new dream reality, moment by moment. Everything always aligned to my next desires.

(That's how we create our reality! We have a desire, we speak it, and take inspired steps... and our reality aligns to bring it in. It can be that simple.)

Yes, of course, there were moments that weren't all sparkle and glory. I had guilt, sadness, wondering what the EFFFF I'm doing...! And all these things were simply inner voices and feelings for me to see, face, and heal. All part of my evolution. In transparency and truth.

No matter how challenging it felt at times, I kept playing with all the concepts you see in this book through this challenge (and other life challenges.) Curiously, while doing self-care, step by step. By doing that, I kept finding more and more gems, inner trust, and more life-sparkle!

I don't feel lost anymore.

I more and more know myself!

I more and more stand up for myself!

I more and more create my sparkle dream life!

And fears keep losing more and more of their power.

Fears are only based on what has been,
on hypothetical outcomes
and not on what's truly possible!

At the time where I'm writing this, I'm in a new relationship with a guy who totally adores me. We have butterflies and magic on all levels, and I found an amazing supporter in him. He understands me, in all my big visions and travels and universe sparkle explorations. I feel full freedom energetically. Lots in common. Music! Romance. New love.

The universe always recreates our world to our wishes. I'm currently in the rainbow behind a storm. I'm in my new paradigm. And that, my friend, is something you can do, too, moment by moment.

What is your truth? What is the sparkle rainbow life you want?

from sh!t to sparkle
_my spirit journey beginnings

how this chapter helps:

This is if you're wondering how I came to where I'm at today, how I found access to so much sparkle, how I went from being only rational to opening up to universe guidance — even finding the support of my spirit guides! And living a more and more magical life!

This is my spiritual journey to this moment!

(P.S. I won't try to convince you of anything or promote any religion. This is my story. Follow your heart to your own truth and experience!)

(P.S. 2: My spiritual journey didn't start that long ago; it's been only about three years! And before then, I would pretty much only believe what I see!)

So! Time warp! Blast into the past!

story time!

Back when I was working in what felt like "the dungeon" of a Swiss life insurance company — and later when I hustled in New York City (see my stories in chapter "Permission to NOT sparkle") — I gave my power away to all kinds of places and people and things.

I had NO CLUE what it meant to live in sparkle, and happy, from within.

If you could have heard my mind's voices back then, you would have heard things like:

⭐ "This life insurance job and my office education is <u>a smart career choice</u>. Since the art schools didn't take me, <u>I have to</u> do this."

⭐ "My best friend knows what's best for me (she actually kept saying that!) <u>She knows things better</u> than I do. I better listen!"

⭐ "My best friend can't afford a car right now, and I want to go with her to Germany every weekend to dance! And party! She also can't drive, so <u>I have to</u> buy a car, and <u>I have to</u> do all the driving. And <u>I have to</u> do all car payments." (Again, my silent mind voices)

During that time, I WAS following what I THOUGHT would bring me happiness, which then meant driving 4.5 hours one way each weekend to U.S. army Country Music dance clubs and a dance team in Germany.

In principle, that was great, but I was <u>not</u> doing it from a place of inspiration or power, but following my inner "should voices." And what my then best friend suggested. Following HER footsteps.

Instead of speaking up about what I truly wanted and trusting myself.

Also, I was not doing any self-care. I didn't set healthy boundaries. We'd leave right after work and come back right back into work on Monday mornings. I was driving sleep-deprived. Getting myself deeper and deeper in debt. Also having several boyfriends in short amounts of time (and judging myself for it.) Grasping to find happiness. Trying to find love, but not knowing how. Not liking myself in the mirror. It was a dark time.

I was in the wrong job, the wrong relationships, and not speaking up. I was just reacting to and following whatever was happening around me. Even if it was NOT what I truly wanted.
It sucked!

When we ignore the voice of our intuition and hearts, we hurt ourselves! It can feel like we want to blow up!

One day — and today, this is funny for me — I had a total snap moment.

I blew up.

It was after a really crappy day at my life insurance day job, where I handled death and injury "cases," taking complaints all day from annoyed customers who were waiting for their money. I felt like I was in a dungeon, and no matter how long I worked, the number of files never seemed to go down. And customers were never happy! It was NOT my zone of genius — more like my zone of hell! (My zone of genius is ART!)

(Yet of course, it also served a purpose to do all this in my life path. Like giving me a great story to tell you here. And finding all kinds of gems for myself later here. Like learning to follow my HEART! Do jobs and things and go to environments that light me up!)

But there I was that day, with all this stuff going on in my life, AND another horrible day at that job that I hated, just wanting to get home.

I was standing on the platform waiting for the train. I remember it was actually a nice day, mellow weather, people were chill, even birds were singing in between trains! Yet, I was in a cloud of shadows. Hating my life. All of it. Picture a cartoon with a storm cloud all around me.

Then I saw a candy bar machine and thought, "Great! Swiss chocolate! Let me have one. That'll be a light in the tunnel in this moment!"

Has it ever happened to you that your life seems to suck, you think it can't get any worse, and then ANOTHER crappy thing comes along?

I'm sure it has! Well! Can you guess what happened next?

The stupid candy bar got stuck.

That's when the whole happy train station scene came to a full stop.

Ohhhhhhh, NO, you didn't. I stared at it. Like in slow motion, a deep inner anger started to gurgle deep down. Like through old drainage pipes of an old house, it began rattling, got louder, and started shooting up.

Then I blew UP.

In full primal mode at this time, I lost it.
I kicked the darn candy machine.
Once. Twice! Hard!

Then time un-froze. Everything around me seemed paused but suddenly also alive. I noticed people around me, all eyes on me.

You know, like in a movie where an actor does something totally crazy and suddenly stops, realizing that everyone is staring? That was me! I suddenly realized what I'd done! How embarrassing!

I was out of control!

Ashamed and feeling very small, I stuck in another coin. Finally got the candy. I paid for it. In more ways than one.

That was a wake-up moment!

That was one of my darkest times. Not knowing who I was, far from being spiritually aware, not doing what I wanted, not following my heart.

Looking back, I see that I could have taken the reigns then, shifted into curiosity, and looked deeper. Allowed myself to shift into CHOICE. To ask myself what I truly wanted. Then chose that. Claimed my sparkle.

Sadly, I didn't dig deeper then. So I created more experiences like this.

(Apparently, I wanted to learn more angles in this lifetime of how to reclaim my power. Ha!)

I did start following my heart soon after that though. Which meant leaving that job for a USA dream summer guest ranch adventure. And then finding my first design job soon after that — even without having had official diplomas or the so-called "necessary" design school experience.

Hello there, Swarovski! I became a graphic designer there in 2000 and got to design all kinds of things! Talking about claiming more sparkle! Grin!

Several entrepreneurial (now follow-my-heart) adventures followed: I illustrated for women magazines and designed book covers, then designed for brands in the fashion industry and wedding industry, even sparked a special Lucite jewelry line during a rooftop photoshoot in New York! Which landed me as an emerging designer at Phoenix Fashionweek!

Anything is possible! And my jewelry line was actually called "Possibility!"

Fast forward to January 2016: I started to feel a soul calling to emerge, to begin giving back. To inspire others — even the planet! — with my work. Somehow! I just didn't know details yet. Or how to make this into a bigger business. (Um, YES, we get to do our soul-calling AND live in abundance! It doesn't have to be either-or! All desires are possible!)

It was January 1, 2016. I was in the baby shoes of a new business. And at another new beginning. I was living in the USA at this time, on beautiful Kodiak Island, Alaska. I had just asked a man to marry me (G!)...

...but he replied "no." He loved me, he said, but wasn't ready...

Snap! There went my happy life movie reel halting to a stop again!

It felt like another "ground zero" kind of scenario. I instantly packed my things and temporarily moved in with a friend. I didn't know what was going to happen. Whether "Mr. Right" would say yes, how long it would take for my business to blossom... I was again waiting for "life to begin."

One of those days, alone at my friend's apartment, I noticed the movie *The Secret* on a shelf. It seemed to be beaming at me. It looked interesting!

Setting aside all that was happening in my life for a moment (this time not kicking and screaming and destroying things!), I allowed myself to be curious to explore the movie's very unusual promise.

There was a secret to life that would make everything magical? What?

Everyone is different, I learned later — some are widely intuitively / spiritually aware already as children. Others, like me, live almost a whole life in human rational (things have to make sense!) paradigms, doing things how we're taught, how "it's supposed to be done..."

Until something opens our eyes to something bigger than us. And we get curious.

That movie sparked that curiosity for me.

So I stepped through that door into that new world and began exploring! Following the curiosity key! Which, for me at that time, meant having fun with book treasure hunts at the local library.

First, I wanted to learn more about the topic manifesting. Denise Duffield-Thomas' book *Get Rich, Lucky Bitch* book inspired me back then. How did she manifest her desires? And her dream business? I was intrigued. Then I went on to read more and more books, from self-awareness, psychology, to inner growth — even some quantum physics.

I simply kept following what intrigued me.
That always brought me to the next step.

One day, without intending to, I had my first spiritual experience.

I was dog-sitting with a sea view, no internet, and a pile of inspiring books. And two sweet lab doggies. I opened a book on the inner critic — this inner voice that we all have that can cause such havoc if we let it! I don't remember who the author was, possibly Shakti Gawain. There was a meditation to hold an inner dialogue with your inner critic, and I dug in.

Then a curious — and slightly shocking — thing happened.

First, all seemed "normal" and right in line with what the book described: I visualized talking with my inner critic, imagined a lovely internal conversation with her, and actually felt like she was agreeing to become my cheerleader. Cool! Then I got a fleeting visual in my mind of a woman with long black hair and a veil.

I felt inspired to also ask her name. At first, in my mind, she seemed to answer, "it doesn't matter," but I insisted. I was curious! Finally, I got the name "Alaya." Which I had never heard before. I was like, "Okay..." and got curious again: Did that actually mean something?

Because I had no internet, I texted a friend to Google it.

What she texted me back was astounding: She said the word meant "one of the highest realms of consciousness" in Buddhism.

I was shocked. How was this possible!

I couldn't explain this rationally. I didn't know much about Buddhism, had never heard that name or definition before, and I certainly didn't choose that as my inner critic's name — how could I? I literally had no information to come up with that on my own. No internet!

What was going on?

Spoiler alert: years later, I found out (through another psychic coach who validated it) that Alaya is actually one of my spirit guides.

Back then, it was a big spiritual opening for me. A confirmation from the universe. That there are things we cannot rationally explain. There's more than what we see. And the experience actually felt so good! Inviting! Even magical. I felt giddy to learn more!

As I continued to follow what intrigued me in life, I found more insights, more gems, and more spiritual WOW!s, one by one.

Sometimes for longer stretches, life seemed to just trundle on normally, but then suddenly, next big sparkle experiences and "what just happened???" moments would pop up in my life.

And it was always when I was ready, and asked, for more sparkle!

Here's another such story that was a new door for me into a new world and a next level of inner growth and awareness.

This time it started with my business. I had hit a glass ceiling with my income. I had been trying to do things the cheap way, learning from free offerings and figuring things out on my own. I wanted to grow my business to the next level, make more money without spending anything. (Hint: That doesn't work.)

One day... now happily married, and it was, I think, 2017, I got an email that GLEAMED at me as THE THING I needed. You know, one of those universe "Helloooo!! Look at me!" things.

It was a next door for me! (Looking back at this moment, I see this!)

It was an email from author Denise Duffield-Thomas. (Yes, the same *Get Rich, Lucky Bitch* author I had started my spiritual journey with!) She invited me to a webinar to attract more clients. Which was about to start happening in just a few minutes. Perfect. (No time to think.)

Did I want to say yes to universe support?
And did I want to say yes to myself?
And to my ask, of growing my biz?

Yes! Yes and yes!

So I hopped on to see it.

Things happen for a reason. Right? That's also why you're here!

(That being said: Is there something here for you right now, standing out as inspiration? Pause, get curious, and listen to your inner guidance!)

(Stop this program right here for ice cream if you need a break. We'll be here when you're ready to continue.)

That webinar was EXACTLY what I needed.
And it promised EXACTLY what I was looking for.
And it cost EXACTLY $1,000 more than I thought I had.

(I thought I had "zero." I was playing small)

But I said yes. I didn't make money an issue. Decided to follow my heart. I put it on my credit card. Even though it felt like a lot! It was a big jump for me at the time. But I felt the heart-call, and so I did it.

> ## Saying yes to our heart always leads us to our next level. Always to more sparkle, eventually!

One big win turned out to be that I met Kavita Singh in that program — whom you've seen appear in several stories in the book by now. She later turned out to be a soul-mate sister of many lifetimes. And we ended up doing many things (and much bigger things than I had done before) together in business! Like getting paid $10,000 by a client for a month of coaching! Something I would have never fathomed possible before!

Had I not listened to my gut with this webinar and the $1,000 price tag program but instead allowed my inner voices to hold me back ("that's too expensive / too scary / crazy... blah blah blah"), I would have held myself back from getting my sparkly wishes. I would not have gotten all the magical support that I got once I said YES to my gut and moved forward!

That was another lesson for me to be brave. And to always take bold action — from my heart. Even if that feels scary!

Which spending $1,000 back then did!

So, what other magic did I find, following my heart's lead at that time?

A FREE trip to a powerful business retreat weekend to Los Angeles! That's what! And an event that was gifted to me for free! Even the air ticket was free — I suddenly found airline miles I didn't remember having!

At that weekend, a next follow-my-heart door (and challenge) was waiting for me. An invitation to a next-level high ticket and high-impact coaching program.

Which, again, feltEXwhat my heart wanted me to do.
Which, again, felt ENTIRELY and VASTLY out of my comfort zone.
It cost $27K. Which, again, was exactly $27K more than I thought I had!

Yet, I said YES to myself and my dream.
Before even knowing how I'd pay for it.
I was literally shaking and saying yes through tears!

My "human" (as opposed to my higher, fully aware, fully sparkly self) said, "You're crazy! That's ridiculous! Reckless! Not safe!

I was questioning whether I was CRAZY. What the heck was I DOING!

Yet it felt right. I had meditated on it. My heart had said yes!

Guess what. The next day, the money showed up. I had totally forgotten (and not seen, in my fears!) that I had already had it, as retirement money! So I chose to invest some of that money in me.

Whenever we say yes to ourselves, our desires,
and follow our heart, possibilities
and resources always show up.

So, what happened after my next-level-of-big-investment and "YES" to my heart and my desires and dreams?

I was introduced to a whole new world of intuitive coaches, and I discovered that I — yes me! — actually already had intuitive coaching superpowers! That program and me saying yes to me gave me the gift of discovering and trusting more of me. Which is priceless if you think of it!

(Side note: we're all intuitive by nature, it's just not always claimed!)

I remember when I landed in that world, what a shell-shock that was!

I had no idea what I was getting myself into.
And adventure, that's what! That always
happens when you follow your heart!

At a pre-event cocktail meet-up I had organized on that weekend in LA, one lady, in particular, stunned me with her unusual ways: She introduced herself warmly with "Aloha" and a strange hand gesture: forming a circle with two fingers in one hand, and pulling on it with two fingers of the other hand, trying to break it apart (as if that meant something!) Then she described to another lady that she saw wolf energy around her. As hello.

What???!

Today I understand that the thing with her fingers was muscle-testing, an easy and effective method to get yes or no answers from our own subconscious. And she was intuitively reading the other woman.

Back then, I was slightly freaked out.

(But, since I didn't get any bad vibes from her, also curious.)

The next day I would be entering a room of 500 such people.

Was I ready for that? No. But discomfort comes with adventure!

Funny enough, I would end up sharing a room with that very Aloha lady (Who today is an old trusted coach friend, and I totally support her in her very powerful and important inspirational work on the planet. Jade Rehder is her name. Look her up.)

So! With that next-level high ticket coaching program (which, by the way, was sold at that free event — total strategy, of course. I could have guessed. Well, it worked!), a new world opened for me.

That program turned out to be incredibly powerful for me: I learned methods of intuitive coaching, of visualizations and meditations that gave access to more inner freedom and superpowers, I learned more and more of who I was and how I can use my unique gifts and what I love to do to positively contribute to the world.

I was surrounded and guided by amazing coaches who were rocking their successful coaching practices and were super intuitive badasses.

And who were actually making money. Not like before (when I had listened to my inner fears around spending money), where I had moved in circles of people who had also tried to get things the cheap way. (Instead of the "follow the heart way," which might also involve investing money.)

These people all had invested (and kept investing) in their education, their business, and themselves. These people kept saying yes to themselves.

One, in particular, I want to give a huge shout-out to, who inspired me greatly, was coach Jenn August. She was the cheerleader I needed back then who tickled my superpowers awake in me and encouraged and empowered me through her transformational (and very intuitive) coaching sessions. On how to hear my own wisdom and use my gifts!

I also got powerful strategies, systems, and tools to build my business.

Nonetheless, within a few months of starting this big coaching program, with all the support and the amazing high-level coaches, it started feeling heavier and heavier, until I felt I was grinding to a halt.

It was kind of like when you set a boat to sea, ready for the adventure...

the beginning!
so light! exciting!

I set my dream to sea... and of course, I started to take action. I needed to do stuff, to move me forward, right? (P.S. note my inner "should" voice?)

to do list

That idea of taking action was great as a principle... but something was not right. Things got heavy. Too many to do's! I felt like I was sinking.

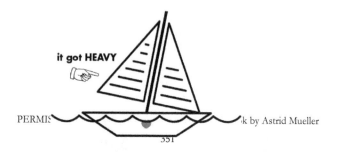

it got HEAVY

At first I had no idea why that was! So I decided to pull the plug. I needed a break! I stopped showing up to the program, even doing the work. Even though I had invested SO MUCH MONEY!

(P.S. notice the pressure I put on myself here? More inner voices!)

I started going outside a lot, and allowing myself to rejuvenate.

What happened next was quite surprising to me.

(Looking back, I think it was a next spiritual growth moment for me!)

I had a magical intuitive (and spiritual) sparkle moment by the sea.

Around that time, and before that, I had been looking for a marketing idea that felt right to promote my brand consulting business.

In the program I was in, and in other places online, I was seeing a lot of things that had already been done, like "do a webinar!" "make a Powerpoint!" "This has to be professional!" "This is the system that works!" I had a lot of "should voices" in my head.

None of the ideas felt right for me. Yet, I put a lot of pressure on myself to try all these things. Once, I spent two days (!) on a Powerpoint presentation. (How long?!! Exactly!) And it didn't even feel like me! I hated it. Business shouldn't be that hard! Or make me feel this bad!

So I went for more walks by the seaside and started asking myself, "Isn't there a better, more feelgood way?"

One day, strolling on one of the beautiful beaches of Kodiak Island, dogs running around me, playing, I asked myself this question again. "What could I do that feels like FUN, EASY, and magically brings customers to me?" And then let it be and soaked up the amazing scenery and sun.

That's when the amazing thing happened: I got an idea. And it wasn't from my head.

It might have been from my intuition, "the universe," or my spirit guides! But who knows! It was a great exciting idea I had not seen done before!

(P.S. look up the BE PLAY DO formula chapter for more about getting into this zone of getting magical ideas!)

The idea felt amazing. And JUST right for me:

I was going to create a game challenge and a card game, play for a week online with clients, where they could experience my teachings with easy daily video prompts. And they could also win stuff!

With my design background, it was so easy. I created a card deck that very afternoon, sent it off to print (I didn't need to know all details yet, just put numbers and letters and symbols on my cards and made them pretty — I trusted the rest of what I needed to know or do would show up later.)

And I announced the game challenge just a few days later.

Yes, without having all the details yet!

And guess what. Instead of just a handful of people, like four or so, showing up to a webinar that I didn't even like doing...

39 people joined the game, and they played daily, A LOT.

The whole thing was a blast. For me, and for everyone!

And at the end of the week, they had experienced me, knew me, were excited to do more with me. I had warm potential customers. Who had just experienced a lot of value and a lot of fun.

How's THAT for a marketing pipeline!

My mind was blown!

Back to the boat analogy: This is what made all the difference:

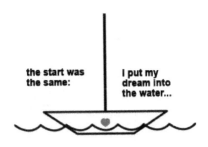

the start was the same: I put my dream into the water...

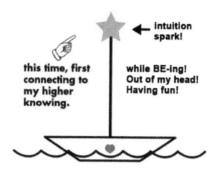

intuition
spark!

this time, first
connecting to
my higher
knowing.

while BE-ing!
Out of my head!
Having fun!

then taking
inspired action
from there
(just few!)

perfect ideas
had landed!
Lighting up
my heart!

and off I went!
now sparked by
inspiration! with
a lit-up heart!

and with
universe
help! a
new sail!

I had a big epiphany then:

All my actions didn't go anywhere magical if
they didn't come from my intuition
& own inner knowing!

I realized that when I just took advice from others as "that's how it's done" and tried to replicate what they were doing... it didn't work. I had to listen to my own guidance, and intuition, and do things in MY WAY, in a way that felt right.

And I also saw that

My intuition always leads me to my best ideas!
And to the things that light me up!

I've seen numerous coaches teach systems that work for them and then sell their principles for lots of money, telling people, "this is THE solution! Do this and you will ____ (insert whatever it is you want!)."

Yes, I believe that we can learn from others and learn skills and methods of doing things... but if we simply try to replicate things from others without listening to our own hearts, it won't work!

We aren't meant to be robots. And to simply
replicate systems. We have to do things that

light us UP and do things our way!
Our own unique sparkle way!

I believe that the universe WANTS us to be empowered and do what
brings us joy. It also wants us to do things in a way that works for US.
Because that's when we shine in our own brilliance! That's when we use
our own superpowers! And create things that have never even been done!

That's the zone of innovation. Of genius. Of true sparkle!

We only find magic and true sparkle if we
learn to trust ourselves that we ultimately have
our best inner guidance.

I realized another thing on that beach. Another gem!

I did not FIRST fully take care of myself (like I did at first in that
program, all those long to-do lists! All the pressure I put on myself! I
often forgot to even take lunch!), I actually did way LESS, not my best
work, I wasn't happy, and I was missing out on my actual best ideas.

When we take time to BE and PLAY,
our intuition comes through,
and we get our best ideas!

That moment by the beach, and this whole time of unplugging from the
action-packed coaching program, with lots of time in the sun, on hikes,
playing with dogs, and being outside, then really got me curious:

How much more magic may I experience when I make time to BE and PLAY, having FUN a FOUNDATION of my life AND MY businesses?

And what if I decide that ALL I do feels like FUN?

I actually decided that on one of those hikes I took during that time!

I also looked at the other side of the spectrum. Actually hustling to get things done. I kept pondering... Do I ever even WANT to hustle? Can hustle feel exciting? Can it be beneficial at all?

As I'm reviewing this book, my take on it is that there is a really great beneficial positive kind of hustle. Like when I feel I'm on a roll! And I can make even not-so-fun feel good. Like by making it a game!

I also see the unhealthy kind of hustle. (I pressured myself for so many years! All those should voices! The not taking care of myself!)

I feel there's a thin line between this good hustle kind and hustling from inner pressure. And the line is our inner awareness. Knowing whether we consciously choose to do something from alignment and joy, and after we fully take care of ourselves, or whether we do them from inner pressure, and on autopilot.

Catching those inner pressure stories will bring you to more sparkle!

Don't feel bad. A lot of these hustle-pressure stories are culture-based.

The idea that we have to work hard to survive has been a concept that has been lived and passed on by many of our previous generations. My mum, for instance, was born right after world war two. Experienced scarcity. And of course, she passed it on in her lifestyle choices and language in how I was raised. I'm not blaming her. It was her story!

Yet it was for me to catch those stories and notice which ones were hers and which one I choose to live by as mine.

Think about all the sayings you've heard from your parents or grandparents about how you have to work hard to make a living? Did you ever notice how many such old sayings are part of your current culture's language! Part of pop culture?

Like "you've got to work hard for a living." Or "you have to earn a living." Geez. What? So that you're worth to live? What are we telling ourselves subconsciously? Words are powerful. They influence how we live. How we feel. Even our health. It's good to pause and think about what we say and what we think, and then tweak to sparkle, as needed!

There's also current western culture that really seems to praise busyness.

God forbid, we "dare" to be "lazy." What does lazy even mean? Where does all that "work hard pressure" come from?

What if being "lazy" was a good thing? A nurture ground of genius?

play prompt:

How many sayings that praise hustle can you think of?
How many of those do you live by that make you feel GOOD?

Catch those sayings. And then choose what you really want to live by.

There is much scientific evidence today on how creativity, rest, and PLAY, will skyrocket the quality of our ideas and the quality of our lives.

It is also widely known today that if we solely rely on our rational thinking, we're actually not using our whole intelligence.

Leading-edge companies like Google design whole work environments based on this knowledge. To spark the inspiration in their employees and allow them to thrive! And they know that this gets them the best results!

To fully sparkle, we must use our whole intelligence. Which includes our left brain (linear) and right brain (intuition and creativity.) And it all begins with our hearts and intuition. All magic starts there.

THEN we can use our logical mind to take the inspired actions and make our dreams real!

Intuition is the key to spark our brilliance!

The magic starts with opening our hearts, our awareness, and also being open to knowing there's more wisdom outside of us. We don't know it all. Really. That's what I realized, more and more.

And so I continued to stay curious and open up to universe magic / spirit / a higher awareness, more and more.

Here's a live example! I'm currently staying at a friend's mansion.

As I just passed the piano-and-fireplace framed seating area on my way to the pool... (Yes, the magic has blown up since I started writing this book! Doing business from the pool, world travel, clients saying yes to paying 10K a month...)

... I spotted a beautiful playful card deck with hanging cards on a stick that you could flip, and then they'd form a unique, inspiring sentence.

I asked the universe: "Show me what I need to see for my book right now, as I'm wrapping it up." Check out what sentence I got:

Know the wisdom of
the art created by
epiphanies.

Isn't this so perfect? It's like the universe is validating this whole conversation. That's where the magic is! In epiphanies! And they come when we make space to hear our intuition! When we get out of our head!

And when we first play and fully take care of ourselves.

play prompt:

Think of the biggest problem / challenge you're trying to solve right now, in your life or your business.

Then do something playful! Let it go! Get out of your head!

(You can do anything playful or use the "Permission To Sparkle" game!)

(Ice cream break.)

Then, when you got your epiphany (without trying, simply letting it come), ask yourself: what one action can you take to move forward?

If you don't get your answer right away, just do something else. You'll get your intuitive AHA. When you stop thinking about it!

back to my story...

(Of how I allowed myself to open up spiritually more and access more and more of my sparkle)

Here's how I discovered my gift of intuitive drawing, which I later powerfully used with clients, even for business strategies:

That came from another universe input: In an Akashic records session with Kavita, the message came through for me to simply start drawing during client sessions. And that it would mean something.

I had NO idea how that would work, but I dared to just do it — no matter what a client would say. And I JUMPED into it right away.

P.S. A hot tip to bring more sparkle in your life, pretty much instantly:

When the universe gives you an action idea,
and you feel it's right, do it.
Right in this moment.
Don't postpone it.

(That moment, when we're in that energy, is the best moment to take action! Think of it like a portal to more sparkle. And it's right here!)

In my example, I got the opportunity to do that inspired thing within a few hours. It was in a coaching call that day with a client. I jumped on it! And simply asked a coaching client, "Hey, I just got inspired to draw while we talk. I feel I'm supposed to do this. Okay?"

Guess what. She said, sure! Fire away!

And then more magic happened:

What I kind of judged as crazy (although I didn't give my mind much space to hold me back or bully me) ... actually meant something to her.

The colors and the composition were a beautiful metaphor for her life and business at the moment, she said! And from the drawing, she received a powerful message of inspiration of what to do next!

What? Well, that was cool, I thought!

And swoosh!! I had received a next universe gift! A new thing that was fun that I could do with clients! That was also powerful! How awesome!

Shortly after, a next universe blessing showed up:

I realized that I ALREADY had a book on intuitive drawings. The resource was already here! (And now it was the time for me because I had followed my inspiration and said yes to doing it!)

I had totally forgotten about this book. Apparently, it hadn't been the time for me to dig in until this very moment. HA! So I started reading and instantly upleveled and made my drawings more powerful.

Thank you, universe!
We're so supported! I'm telling you!

Next, I took the inspirations of the book to make them my own, play in my own style. I added sparkles, stickers, and scrapbooking elements — I just did what felt good to me, and fun.

I realized all this came naturally to me! It felt like home!

Yet, we ALL have access to intuition; we simply all have different areas of natural strength to start out. For me, it was visuals because I'm a designer. How about you? How do you most easily hear your intuition? Sight / Sound / A Feeling / Inner knowing / Dreams / ... stay curious!

I started doing more such intuitive readings with my clients. I felt the magic. And the clients got more clarity! We all had more fun! Because I was playing more with my superpowers and in my zone of genius!

I was living and sharing more of my true sparkle!

Note that I did NOT have any certificate. I didn't need it. There's a time and place for certificates, but don't get them for the sake of it or because you think you need it to prove anything...

As you see, all I did here was take action based on spirit guidance I got, then take a leap of faith of just try it out. And that can be enough!

Are you ready to let more of your magic and sparkle out?

play prompt:

Take a moment to listen within, and ask yourself:

What magic, what superpowers might be slumbering inside of you? What wants to come out, to come to the world that feels fun and so NATURAL to you?

Now you got a glimpse into how I started and how I started unfolding my superpowers. You see that it all started with curiosity and being open to receiving answers. I always got next resources. Next epiphanies.

Close your eyes, hand on heart. What is your intuition telling you about your superpowers, and what you can play with more, right now?

sparkle tip:

Energy is more important than content.
Energy is everything. Take action fast from
that spark in your heart. Even if it's imperfect.

Like I did with my drawings!

intuition tip:

Intuition is that FIRST (often really subtle) little idea that we get. The
mind comes SECOND.

Act right away when something feels right in your heart! That way, fear
voices and inner rabbit holes won't catch you or trip you up.

And if you do get fear voices to "catch you," you can turn it around and
be curious, as always, and say HA! I see you! And catch them yourself.

And then you take your inspired actions anways.
(And/or work through your fears and limiting thoughts, as feels right,
while being kind to yourself! It's not a race. It's a sparkle game!)

What next sparkle step are you inspired to do now,
in your own life adventure and spiritual journey?

living a
sparkle life

(What my life looked like with more sparkle
and additional magical keys I found to get there!)

what my life looks like with more **sparkle**

how this chapter helps:

I wrote this chapter after having conquered some of the bigger life challenges you saw earlier in this book: Here, you'll see what happened and how I now live more powerfully, with more joy and more sparkle!

And what that looks like in my life when life brings me challenges!

Get inspired by my stories, and keep playing with this book (and the game!) to also bring more and more sparkle into your own life!

story 1: living in truth

It's fall 2019; I'm in Houston and just saw my soulmate D again. Yes, the one who had catapulted me into the realization that I had to leave my marriage (see earlier chapters in this book.)

It's a new beginning, and I'm in a new space.

No one or no thing has power over me.

I feel I'm in a dragon's nest.

Ready to fly free.

I chose to see that soulmate, dance with him, and to feel the sparks that were totally there. And I was fully transparent about everything with my new boyfriend in Alaska. Sharing everything. Including that — at first — I wasn't sure what would happen when I'd again see this soulmate.

I ended up choosing not to go beyond friendship. It would have been really tempting to follow the sparks of our connection! But he was in a relationship I didn't want to interfere with, and I also didn't really just want a temporary "hey I'm in town," one-time relationship experience.

I chose to simply dance with him (as often as possible!) and to spend time with him that way. Simply as dancers. So I went to all the dance classes he held while I was in town, and I also booked a private dance lesson with him, fulfilling a personal childhood sparkle dream of mine:

I always had this fantasy to be able to dance with Fred Astaire! Like Ginger Rogers! This private dance lesson with my professional dancer soulmate friend fulfilled this dream for me this weekend.

My own version of it.

And I enjoyed every minute of it.

Did I ever say anything is possible? It is.

And the magic of this story, for me... as we talk about living in more sparkle: I feel my sparkle. My strength. Like I can do anything. Be anything! I am beginning to fully trust myself!

Because I'm in a new world where I live and speak my truth! Where I design my reality, not by someone else's rules, but MY truth.

I choose to see this as possible, speak my wishes, and then allow them to become real.

I feel strong. Like I'm in a dragon's nest, still seeing some of the after-birth ("you can't do this or that" stories...), but I'm not affected by them anymore... I'm starting to feel free!

Reborn as free as a dragon! Ready to fly in the rain.

By the way: I found this head-less Halloween bat yesterday in the garage at the Houston Museum of Natural History in Houston. Yes! I also see universe signs everywhere now that I live in more sparkle!

I felt this was not just a fun synchronicity but also a sign to show me that I'm on the right path. My path! A sign of celebration! I'm not following limited stories of my mind, but spreading my wings! And flying in sparkle!

Yup, there are also sparkles on this thing. LOL.

As I look around at other people's lives and their stories, and look at mine, I'm starting to see a big difference. Not with eyes of comparison where one thing is deemed better than the other, but eyes of observation.

I see most people still live by some kind of limitations and fears, giving their power away to how things are/should be/obligations/ circumstances. Choosing by how things are done, or "expected to be done," instead of what they would really want, "if anything was possible."

And it is. We don't have to limit ourselves.

So what happened when I had told my boyfriend in Alaska about seeing my soulmate? When I told him that I'd dance with him? And that I'd choose moment by moment what feels right? Speaking my full truth in full transparency, living in pure honesty, and freedom?

And he was actually at peace with it.

(I'm rubbing off on him, he said. Funny! And I can see that. He used to draw in all kinds of drama in life. Now (having been around me and my more and more sparkly joy ways of living...), he's also more calm.)

This is not to say that everyone around us is always ready for this kind of uncertainty. He could have freaked out. Broken up with me. I didn't know what he'd do. What's important here for me, though, is that I stayed in my truth and spoke my truth and my desires, even without knowing. And I was okay with it.

Knowing that I'll always be okay (at least eventually) when I follow my heart.

I didn't use to be this bold or brave years ago. This is a true celebration for me for a more sparkly and powerful way of living.

Does that mean I don't love my boyfriend? Or don't love either one of them? No. It means I'm committed to my truth, to following my heart, and to living in sparkle. And I choose to not buy into fears but live in trust and without attachment to outcomes.

Does that mean that I'm now hopping all over the place, starting relationships everywhere, or just following feelings, getting intimate with people whenever I feel like it?

No.

Yes.

No.

(Did some of that trigger you? Good. What came up? Be curious.)

(The question doesn't matter. What matters is our reaction to things. Because that points to our own inner desires and beliefs!)

play prompt:

Journal. What was your mind telling you as you read my story? Are there any stories of judgment about how I'm living, thinking, being?

_____

_____

_____

As you take your eyes off ME, turn your eyes on YOU.

What do all those stories mean to you about YOU? What are you telling yourself of what you would, could, should never do? Why?

_____

_____

_____

Now, if all those concerns weren't real... what's YOUR truth? What kind of relationships/life would you love to experience? If there were no risk, no fears?

And what is your mind telling you why you canNOT have that?

_____

Let that pen flow. Catch your own limitations. Those are gems. You can choose to let them go. And make your own rules.

And choose to be a dragon. Claim your truth. Trust that the universe will realign in a way that's for everyone's highest good.

(Yes, that includes you.)

Now go back for a moment and read my last paragraph right before the YES. NO. YES. There's another reason why it doesn't matter. Look at the paragraph with new eyes.

See something?

It's tainted. By societal norms, by expectations we carry of how we should live, of what we make things mean. Tainted with judgment against others who live freely. Potentially you had some judgment come up against me and my choices. Based on whatever society conditioning you've been living in.

Allow yourself to suspend everything.

So what! What IF I (or you) chose to love-hop all over the place?

Allow yourself to live freely and express and live all your desires.

Really, who cares. (More often than not, people don't.) And if they do, give yourself permission to live your own truth, even if your worst fears or nightmares came true. Because you know what?

What I've found is that the worst nightmares and fears are usually the ones we create for ourselves. We imprison ourselves! That's living with secrets, not fully freely IN JOY... and that is like a DISEASE. Like the word says. It will eat away at you.

Why should you NOT have ALL that you desire?

I recently came back to a story I experienced as a child around Christmas. I wanted a particular set of colored markers. And my dad got me markers! But they were not the right kind. They didn't light up my heart. I had really set my heart on those particular other ones. I began to cry.

I didn't want to make my dad feel bad then! I appreciated his gift! Yet it also didn't make me happy! I felt so bad telling him!

Five-year-old me ended up telling my truth to dad through my tears. I really wanted those other ones! The round ones. Not the ones with the weird design (I was already a designer at heart back then.)

I was so sad to have to tell him. Thought I would hurt his feelings. (Society conditioning too! "You should be grateful for gifts!" Right?)

Guess what happened as his baby girl sat crying on his lap.
Of course, he wanted to see me happy. And he was glad I spoke openly.

And, as it was possible in this case without a problem, he ended up getting me the pens I truly wanted!

I was actually not being a brat or ungrateful! (The voices I could have listened to in my head! Of course, those things CAN be true, but they weren't here!) I was simply speaking sparkle. Saying what I wanted.

We have to choose this same kind of truth and openness about our desires for ourselves. Only then are we giving ourselves permission to even have the opportunity to get what we truly want!

We do not have to abandon our desires because of inner voices. Those inner voices are simply stories. We don't know how others will react. And it doesn't matter. What matters is that we don't abandon ourselves.

play prompt:

Where are you currently not allowing yourself to ask for your own perfect "Christmas gift" (a thing / experience that would make you feel sparkly?)

What do you think would happen if you spoke up? What do you think people would say? What are you making it all mean about yourself? In what way are you not feeling safe? What are your mind-stories?

_____

_____

Whatever objections you got, they're all inner stories.

Whatever you THINK will happen is always just an assumption. And even if.... so what? Speak your truth, and you'll find inner peace.

That's what matters.

play prompt:

Let's make this last question a play prompt. You have an objection that says you cannot currently have something you want. Simply say:

So, what? Who cares?

Keep asking that question until you get to the bottom of your stories! (Keep asking "So what? Who cares?" to every objection your mind has until you feel that's your deepest inner story and you've got nothing else.)

(When you catch THAT one, you can claim some serious sparkle freedom!

Write all those stories on a separate sheet of paper, and then burn them!

story 2: speaking full truth, learning gems...

As I'm publishing this book, I am more and more detaching myself from what (I think) others will say, and I am choosing to live in my truth, whatever happens around me.

I also let go of taking responsibility for other people's feelings. And no longer hold back my (kindly spoken) truth in order to protect others' feelings.

I've come to believe that it's actually serving people more if we TRUST they are always okay and that they deserve to hear our truths.

Because only truth gives others the opportunity to know what's truly going on, and then also to choose from their own truth!

Here's how I learned this the hard way:

When I realized I had to leave my husband because I felt I had outgrown the relationship, I had to say it. Even without knowing details. Or knowing how I would live.

When I realized that I need full freedom without any constraints whatsoever, even in relationships (that came up for me after we were already divorced, and kind of getting back together), I chose to tell him. I didn't want to hold back my truth anymore. And couldn't.

When someone showed up in my life in Alaska who I felt like cuddling with, I told my then-ex-hubby about that. When that someone and I got more intimate, I told him as well (because we were also still in a relationship of some sort). "Hey, this is now happening, just so you know." I wouldn't have continued to explore an open relationship paradigm with my ex-hubby had he not agreed to it.

I did get challenged with a next truth level there because that someone happened to be a close friend. I bumped up against a new challenge:

Was I ready to ALWAYS live in my FULL truth?

The universe brings us such play situations, really, to see if we're YES!

There was a situation where I wasn't YES yet!

I didn't tell my ex-hubby the NAME of that other person. I felt that would be too harsh. Back then, I took responsibility for my ex-hubby's feelings. Assuming. Protecting. Thinking he would NOT be okay.

It turns out, even that AGREED-ON secret backfired. A huge ball of drama and pain ensued over the next year BECAUSE of it. He felt betrayed in so many ways, and TWO friendships broke. To this day, he hasn't chosen to allow for healing what happened then. All unnecessary.

Looking back, it made no sense to keep the truth of the name a secret.

The tough and true-love thing for me would have been to also say that friend's name. Because that would have given my ex-hubby clarity and a clear choice.

True, it would have been painful, but it wouldn't have felt like hidden secrets not spoken to your face. Which is where he felt the betrayal. (Even though he had said he was okay with not knowing the name!)

From this story, I've come to the conclusion that NO secrets and ONLY truth is the ONLY true free — and sparkle — way of living.

Because:

* Secrets eat away at you and cause pain. Truth allows to free everyone and — after tough love moments, you can actually heal.

* Sooner or later, truth always wins anyways. So why hold back and create unnecessary delays and pain?

* Who feels BETTER about finding out something hurtful AFTER time has passed, really? Not me! Does finding out later make things better? No.

* Secrets are not fair to anyone. Don't our partners (and anyone in our lives) deserve the full truth? How do we know they wouldn't be okay with the truth? Or that an even better solution could show up as a result of it? Heck, I want to know the truth!

Truth allows for alignment of what's truly aligned. Holding back truth actually prevents true alignment.

* How can we assume we KNOW what someone would say or do? That's actually super patronizing, or like playing God. Even with good intentions. And if you're on the receiving end, that really sucks. I'd really rather know the truth. Because that's empowering to me. I get to choose.

★ And then there's the assumed outcome and fear we may carry to want to hold back truth... What if the other person holds the same secret or already knows about ours? What if they'd actually be *relieved* by hearing us say it out loud?

With all these scenarios, it boils down to two things:

Secrets hold us back from OUR OWN inner freedom. And they eat away at EVERYONE involved in the situation.

With all the "no"s and heaviness that may emerge as you read this, here's an awesome positive side coming, and you'll guess it:

All those stories that are boiling up inside of you as to why you should KEEP a secret are simply shadows, holding gems, and learning lessons for you / ourselves to see and release.

Fear of what the person will say or do? I found that it's most sparkly and magical for everyone if I dettach from the outcome. This helps me reclaim my power and feel peace. (And allow others to live in their own sparkle and free choices.)

I now live with this sparkle recipe:

1. Speak my desires (kindly) in transparency and truth.

2. Allow the universe to surprise me how these desires will manifest. (Note: sometimes they don't because something else, or at another time, is to our highest benefit!)

3. Then I let it go! So that the universe CAN actually surprise me. I keep learning not to try to control everything.

I have another story about truth (and how not speaking it hurt me).

Here's what happened to me personally, on a physical level (!):

story 3: holding stuff in — health challenged

When I held that one secret of the earlier story in (not revealing the name of my cuddle-buddy boyfriend even though it was agreed that I would not share the name with my ex-hubby), that secret was eating away at me.

Not just in my heart and mind but also in my body.

I literally started feeling it as physical pain at some point when I was not living in pure heart, pure truth alignment! It began as constriction in my chest, a weird pain on my right ribs that happened more and more often. Sometimes it was almost a sting. Eventually, I actually saw two visible, strange, elongated bumps right under my skin!

They almost looked like a protruding claw under my skin! Somewhere I have a picture.

How's that for a strong sign that something was gnawing at me!

That was my first powerful experience of my body giving me clear, powerful messages as guidance. To STOP doing something! Or to do something differently!

Physical symptoms, I now believe, are almost always somehow traceable to a deeper inner root of suppressed negative stories and emotions or messages for us when we don't live like we truly want to live. Our bodies can show us things we can heal in our energy field, learn, or forgive and let go. And nudge us to change our lives so that we feel happy, sparkly! And joy.

(Read the work of Carolyn Myss if you're intrigued to dig into this more. She's studied how illnesses relate to inner causes and specific emotions, both from the viewpoint of modern science as well as medical intuition.)

play prompt:

If you have some body issues and are wondering what they may be all about. Ask yourself, "what might my body or this symptom be telling me here? What may be the message, the metaphor, for my life here?"

What does my body want me to change in my life at present or see? What story or truth may I be holding in?

_____

_____

In my case, I cross-checked with an intuitive coach in my inner circle, who reaffirmed what I already sensed: that this claw-looking chest thing, right under my skin, was here to show me that something had literally gotten under my skin. And that something was gnawing at me. It was actually pointing right up to my heart! A potent metaphor!

It had everything to do with me holding in that secret of the name.

So! One day I chose to free myself from the whole conundrum of how things SHOULD be done, (spare his feelings, you can't possibly tell him it's a close friend, that would be terrible!), not trusting myself (I wouldn't know how to handle him seeing so sad!...), not trusting that he'd be okay... etc.

I just stopped. And asked myself, very clearly:

If none of all that mattered, what do I WANT?

play prompt:

(Quick story break! You can ask yourself this same last question, pretty much with whatever conundrum you might currently have going on!)

If none of your current concerns mattered, what do you really WANT?

Doing this for myself here, I was taking all spinning thoughts out of the equation. Simply tuned into my deep heart's desire.

And I realized and spoke it out loud:

And guess what.

Within an hour, I got a text from my new flame that my ex-hubby was at his place, that he knew everything, and that I should come over and bring whiskey. And that it was all okay.

WHAT???

It felt SO GOOD to have it finally out in the open. And to also have such a mellow — even (at least then) humorous — way of this unfolding!

Yes, it takes GUTS to speak truth at all times. To BE what you want to be. To ASK for what your heart asks for. To CLAIM your full freedom.

Hence my symbol of the gutsy dragon. To live in true sparkle takes guts.

But guess what.

It's your birthright to live in full freedom. (And everyone's birthright too.) Truth makes that possible.

What IF you can have it all? (Shadow alert! Assuming we cannot have it all holds some limiting thought paradigms! For example, we might think that we have to choose. Or wait for something to happen before we can have something. Or that we don't deserve something...

What if you can have ALL that you want NOW?

What if you can have (insert your desires) _____

AND _____

AND _____

AND _____???

And what if ALL that is possible and totally okay?

What if it's MORE than okay?

What if there's MORE than enough for everyone?

What if you actually EXPAND everyone's abundance by giving yourself permission to receive everything you want?

What if living your pure desires, and allowing yourself to receive them, would actually make you a sparkle life role model for others?

And inspire them to give themselves permission to also sparkle that way?

What if us being in pure ABUNDANCE energy is inspiring everyone else also be in pure abundance energy as well?

What if us being in SCARCITY energy also inspires others to hold back?

It all starts with ourselves.

And we get to choose to live our pure desires or to hold back.

What I find now is that the universe ALWAYS realigns. Whether we ask for what we want or for a limitation. So why not ask for what brings us happiness, in full truth, and full openness, and for real?

What would the world look like if we all gave ourselves permission to ask for all our desires and therefore inspired everyone to do the same?

Ponder this for a moment! Really!

What kind of role models are parents who give themselves full permission to fully soul-nourish themselves and live in full, happy creativity, joy, and abundance? What if they can do that for themselves and also include their children, to experience the same?

What if there's always enough time?

What kind of role models are parents who starve and sacrifice themselves in order to save others, always putting others first?

Which of these models — sparkle or starve — might be more sustainable?

We can all sparkle.

play prompt:

As you read through these last thought prompts, is there an area where you tend to put others first before nourishing yourself? What true desires may you have been suppressing because you think you can't, and others come first?

And then... as you become curious... How may you nourish yourself first, AND everyone also gets to sparkle for themselves?

State your desires, and then let it go for a moment. Give space to the universe. Solutions and ideas will come to you. Yay! Sparkle for everyone!

story 3: feeling strong with truth and sparkle

A few months ago, I had a friend who currently loves to take debating classes at the Harvard collegiate level and blast really intense "accusations" at me, even with raised voice, about how she perceived me based on something I said. Even though I felt the energy of her own agitation, I was able to observe the situation and not take it personally.

I stayed in curiosity. Listened. Discerned between her story and where I felt I could learn some things or shift how I did things.

It kind of felt like me being a magician, almost seeing this intense energy blast toward my direction. Yet through my practice with sparkle and shadow catching, I was able to keep this ball of thunder energy in the middle of our conversation instead of soaking it up and getting upset. Or feeling like I had to run away. I was standing my ground. I was okay.

I was speaking my truth calmly, not taking up her energy, and eventually, her heated agitation calmed down, and we both upgraded our views based on each other's truth and experiences.

With all the sparkle practice, I'm noticing that now also my inner fear voices don't matter as much anymore! True: sometimes I get caught in them still! I have to be on my toes! (That's when it can become fun to play the shadow catch game! See page 43.)

But I keep coming back to my voice of highest alignment. My inner truth. Which is a voice and feeling of pure possibility, of calmness, of peace. Even excitement! Sparkle! Joy! It's pretty amazing!

That brings me to the next sparkle life story of what I'm experiencing:

story 4: sparkling with and through cancer

In September 2020, I got diagnosed with breast cancer. A fast-moving kind. Stage 4. I did have a freak-out moment at the beginning, yet — thanks to one of the coaches I was working with at the time — I was able to catch that it was the fear energy of the clinic that had gotten to me. And fears of conditioning around the word cancer. Society conditioning!

I actually got intuition and spirit guidance that I will be okay. And I trust and know now that I will be. No story or supposed outcome someone thinks might happen — even if it has been like that in a million cases — has to be my reality. (Or yours.)

If I believe I will heal, I will heal.

If I believe I will not, I won't.

That's how I operate now. And I choose obviously to sparkle! And thrive! And so, I have been sparkling through my healing experience.

Yes, there have been downs and challenges, obviously. But I've found a unique way of sparkling even THROUGH and DURING crazy challenges. Even through chemo. Making the best of it. Finding joy in moments within it and through it.

I kept applying ideas and play prompts I've been sharing in this book.

Another book will be coming, especially from my cancer healing experience. See also the last chapters, where I share more magical keys that helped me to sparkle even through such challenging times.

There are no limits.
Only the limits we put on ourselves.

To fully claim my freedom, I had to boldly dare to live in my truth.

Kind of like dragons, flying bold, daring, free.

That's how I keep finding rainbows.

And more sparkle. Through any

and all challenges.

In what way are you currently not fully living in sparkle?
Where can you turn up your bravery volume and act like a dragon?

What superpowers may you already have inside of you,
that you can simply activate and fly like a dragon?

What support may you already have at your fingertips,
to help you make that happen?

Take a baby dragon step now (or a flight!),

then allow the universe to show you the next steps.

how I finish stuff when it gets **tough**

how this chapter helps:

If you're like me, starting things can be easy. Keeping going — or lo and behold! Finishing things! — can be a whole different story.

I wrote this chapter live role modeling how I kept rolling forward with the book and then also how I finished it.

As you've seen, I wrote this book as life happened, while IN the story, or right afterward. It truly is like that with the universe: when we ask and are curious about something (like me, being curious about the topic "Permission To Sparkle," and wanting to write this book), the universe brings us stories and scenarios to support that topic.

That's EXACTLY what happened with this book, and that's how I allowed myself to get inspired. I always knew when something from my life would become yet another chapter, and whenever I felt that call, I followed the inspiration to write.

Even if that sometimes meant waking up in the middle of the night.

I never allowed any heavy energy to MAKE ME write.

As I began writing this chapter in July 2019, I was nearing the completion of the book and starting to feel less and less inspired to finish the book. Suddenly it felt like hard work, not as playful.

So what did I do? I shifted into play.

rolling forward with play

To help me wrap the book project up with ease, I asked the universe for help and then simply wrote all that was going through my mind. I made it an "Imperfect is perfect! Just let it all out! " writing game. That's a beautiful recipe to get unstuck (and also to allow universe support.)

(I could have deleted this next part because its main premise was to get me unstuck and roll forward with writing again. However, I felt inspired to keep it, so you can see my internal dialogue and how I allowed the universe to playfully inspire me! And how it all helped me roll forward!)

Here's how I started, simply stating my wish to the universe:

Dear universe, dear book: please help me wrap up with ease. And please help me know when all the magic that's meant to be in here for the readers is here, and the book is complete.

So! What is it, sparkle book and universe, that you still want me to share before we're complete?

Your story. Your magic. They need to see it.

This is easy. Your story is one chapter, the spirituality one, how you got here. The magic part, they need to experience you. Invite them in.

(And with "they need to," we don't mean they have to, from a "should" energy. On the contrary. Like you, we call them to follow what makes them feel sparkly. If they're curious to experience you, and it feels sparkly to them, they shall follow that bling-bling.)

Cool! That feels easy!

(By the way, following that universe hint, if you want to experience me more, come to my website and follow what tickles you there. By the time you read this, you'll probably see my new website there! Notice, I'm building my Ferrari as I'm driving... going live before having all details. Try it!)

Anything else, universe and book?

(I feel they will point me to a few notes, pages, and chapters that call for adjustment, and I trust that I'll know and feel when the book is complete.)

Universe, is it that I shall wrap up the book tonight? On July 4, 2019?

We'll let you make the call. Do what feels inspired.

Ah! I'm noticing an inner voice of perfection, and the teeter-totter of "there's always more! I can't stop!" and "it's complete."

Yes, there can be sequels. When it feels complete, it shall be complete.

I go on asking, "How can the readers play to be sparkly? What about the tools? Aren't those missing?"

Go look.

(So I did. And as I started reading it, suddenly I found the words to complete that chapter, and all came together with ease.)

1:11 am on July 5, 2019:

I feel I got this! The tools chapter is complete! Next, I'm inspired to wrap up the sparkle productivity chapter, and it's called the Sparkle Miracle Formula of BE PLAY DO. All is coming together magically, woo-hoo! (Cheering myself on as the mojo is returning.)

Also, my story — I'll add that next. Feeling it almost wrapped up — and more and more powerful — thank you, universe! All in divine timing. Permission for imperfection. Permission for future adjustments.

For now, it still feels open. Having fun. Staying curious.

Letting it flow.

Thank you, universe, for giving me intuitive answers as I'm writing, helping me to wrap up the book!

You're welcome! This is important. This is role modeling for others how to listen within. flow forward. co-create with the universe... how to stay and get back on the sparkle path... you're role modeling how easy it can be!

playing through avoidance

Writing a book — and publishing it — is such a great learning opportunity for inner mastery. Of course, I hit more roadblocks, and not all was easy. Because I'm super resourceful and allowed myself to be supported, I kept finding more help and ideas. Sharing them here for you as an idea list: take what works for you, and roll with it!

- ★ I did a BETA group, a free one, where people could experience the book along with live group calls while I was writing it.

- ★ I got guidance from other coach peers who helped me get unstuck and find next strategy steps.

- ★ As I lost my mojo again, I did another BETA group, this time a paid one. This time with the intention to finish the book.

- ★ I lovingly got my butt kicked from peer coaches when time rolled on again, and I still hadn't finished it.

- ★ I teamed up with another writer to set a launch date and write the book while cheering each other on.

- ★ I hired an editor to read the book for content and structure and gave her a timeline. (I was planning to self-publish.)

- ★ I spoke with other book publishing professionals to consider hiring them too, and we discussed best options and a timeline.

- ★ I drummed up pre-launch excitement together with the other writer I had teamed up with, and we did a fundraiser.

And then what happened?

She finished her book and published it, and I fell off the wagon again.

I got as far as finishing my book in the rough, sending it to my editor, and getting it back, with a few wonderful notes, and fairly easy comments for suggested corrections. Almost ready for publishing...

You'd think I would have just kept rolling, right? Wrong.

It started collecting dust again. So what happened from here? And what helped me actually finish it?

- ★ I talked myself into being busy with other things. (Translation: I was avoiding it and procrastinating.)

- ★ I started having people ask me about it. (I still was having very convincing reasons as to why I was not currently writing.)

- ★ I watched my colleague publish hers and internally cringed about my own lack of action. Starting to judge myself. Yet still avoiding

- ★ A friend invited me to a book-writing workshop, which was great! I got more inspiration, and everyone cheered me on — yay she's almost done. (Wow! And that made me feel good!) And I also felt like a fraud. Because I was still not continuing the wrap-up of it.

★ Another coach friend had another book-writing workshop to help authors wrap up and publish their books — and I attended and loved it! And used it for my NEXT book that I had started writing. More avoidance.

Until......

A coach colleague spotted that I probably had some inner stories lurking. Because I seemed to really stretch out the completion of this book.

(Hint: if we keep avoiding something that we actually want to do, there's something deeper going on for sure!)

So she called me into the room to look at my business (the book was just one telltale sign of where I was avoiding things.) What was happening was that I really had done all the things, felt I did all the things right, yet I had GRAZED OVER some DEEP STUFF.

Which had kept me avoiding.... a next level of sparkle.

Like finishing the book. Like increasing how much money I made with my business. As we talked, it became clear to me that I had been avoiding ALL KINDS OF THINGS. And spinning in circles in all kinds of ways.

I had hit another glass ceiling. Yay! Another opportunity. Of course. So what did I do?

Say I'M DONE WITH THAT! Became curious. And invited universe support. Which here had shown up, as one resource, with this coach.

So I hired her to help me see my trees for the forest again and get to the foundation of things. She became a guide for my deep not-so-fun path that I had been avoiding, helped me to uncover some deep (totally unhealthy) subconscious patterns I had been running and let them go.

Like... I had been running my business from the playful energy of a princess — not as sovereign who takes dreams and makes them real.

That princess had been so great at dreaming and starting things... but avoided finishing things. (Which this inner archetype is not supposed to!) Children are meant to play. They can't run a business.

My queen needed to start entering the game.

I also uncovered a bunch of messed-up dependency patterns where I had literally subconsciously kept recreating ground-zero poverty-like scenarios to be rescued, again and again, by either men or family, bailing me out... I was afraid to stand on my own feet because...

What if...

I suddenly became bigger and more successful than anyone else? Would everyone leave me then? Or judge me? Would I no longer be loved?

Better stay small and relatable.
As if relatable means being loved.

I had to untangle a bunch of mind-stories here. Because really, who knows! I was assuming what would happen — based on made-up stories!

And also, what if...

I really suddenly was not loved? Hypothetically? In what ways have I been clinging on to feeling loved? I discovered that I had an unhealthy way of playing small, and then feel being taken care of, and misconstrued that for "hey! Look! I'm being loved." Truth was, I was loved no matter what! And no one who loves me truly, wants me to play small!!!

Also... I had to discover that I had to truly love myself, independent of who or what was in my life. And then suddenly... I was independent! More sparkly! Making choices not out of fear, but freedom! Me being me!

I also asked myself, "What if... 'the worst-case scenario' happened?"

What was that, at this time, for me? (What was my story? Of course, this is always subjective and simply a fear. We never know what will happen.)

I had to face those fears and start trusting myself that no matter what. That I'd always be okay. And always lovingly take care of myself. That I'd always find resources, find next steps; there would always be some way.

I did a lot of untangling! Really did some deep diving.

And then, at some point, I pulled the plug. And chose to leave the shadow-quest and simply focus on SPARKLE and JOY again.

Both these approaches helped me. Both in their ways! I found there's a time for deep dives and a time to simply focus on what brings me joy. Both actually helped me spot old stories and change them to sparkle!

When I shifted my focus on JOY, I also discovered that I really activated my juices for life again. My bravery. I actually energized myself also to move forward — simply by playing!

One key thing I did always have to do, though, was stop bullying myself internally. No more pressure. I had to be kind to myself and take care of myself, no matter what's going on. Do the things that nourish me. Body mind soul. The BE part! Remember the BE PLAY DO formula?

THEN...., after this being, and taking care of me, the PLAY...
And soon, I'd be rolling forward again!

And if I didn't? If I kept avoiding things? Then yes! I could bring those facet glasses back and look closer to see if there were more inner avoidance shadow mind games at play holding me back from bringing more sparkle into my life. Either way — there's nothing wrong here. It's all a life adventure game.

Are you spinning the wheels? Never finishing things? Then look deeper. What's behind your avoidance? Great time to become curious. Once you see through your illusions, you can hit PLAY and roll forward again!

more magical keys to
sparkle when it's tough

how this chapter helps:

In this chapter, you'll find six additional magical keys that helped me bring sparkle to my journey and meet even SUPER challenging moments with a sparkly, can-do attitude!

Get inspired how you too can amp-up your sparkle superpowers to turn ANY difficulties you may currently experience into opportunities!

I'm penning these closing words in April 2021 while healing from cancer. I've found out that the way I've been navigating this very big health challenge apparently is extraordinary: Many people and also my doctors told me that I'm not just sparkling in hindsight and coming out of the hole after a deep winter of hiding and healing — like many patients seem to do. I seem to have a knack to navigate through it all powerfully — even with joy — while I'm going through everything.

Of course, this also affects my healing. Which has been powerful and fast. I've been feeling way better than, apparently, most patients do, even through chemo. Even my blood numbers have improved while going through chemo (apparently unheard of – my oncology doctor was stunned), and my tumors have been shrinking on a fast track.

While I (mostly) have been feeling okay or even sparkly.

I'll write a book with more details about my cancer healing journey. Here, I'm sharing what I now see as a few keys that helped me sparkle — and thrive — even through this challenge.

key: trusting I'll be ok

In the very beginning of my cancer journey, I got spirit guidance that this cancer experience will only be "a blip in my journey." I fully trusted that. And this full trust has been a huge rock and anchor for me in my journey.

It has helped me not to go down rabbit holes of researching the "what ifs" of cancer, to not worry about it, and to simply see this journey as something that I'm going through right now, but it's not defining me. And not the end of me. It's temporary.

If you can also find the trust that you'll be okay through and after whatever is challenging you right now... then you can do anything as well! And the thing loses power over you.

I found my trust through spirit guidance relayed through a spirit guide coach and medium, Lois Warnock. You can find spirit guidance too by praying and hearing your own answers through your own connection with a higher power and the universe.

And you can also find that trust within yourself by deciding what you want to experience:

key: deciding what I want to experience

There are numerous accounts of cancer patients who decided to experience their kids graduating or to actually fully heal... and then it happened. Because that's what they wanted and decided. And their body concurred. Our mind is a powerful thing!

I decided at the beginning of my cancer journey that a) of course, I will heal! And b) I decided to see my healing journey as a "CAN-cer spa experience of healing into love."

Viewing it from this angle, my chemo became a "crazy-ass deep cleanse." The thought of letting go of a breast? A boob job and rejuvenation. Skin issues because of chemo? A "red carpet treatment." (The cancer-specializing dermatologist I go to actually calls it that!) All my hair falling out, even my lashes? Magnetic lashes made me feel like a Hollywood diva. Especially when I added a pink wig! Fun!

key:humor

As you see, because of my reframe of cancer healing to a "spa experience," I actually found quite a bit of humor in the journey.

And, of course, humor is sparkle. Humor heals.

Humor improves everything!

How can you reframe whatever you're going through now to a more fun and humorous thing?

_____

_____

What do you decide you want to experience?

_____

key: joy

At the beginning of my cancer healing, I was still in the middle of working with coaches for my business and for my inner empowerment. Because our inner empowerment and mindset, of course, is the core of our life and our business. When I'm empowered, I can do anything!

The area I was focusing on was catching shadows. Like I've also talked about in this book. And it's great! It helped me so much!

HowEVER. There came a point where I realized it was enough.

I realize I felt aware enough and knew enough about my shadows and inner stories, and it was time for me to shift my energy. Because too many shadows (and the fact that I felt I was never done! As if something was wrong with me) was not healthy. I literally felt how focusing on shadows made me feel heavy and didn't feel good in my body, whereas when I focused on joy, my energy shifted. I felt good.

Which is the energy of healing.

So I decided to stop with the shadow work and focus on joy.

I dropped all my coaches and surrounded myself with new people and creativity.

I decided to only choose things if they brought me deep joy! Which, of course, can sometimes mean doing things that are not instant fun but lead to deep joy! Like me doing the final edits of this book. Seeing this book in your hands and just thinking about it sparkling up people's lives does indeed give me big joy! It's what I really want.

I can still catch shadows now without making that the main focus. My focus is now joy. And as they say:
What we focus on, grows!

key:play

In my cancer healing journey, playing has been a key ingredient to feel better, heal, and make it through challenges while feeling more sparkly. I brought creative things to my chemo, even sparkles! Of course! Put on hot lipstick and unicorn slippers at the clinic. I also just got myself more musical toys.

Anything that got me moving, dancing, singing, playing... helped me so much! Play makes everything better. Even challenges.

Play also helps us move forward when we're stuck and do scary things when we think we cannot do something! Like when I go to procedures, and I'm scared, I bring music in, and sometimes I sing along with it!

Yes, this just happened. I sang to Joss Stone while I was being poked and felt a burning pain. Yeeeeeahhhhhh, soul shine! It stiiiings! Singing along with it made it easier and go faster. And humor too. Way better.

When we play and see something as a game, we feel more powerful and brave!

Playing also helps us boost and grow our confidence.

The more we play and do (healthy) scary things, the more we dare to do things!

It's a practice. The more we do scary things, the easier they become! My first chemo was scary, weird, and not comfortable. As I kept going to treatments and brought with me more play (I brought things that would positively entertain me with good vibes), it got better and better.

Where play was missing, I brought it to treatments and made them my own experience.

key: (s)peak up

Only you know what you need to peak. To sparkle. To live brilliantly. Or even to feel better in this very moment.

I was astounded how many fellow cancer patients do NOT seem to speak up. I'm truly learning to become an advocate for myself through this journey. To ask for what I need, say what I think... tell my doctors, even clinic leaders! What felt right for me and what I needed for my healing.

Yes, my (and your) opinion matters! As long as we don't push it onto others, of course. It is important that we speak up for ourselves.

I've been speaking up about my insights, my learnings, my needs, my ideas — everything! — throughout my whole cancer healing experience.

When I arrived at the chemo clinic, I was not at ease to start chemo. I didn't like where a nurse asked me to sit. It was right next to other patients, next to a wastebasket full of icky chemo things. So I asked for a different spot. And to speak to a doctor. I asked for what I needed.

When the chair at the clinic faced the corner of a wall? I turned it to face the window. When the fluorescent light and green of the walls almost made me gag, I said so. I turned the light down. Brought my own lights.

The nurses and the clinic manager actually appreciated ALL of it.

And if they had not? It doesn't matter. I'm advocating for myself. If you want something, stay with it. Say it. Don't drop your desires.

What is it that you need right now? And where can you speak up? What additional keys can you think of that you also have for yourself?

list of additional
helpful tools

how this chapter helps:

Over the years, I've done many things for inner growth and empowerment. Here are a few additional tools and modalities for your inspiration. Some are already mentioned in the book. May this serve as a quick reference play list. Go with what calls you. And add your own!

Before you dig in: Remember, your best wisdom is INSIDE of you and comes from your heart. You'll find your own best ideas!

My list of additional helpful tools:

* Counting from 10 to 1 as you take slow breaths, and set the intention to feel fully refreshed and awesome by 1.

* Going outside. Fresh air + nature walks cleanse our thoughts and rejuvenate our whole way of being!

* ONE BREATH alone, when you're stressed out, works wonders.

* Hugging a doggie, a cat, or a human. We all need love!

* Intuitive art for clarity Doodle, draw, or craft something with the intention to get clarity on something – WITHOUT THINKING about it. Just doing it. That's super fun and powerful. You'll find answers from your heart that way. Instead of trying to get answers the HARD way. ;-) Just create

something, even blindly! And then when you stop, look at it and ask questions like "What can I learn here?" or "Show me what's going on here." You'll find your best answers!

* **Drawing, writing, or crafting something to let GO.** Express your feelings without thinking, with the intention to let something go. That's one of my main go-tos: using art. A powerful release tool!
  Important: When you're done, burn or shred the thing to let it all go! That's like a mini ritual. And you'll actually feel more free.

* **Crafting something to invite something IN.** Craft something to represent what you want to invite IN.

* **Journaling.** Even just for five minutes is powerful. Journaling question ideas: "How do I WANT to feel? What do I WANT to learn here? What does the universe want me to see, be, or do today?"

* **Journeying.** Doing a soul-journey visualization to access your inner wisdom. It's kind of like your very own fairy tale meditation where you allow your imagination to paint the story, and get magical answers. Everyone can learn this. Look up IntuitiveByTheSea.com — one of my favorite coaches!

* **Pulling oracle cards,** then listen inside to what resonates. I always get something that serves, then take action from there.

* **Play.** Yes, play! Mentioning it again. :) It ALWAYS shifts our energy! We often take ourselves too seriously! What would you do now if you were a kid? Dare to be silly! Tumble! Or even spit!

* **Letting the inner voices / feelings speak.** Just for a moment. Expressing them (as movement / voice / drawing / writing / talking... even just listening in your mind) often already helps.

- ★ Move! Dancing it all out! Expressing that NEGATIVE emotion is so healing. Often we bottle things up and forget to release. Dance full-out, then breathe. Now, how do you feel?

- ★ Dancing into positivity. Listening to a song that makes you feel like you want to feel and dance to it fully! So powerful!

- ★ Meditating. I often find meditations, searching on YouTube by topic. Like "healing meditation." Then I use what resonates. I also like the CALM app. Try some out. Find what works for YOU.

- ★ Checking in with your body. Sometimes my body needs something. Like to eat! Or my inner child needs play time! Pause, check in with yourself, then do what feels good.

- ★ Ask your spirit guides / the universe / God for support!

If you have repeating stories/voices/patterns, despite your efforts to get past them, allow yourself to be fully supported. It's okay to ask for help. Choose what your heart leads you to. Where you feel empowered.

Here are a few deeper healing and transformation modalities I've done for myself over the years, some as a one-time thing, some regularly:

- ★ Counseling —My first big shift was through a psychiatrist. After I had tried in vain for six years to free myself from a toxic relationship. Six years!! Talking about taking detours. (Please don't ever wait that long to get help.)

- ★ "The Journey" — A visualization method that goes deep and created big shifts and releases for me.

- ★ Qi Gong energy moving classes

- ★ Akashic Record readings — where you get wisdom and answers to anything from the big universe bird's eye view. You get JUST what serves you in that moment. Not more. Always magical! We can also learn to do this for ourselves.

- ★ Visualization Journeys and Hypno Meditations

- ★ Business coaching and Mindset coaching with guides and coaches

- ★ Astrological Birth Chart Reading — Big picture view about my life and my superpowers and how it all fits into my dreams

- ★ Psychic business coaching and life coaching to get fast-track answers and business strategies

- ★ Intuition opening classes to train my own intuition

- ★ Conversation + Visualization with Future Self (you can also do that by yourself by having an inner conversation with both your present and future self. Go to an inspired spot, close your eyes, take a few breaths, then speak to yourself or silently in your mind)

- ★ "Fear Be Gone" energy shifting of old fears through visualization (Coach Bill Baren coined that term, I believe.)

- ★ Working with Archetypes and Shadow Alchemy

- ★ Energy Healing. Reiki. Tapping. Acupuncture...

Know that you don't "need" any of this. You certainly don't need ALL of this. Follow your own path and resources that serve YOU.

I used to get pissed off for a long time, thinking, "does this learning and growing never end?" Haha! But truly, as humans, we actually like to grow and learn. It's part of our life experience. It's a journey. Not a goal.

What do you want?
State your desires to the universe.
Then say YES when the right resources show!

closing words from **merlin**

how this chapter helps:

I feel inspired to invite Merlin to leave a few closing words. In gratitude for all the wisdom that I received in the last year and while writing this book. My life truly has been an adventure — now penned here — an interactive galaxy ride of going from "Permission to Sparkle" to freeing my inner diamond, to now, as it turns out, flying with dragons! Ha!

So! Let's see what Merlin says!

Tune in to your inner magic.

You all got this.

You've just tapped the surface.

Dig deep.

It can be fun.

What fish can you find in that aquarium?

Follow the birds, the fish, whatever calls you.

The inspiration. The nudges. The play prompts.

Inside this book and outside.

We're talking about your life.

Do it in your style.

Dare to break your rules.

Know you're always safe.

You rock.

Anything else, Merlin?

No. Enough words. That's it.

Take action. Run with it.

Choose to see all as play!

Use the game!

Follow the play prompts!

(that was also JC (how I call Jesus) chiming in)

Today is tomorrow.

Time is an illusion.

What matters is only the now.

Claim it.

Create your future.

***

And that feels like the end of THIS book.

Stay tuned for my next books.

To fly with the dragons.

Free. Wildly. Boldly.

Through rain,

Into rain-

bows.

pass the sparkle on:

Are you inspired to do more with this book and to play with others?

Or to bring more sparkle to a group that you play in,
or to your own special cause?

I love to inspire people to sparkle.

I have this vision of sparkling up communities all over the planet!

I love to play with this book and game in groups and in public to inspire!

On my website, you find access to resources and sparkly play possibilities.
You can also contact me about how I could show up in your group or
your media outlet to help you enhance a special,
meaningful sparkle cause of your own.

It will be my honor to help you enhance your sparkle
and pass the sparkle on!

Much love!

AstridMueller.com